Musical Growth and Development

Musical Growth and Development

Birth Through Six

Dorothy T. McDonald
University of Iowa

Gene M. Simons
University of Georgia

Schirmer Books
A Division of Macmillan, Inc.
New York
Collier Macmillan Publishers
London

Schirmer Books
A Division of Macmillan, Inc.
866 Third Avenue, New York, N. Y. 10022

Collier Macmillan Canada, Inc.

Library of Congress Catalog Card Number: 88-4106

Printed in the United States of America

printing number
1   2   3   4   5   6   7   8   9   10

Library of Congress Cataloging-in-Publication Data

McDonald, Dorothy T.
    Musical growth and development: birth through six/Dorothy T.
McDonald, Gene M. Simons.
    p. cm.
"Songs and Movement Activities: Sources, compiled by Claire
McCoy": p.
    Includes index.
    ISBN 0-02-873070-4
    1. Music—Instruction and study—Juvenile. 2. Child development.
I. Simons, Gene M. II. Title.
MT2.M39 1988
780'.7—dc19   88-4106
                                              CIP
                                              MN

To the memory of Gene Simons, who
contributed much to our knowledge
of musical growth and development
in early childhood

Contents

CHAPTER 8: EVALUATION OF PRESCHOOL MUSIC PROGRAMS 175

CHAPTER 9: MATERIALS FOR INSTRUCTION 191

APPENDIX A: TEACHER SKILLS: USING INSTRUMENTS 269

Preface

*Attend! We are now beginning. When we get to the end
of the story we shall know more than we do now.**

    I have a colleague who has described two ways of teaching music methods classes. She tells her students:

> I can give you a recipe for an excellent omelet. You can follow the recipe, step by step, and produce a very fine omelet. Your friends will no doubt ask you for the recipe and will compliment you on your culinary abilities. But with one recipe, you will be able to make only one kind of omelet. Your omelet-making expertise will be limited.
>
>   On the other hand, we could study and discuss together the basic principles of omelet-making. We could examine the fundamental ingredients, gain insights about the proportional balance of the various ingredients and determine their effect on the finished product. We could then formulate the most effective methods of stirring and mixing, decide on proper pan temperature, and make decisions about when the omelet is ready to be taken from the pan, and when to serve it. With this kind of knowledge, you can make many omelets; you can create new omelets! Your omelet-producing expertise will be limited only by your own creativity.

    So might a book dealing with the teaching of music to young children be described. It may be a recipe book—containing all sorts of fine activities and lesson plans. Such books are valuable and should be part of every early childhood educator's professional library. To use these books effectively, however, a teacher needs fundamental knowledge about the "ingredients" of musical development, so to speak. Also needed is information concerning the "stirring and mixing" of other aspects of child growth and development that affect musical growth. Other useful

*M. G. Weiser, *Group care and education of infants and toddlers* (St. Louis, MO: C. V. Mosby, 1982), p. 1.

information includes how to "serve" musical experiences to young children.

This book was written to initiate dialogue among all those persons to whom early childhood music education is important. Its basic premise is that the knowledge about young children's musical development that has been provided by research and study is useful information for all educators. In the field of music education, as in all important undertakings, knowing where we have come from, where we are, and where we are going is necessary.

The general outline of this study may be sketched as follows. Chapter 1 focuses on the historical heritage of early childhood music education and its present status. Chapter 2 presents theories of child development and learning, with their implications for music instruction. Chapter 3 presents information derived from music developmental and instructional research. Thus, the "ingredients" and the "mixing and stirring" of effective music education can become part of our information base.

A book proposing to assist in the nurturing of musicality, however, should offer suggestions about "serving" the finished product. Chapter 4 deals with preparing a musical environment that fosters learning; Chapter 5 discusses instructional strategies. In Chapter 6, suggestions for teaching music to children with special needs are presented; in Chapter 7, selected methods of instruction are described. Chapter 8 addresses the topic of evaluation, a process that enables us to take a realistic look at the effectiveness of our music programs.

The final chapter in the book contains many songs and musical activities that may be used in implementing an effective program of musical instruction for our youngest learners.

A completed textbook is the result of the efforts of many persons. Because of the untimely death of one of the authors of this book, the task of preparing the final manuscript necessitated calling upon colleagues to help complete the work. I am indebted to Dr. Kate Gfeller for her contributions to Chapter 6, which deals with music instruction for special-needs children. I want to express my gratitude to Dr. Claire McCoy for her work in preparing Appendix B, "Songs and Movement Activities."

Pictures add immeasurably to any book about children and music. Teachers whose cooperation in providing photographs of children engaged in music activities are much appreciated. They include Susan Conolly, Dr. Darlene McNulty, Ruth Seim, and Mary Anne Sims. I also want to thank Jeffrey Aaron, one of the photographers, and the many parents of the children.

I am grateful to my typist, Elizabeth Voss, for her typing, retyping, and re-retyping of the manuscript.

The plan for writing this book was that it should be of wide scope, draw largely on research-based information, provide foundational information, and offer practical suggestions for early childhood music teaching. If this plan has been accomplished, those who strive to help young children become musical will find this book useful.

Dorothy McDonald

Musical Growth and Development

Chapter 1

Early Childhood Music: Past and Present

Since music has so much to do with the molding of character,
it is necessary that we teach it to our children.

—*Aristotle*

That music can contribute to the quality of children's early life experiences would be disputed by few persons involved in the education of young children. Teachers have always been aware of the ability of music to soothe, stimulate, excite, or entertain children. It is a rare teacher who has not sung a quiet song to ease a fretful child, planned a vigorous rhythmic activity to release pent-up energy, or played a favorite record to bring calm (or, perhaps, an energetic response) to a classroom. Music is such an integral part of early childhood that it is difficult to imagine children in an educational environment that does not include it.

Why is music considered a rightful part of childhood education? Many reasons have been put forth. One group of educators, delineating the place of music in "good schools for young children," has described music activities as contributing to emotional growth "by providing pleasure, joy and creative expression"; to perceptual growth by "developing listening and auditory discrimination skills"; to motor skill development by helping children realize "gains in physical development and use of (their) bodies"; and to vocal growth by helping them "increase the range and flexibility of (their) voices" (Leeper, Dales, Skipper, and Witherspoon, 1974, p. 374). These contributions of music to a child's education can be found, stated in various ways, in most textbooks concerned with early childhood educational curricula.

Music's role in social development has also been cited. Foster (1965) wrote:

> Music has an integrating power on the individual and the group. The withdrawn child tends to relax his guard and is more ready to participate with the others, while the hostile child seems to be less aggressive, so that each is helped to become a contributing member of the group. Here is one task in which all can cooperate to produce something mutually pleasing. (p. 374)

Musical games may be the first social experiences in which a young child shows inclination to participate and share with others. While children younger than three or four generally engage in such activities with an adult, the fun of joining a game with others gradually attracts even our youngest children, and thus social exchanges and cooperative play skills begin to develop.

Less functional, perhaps, but equally important is the role of music in introducing young children to their cultural heritage. Although there is little understanding during these early years of the "long history of music" or the significance of music to ethnic groups different from their own, preschoolers who learn to distinguish and enjoy folk songs of Appalachia, Spanish-American tunes of the Southwest, or the country ballads of the mountains and plains, have taken a big step in becoming aware of the historical and cultural records left to them through the music of the peoples who first settled our country.

Many educators see the role of music as a powerful tool for teaching cognitive skills. There are preschools today where music, because of its appeal to children, is used for rigorous reinforcement of cognitive operations, such as learning the alphabet, number seriation and take-away, add-to concepts, and meanings of conceptual pairs such as up-down, in-out, over-under, above-below, fast-slow (Bereiter and Engelman, 1966).

All of these are important reasons for teachers to plan quality music experiences purposefully for their young students. But perhaps the most important role of music in education is what it can add to the aesthetic component of a child's life—the development of sensitivity for the feelings, impressions, and images that music can convey. As Hymes (1981) reminds us, "Our experiences today make it abundantly clear: We need children with better sensitivities fully as much as we need better informed children. Today's education makes a major error when it concentrates on knowledge alone" (p. 29). Musical experiences, which stimulate imagination and stir emotions, can make a unique contribution to this aspect of educational development.

In spite of this rather general consensus about the value of music, it is impossible at the present time to describe a "typical" preschool or primary school music curriculum. Part of this is due to the variety of educational settings wherein early childhood music education takes place. Today's children, in the first half-dozen years of life, may have been "in school" from birth onward. Day-care centers may have been their first school. The proportion of children who attend day-care centers has increased enormously during the last decades. Many such centers provide comprehensive care for children of all ages. At age two or thereabouts, many children are enrolled in nursery schools or early childhood centers, which generally serve children from two to five years of age. At age four, they may attend a prekindergarten class, which may be privately run or a part of the public school system. At five, most children enter kindergarten; at six, the first grade.

The music experiences in these preschools are as varied as their settings. The prekindergarten or kindergarten child may have received music instruction from the music specialist who plans the curriculum for the entire elementary school. In this arrangement, music periods are generally planned for specific times each day or week, when the specialist will visit the room. When the planned music period is over, that is often the end of music activities for the day or week. In other kindergartens, the classroom teacher is responsible for music instruction, and music may be integrated with other curricular activities—an arrangement that permits a more flexible and spontaneous program.

For younger children, a description of music education is more difficult. In most nursery schools and early childhood centers, music is the responsibility of the teachers and care givers, who may or may not have had preprofessional training or musical background. Dependent upon their abilities and interests, most preschool teachers do include musical activities; experiences in singing, listening, and rhythms are preplanned, or they occur spontaneously throughout the day (Figure 1.1).

A relatively recent phenomenon, which must be included in any discussion of the various types of preschool music education, is the privately run music preschool. These schools have grown in popularity and number during the past decade. More than a few of our under-six population have received in these schools quite sophisticated, intensive instruction on traditional instruments—the Suzuki Talent Education program for stringed instruments (violin, cello) and flute is perhaps the best known example of this type of preschool music training. Others, such as the Kindermusik (Heyge, 1980) and Carabo-Cone (1969) programs, provide a varied but nonetheless focused type of music instruction quite different from the general music programs of most preschools and kindergartens.

This brief overview of early childhood music education makes for a fragmented picture. On the one hand, little curricular unity is evi-

Figure 1.1. Young children and music are natural friends.

dent, either among preschools or between preschools and the public schools. While excellent programs exist, they are usually developed within individual preschools or school systems. On the other hand, there is now probably more interest among parents and teachers in the musical development of young children than at any previous time in history. More young children are receiving quality music instruction than ever before. More materials—songbooks, tapes and recordings, instruments—are being produced especially for our under-six population. And more school music educators and psychologists are engaged in the study of the music teaching-learning process as it applies to young children.

Music today is regarded as an essential, desirable component in the aesthetic development of the young child. Has it always been? Where and when did the concept of early childhood music education begin? Where is it now? And where is it going? We will now take up the answers to these questions.

EUROPEAN BEGINNINGS

Preschool music education was born with and grew along with the concept of early childhood education itself. The preschool movement began more than three hundred years ago. In 1659, John Amos Comenius, a Czech educator, published a book, *The Great Didactic,* in which he "shocked the world" by suggesting that "not only was there an identifiable stage of growth from infancy to six years of age, but also that there was an appropriate curriculum for this age" (Weiser, 1982, p. 10). The curriculum he formulated was intended to be carried out in the home—a "Mother School"—and consisted of introductory factual, language, and sensory skills. Also included was music—"to awaken the senses, soothe the mind, contribute to speech production and promote good health" (Monroe, 1900, p. 119). Mothers were advised to encourage infant vocalizations (described as "complaints and wailings"), to provide sound-producing toys for their toddlers ("give them horns, whistles, drums and rattles and allow them to acquire perceptions of rhythm and melody") and to sing with their young daughters and sons ("the more common melodies, . . . including . . . easy psalms and hymns, [to] give them the elements of music") (Laurie, 1892, p. 141). These introductory musical experiences would provide a foundation for later study of singing, music reading, and instrumental instruction (Sadler, 1966, p. 230).

This concept of music as a part of an age-appropriate, comprehensive educational plan for young children was quite singular when contrasted to what we know of music education at that time. Music, as one of the seven liberal arts, was part of a classical education, but was studied theoretically; performance skills were "an adornment for the nobility." *Childhood* music education was unheard of. The goal of music instruction was to develop adult musical behaviors, no matter what the age of the learner. Such training, according to Aries, "explains the frequency, in the families of professionals, of what we now call infant prodigies, such as the young Mozart" (1962, p. 63). But Mozarts occur only occasionally in history.

The theories of Comenius were far too advanced to be accepted by his contemporaries, but the concept he introduced—that early childhood is a unique stage of development, which requires a special type of education—persisted. So, too, did the concept of music as a contributory force in the development of desired moral, physical, and sensory skills, as well as an art form worthy of study for its own sake.

About a hundred years later, the French philosopher Jean-Jacques Rousseau reintroduced the concept that the early years of life were not simply preparation for adulthood, but, rather, a time for living, feeling, and thinking "as a child." Rousseau set forth his theories in two books, *Emile* and *The Social Contract,* both published in 1762. He proposed an education derived from natural experiences in a natural environment, with minimal intervention from adults. Like Comenius, he had definite ideas about the role of music in education. Feeling that music was a "particularly effective way of expressing . . . deepest emotions in a pure and simple form" (Grimsley, 1973, p. 128), he was particularly concerned with the type of music that should be taught to young children:

> I do not disapprove of nurses amusing the child with songs, and very cheerful and varied accents; but I do disapprove of her stunning him with a multitude of useless words of which he comprehends nothing except the tone she throws into them. (Rousseau, 1893, p. 36)

Rousseau was himself a musician, and seemed to recognize "appropriate" musical objectives for young children—"Make his voice accurate, uniform, flexible and sonorous; and his ear sensitive to measure and harmony, but nothing more than this" (Rousseau, 1893, p. 116). He advocated childlike songs for children; if none were available, teachers should create their own—"expressly for him, interesting for his age, and as simple as his ideas" (p. 116).

Rousseau's educational theories created such a furor that he was forced to live in isolation the last years of his life. Yet the concept of early childhood, introduced by Comenius and expanded by Rousseau, was not stilled, and about fifty years later it inspired Heinrich Pestalozzi, a Swiss educator, to devise a curriculum based on these theories and to test it in various experimental schools.

Pestalozzi felt that education for young children should be functional and practical and should enable all persons to become useful members of society. He, too, recommended that education begin at home, at the "mother's knee." He provided guidelines for such a school in *How Gertrude Teaches Her Children*, published in 1801. When the child was old enough for out-of-home education, Pestalozzi's schools offered a more expanded curriculum than was found in most schools, and included "useful" as well as traditional subjects. Music was one of the "useful" subjects, and enjoyed such a prominent place in his schools that he is credited with the "practical introduction of music into the primary school curriculum" (Downs, 1975, p. 57).

Pestalozzi believed that children learn best through experience and self-discovery. Experience should precede theory. Music learning, therefore, should begin with singing. His students were taught many folk and national songs, and learned to sing them well—"singing was not only a means of recreation and socialization, but was taught as an accomplishment" (Keene, 1982, p. 81). Thus did children's songs become an instrument for music instruction. All music theory—for example, instruction in music reading—was derived from the song.

Two of Pestalozzi's teachers prepared a music methods text, in which this approach to instruction was presented. This text, *The Teaching of Music on Pestalozzian Principles,* was published in 1810. The formulation of a method for group instruction in music was an important event in music education, for it implied that music instruction was important for *all* children, and that, if the instruction were well conceived, *every* child could learn to sing and to read music—not just the talented few. Coupled with the belief that music played an important role in the development of moral character, good citizenship, and "harmonious" emotional growth, music's place in elementary school curricula became firmly established in nineteenth century education.

The educator who was to place it at the core of *preschool* education was a student of Pestalozzi—Frederick Froebel, the founder of the kindergarten. Froebel also believed that children learned through experience, or "self-activity." Because young children's self-activity is play, it is from playful activities that learning derives.

Interestingly, although Froebel was not a musician, the book in which many of his theories were presented is a book of songs, verses, games, and "commentaries" to guide teachers' presentation of the materials. This book, *Mother-Play and Nursery Songs,* was described in extravagant terms by one of America's kindergarten pioneers, Susan Blow:

> As a child's book, this little collection of songs and games is unique in literature. As a mother's book, likewise, it has no ancestry and no posterity. It is the greatest book for little children and the greatest book for mothers in the world. (Blow, 1895b, p. 39)

Froebel did not regard *Mother-Play* as a music textbook, however. Believing that moral training was central to the entire educational process, he used music as a vehicle for such training. Each verse or song in *Mother-Play* contained a lesson; given a musical setting, the lessons were more easily learned and longer remembered. Figures 1.2 and 1.3 show his treatment of "Pat-a-Cake." Not merely a child's game song, it became a lesson about the interrelatedness of man and nature. The teacher was instructed:

> In "Pat-a-Cake", the cake suggests flour and the miller; these suggest corn and the farmer; the corn, the field where it grows so wonderfully; its growth, an unseen energizing and fostering power. (Bowen, 1906, p. 71)

Music also was used to help children develop self-discipline:

> It is a good plan . . . to accompany each change (in activity) by rhyme and song; so that the latent sense of rhythm and song, and above all, the sense of order in the human being and child, may

Figure 1.2. "Pat-a-Cake" from Froebel's *Mother-Play and Nursery Songs.*

Figure 1.3. "Pat-a-Cake" from Froebel's *Mother-Play and Nursery Songs:* musical setting.

be aroused and strengthened to an impulse for social cooperation. (Froebel, 1904, p. 267)

At the end of the nineteenth century, music as a part of early childhood education was generally accepted by the educational establishment. Table 1.1 summarizes the reasons why. Music's role was utilitar-

Table 1.1. Music's Role in Early Childhood Education:
Early European Reformers

Name	Date	Nationality	Selected Statements
Comenius	1592–1670	Moravian	"to awaken the senses, soothe the mind, contribute to speech production and promote good health." (Monroe, 1900, p. 119)
Rousseau	1712–1778	French	"to contribute to . . . the extension of enjoyment among the common people, and the glorification of their . . . lives and moods." (Morley, 1910, p. 291)
Pestalozzi	1746–1827	Swiss	"If cultivated in the right spirit, it strikes at the root of every bad or narrow feeling, of every ungenerous or mean propensity, of every emotion unworthy of humanity." (Downs, 1975, p. 57)
Froebel	1771–1852	German	"Much is . . . given to the outer ear, that man all unheeding will not hear. Then call the child's attention to it now, and all his life in joyous stream shall flow." (Alper, 1980, p. 112)

ian and functional, and its importance was recognized. American music educators owe considerable debt to these early teachers and philosophers.

AMERICAN BEGINNINGS

The names of Pestalozzi and Froebel are particularly important in the history of American early childhood music education, for these men's theories, philosophies, and methods had much to do with the establishment of curricular music in our early elementary schools and kindergartens.

Pestalozzi's theories excited much interest among American educators in the beginning decades of the nineteenth century. His method for group instruction in music was no exception. This method was tried out, with much success, in the private music classes of Lowell Mason, a Boston musician who has been called the "father of public school music." Mason succeeded in convincing the Boston school board that such instruction could be carried out in the public elementary schools, and thus, in 1838, music became a part of that city's free public education and soon spread to other cities throughout the country.

At first, only the upper grades received music instruction, but during the 1850s and 1860s it was extended to the primary grades. Historians have suggested that American school music teachers, after the beginning decades, forgot the *real* purpose of music instruction and became embroiled in a pedagogical battle over how to teach note reading:

> No child seemed too young to be exposed to the mysteries of notes names, keys and chords. The music specialist . . . placed the study of music on par with the so-called academic subjects. In 1860 it was expected that two-thirds of the instruction time . . . be devoted to the learning of theoretical principles while the remainder could be spent in singing. (Keene, 1982, p. 179)

"Experience before theory," even for the youngest elementary school students, was apparently neglected.

However, preschool music during the 19th century had another setting—the kindergarten, which was not yet a part of the public schools. The first kindergarten in the United States was in the home of Mrs. Carl Shurz, in Watertown, Wisconsin, in 1855. In 1860 Elizabeth Peabody established one in Boston. Not until 1873, when Susan Blow succeeded in opening a kindergarten in the Saint Louis schools, did it become part of free public education.

All of these kindergarten pioneers were students of Froebelian methods, and the first kindergartens in America adhered closely to Froebel's model. It is not surprising that music has had a prominent role, from the beginning, in our kindergartens. Froebel had established children's songs as an important instructional medium. Early kindergarten educators translated the Froebelian song materials for America's teachers and established teacher-training courses. As more and better songs became needed, a surge of kindergarten songbooks appeared between 1880 and the early years of the twentieth century. When kindergartens became part of the public school system, the Froebelian concept of early childhood music education permeated primary school music instruction and rote songs became important educational tools:

> The early work in the public schools had been confined almost wholly to teaching the musical notation. It was now seen . . . that music must be given a meaning to the child, and that a love of song must be developed before introduction in musical notation could have any significance. (Vandewalker, 1971, p. 50)

Songs found in kindergarten texts were carefully selected; they attempted to be "truly musical and childlike in thought, word or melody" (Vandewalker, 1971, p. 175), according to the editors and authors.

But what was "childlike" music? How did young children "think" about music? And what was a "childlike" melody? During the closing years of the nineteenth century, the child study movement, "an educational fashion among educators and psychologists," began, which called for "widespread and scientific observation and study of children" (Humphreys, 1985, p. 79) in all areas of instruction. Music educators were drawn into the movement, and questions regarding the music teaching/learning process were reconsidered and reevaluated. G. Stanley Hall, a leader in the movement, "exhorted teachers to begin systematic study of their students, . . . and (from) the data collected, to provide (age-appropriate) guidance and training" (Humphreys, 1985, p. 82). An early music supervisor, H. E. Holt, advised music teachers to evaluate their methods of teaching, and to "go to their foundations and ascertain the soundness of the principles upon which they are based" (Humphreys, 1985, p. 84). The era of the scientific study of the child had begun.

THE FIRST HALF OF THE TWENTIETH CENTURY

The child study movement initiated a period of increasing inquiry into the teaching/learning process, in music as well as in other areas of learning. Although the study of the musical development of children was more the purview of psychologists and, to a lesser extent, nonmusician child study researchers (Humphreys, 1985, p. 85), the influence of music behavioral research, begun in the child study era, was significant. Research about the nature of young children's musical responses and musical understanding began to be conducted. Music psychologists began to test, not the effects of musical training on morality and character (untestable, to be sure), but rather the musical preferences, age-referenced responses, and behaviors of students.

THE IOWA STUDIES

One of the first efforts to measure young children's musical development was carried out at the Iowa Child Welfare Research Station on the University of Iowa campus. The research station, opened in 1921 (and listed by the U.S. government Bureau of Education as one of the first nursery schools), included a "preschool laboratory" for children from two to six years of age. The findings from the research conducted at the station were published in a series of reports throughout the 1920s and 1930s. Among the compilations of research studies appearing during these years are three volumes concerned with musical development (Seashore, 1939; Stoddard, 1932; Williams, 1933). The studies reported in these volumes describe the rhythmic and vocal behaviors of three- to five-year-old children. These publications represent a beginning of the efforts of twentieth century music psychologists to provide a research information base for music teachers and curriculum planners, an effort that continues today.

THE PILLSBURY STUDIES

Another pioneer project in early childhood music research was carried out at the Pillsbury Foundation School in Santa Barbara, California, during the years 1937–1951. Students in this school ranged in age from two to six years. The school was established as a laboratory to study the creative musical behaviors of children. A balanced music program was offered, with emphasis on "continuous opportunity for unregimented music-making, for hearing many kinds of music, and for receiving expert musical guidance and assistance" (Moorhead and Pond, 1978, p. 3). Observational records of the self-initiated, creative activities of the children were kept, and from 1941 to 1951 the school's directors published their reports in a series of four volumes. These reports have since been reissued as a single text, *Music of Young Children* (Moorhead and Pond, 1978).

Volume 1 of this project, entitled *Chant,* describes the spontaneous singing of the young children studied—what motivated their song-making, the pitch range and patterns frequently used, what the songs were about, and the type of motor movement that commonly accompanied them. Volume 2, *General Observations,* includes a discussion of dramatic play that evolved from song activities. *Musical Notation,* Volume 3, describes an experiment in teaching five- and six-year-old children to read musical notation. The final report, *Free Use of Instruments for Musical Growth,* is an observational record of how four-year-old children explored, experimented with, and used a variety of percussion and tonal instruments to produce music.

The Pillsbury Studies have been the basis for much subsequent

"Twinkle, Twinkle, Little Star" in Dann's *First-Year Music* (1914)

words, Jane Taylor; music, Arthur Johnstone

Figure 1.4. Two settings of a child's song: "Twinkle, Twinkle, Little Star."

research concerning the creative musical behaviors of young children and "seem today to be no less pertinent to the needs of education than [they were] when the project began" (Moorhead and Pond, 1978, p. 3).

These projects, the Iowa Studies and the Pillsbury Studies, are representative of a new phase in the history of early childhood music education. If music is to remain a lively and viable component of the curriculum, it should be taught so that children not only enjoy it (and

Figure 1.4. (continued)

develop social, cooperative and perceptive listening skills) but also learn something about the art. In the first half of the twentieth century, researchers devoted much effort to this cause, and, if most early childhood music educators were unaware of their work, the editors and authors of the music texts and materials that they used were not, as the contents of publications began to reflect some of the findings of research. For example, early childhood songs in kindergarten and primary music texts gradually were notated in keys that accommodated the pitch range researchers had established as most comfortable for young children, rather than the higher key ranges that characterized so many songs in early texts. Songs about common life experiences replaced the more eclectic inclusions of earlier texts.

You may wish to compare the two settings of the children's verse "Twinkle, Twinkle Little Star" shown in Figure 1.4. The first one appeared in the *First Year Music* book of the Hollis Dann Music Course, published in 1914. The text was to be used in the kindergarten and first grade. The second version is the one we use today.

While the melody of the first version is attractive, one can sense the greater difficulty of the song, both because of the higher pitch range required of the singer and because of the lack of melodic repetition, making it more difficult to remember.

TODAY

The second half of the twentieth century has seen many changes in early childhood education. World War II, which led many mothers to join the work force, necessitated the establishment of many more day-care and preschool centers than had existed up to that time. Head Start, begun in 1965 for the purpose of providing preschool experience for children from low-income backgrounds, further increased the number of young children in educational settings. At the same time, behavioral scientists began publishing much information about the significance of the early years' experiences to children's later achievement in school.

In the last two decades music educators, as well, have become more aware of the importance of early musical instruction for preschool youngsters. Because school music teachers generally are not involved in teaching in preschool settings, little attention had been given up to this time by music specialists to early musical development. With the continued publication of research about the importance of the early years in musical development, however, there have been increasing efforts to "close the gap" between researchers and practitioners, and between music educators and early childhood teachers. Two of these efforts were the Tanglewood Symposium and the GO Project.

THE TANGLEWOOD SYMPOSIUM

In 1967, the Music Educators National Conference (MENC), in cooperation with the Berkshire Music Center, the Theodore Presser Foundation, and the School of Fine and Applied Arts of Boston University, sponsored the Tanglewood Symposium to discuss the role of music in contemporary society. This topic was debated by educators, scientists, sociologists, corporate businessmen, and musicians. A report of the symposium was published by the Music Educators National Conference (Choate, 1968).

GO PROJECT

As a result of the discussions carried out at the Tanglewood Symposium, critical issues in music education were identified, and recommendations were made. In 1969, the MENC initiated the Goals and Objectives Project (GO Project) to address the Tanglewood recommendations. Thirty-five goals and objectives for immediate focus were identified. Several addressed the issue of early childhood music education and the problem of the existing gap both between research and practice and between early childhood music education and public school music education. These resolutions were the following:

- Advocate the expansion of music education to include preschool music,
- Lead in efforts to ensure that every school system requires music from kindergarten through grade 6, . . .
- Cooperate in the development of exemplary models of desirable programs and practices in the teaching of music,
- Promote the conduct of research and research-related activities in music education,
- Gather and disseminate information about music and music education, and
- Pursue effective working relationships with organizations and groups having mutual interests. (Mark, 1986, pp. 58–59)

OTHER EVENTS

Although the objectives of the GO Project have not yet been fully realized, the identification and articulation of specific goals did serve to focus attention on aspects of music education that needed attention, and among them was early childhood music. Since the GO Project, some noteworthy events have occurred in the area of preschool music education. Some resulted from the GO Project; others occurred as a result of an increasing awareness among music educators of the importance of quality music education for young children. Several of these events and symposia are listed here, arranged more or less chronologically according to year of occurrence.

1. The publication of *The School Music Program: Description and Standards* (1974; Music Educators National Conference, 1986) by the MENC. The book contains a description of quality music programs for all grades. An early childhood program is included. (The program description used in the 1986 edition of *The School Music Program* served as the format for "Materials for Instruction," Chapter 9 in this text.)

2. An increasing number of articles dealing with preschool music in the *Music Educators Journal,* published by the MENC.

3. Symposia at various universities and colleges devoted to the discussion of early childhood music education. The Ohio State University sponsored two such conferences, in 1977 and 1979, as part of their *Current Issues in Music Education* series. These symposia brought music education researchers together with administrators, teachers, and students in preschool programs. The papers and proceedings were published by The Ohio State University Press under the titles *Music for the Preschool Child* (Tolbert, 1977) and *Music of Young Children* (Tolbert, 1980).

4. The National Symposium on the Applications of Psychology to the Teaching and Learning of Music, held in Ann Arbor, Michigan, in 1978, 1979, and 1981. This symposium brought together psychologists and music educators to explore the relationships between behavioral psychology and music education. Papers were published by the MENC under the title *Documentary Report of the Ann Arbor Symposium* (Music Educators National Conference, 1981; Music Educators, 1983).

5. The establishment of a Special Research Interest Group (SRIG) in early childhood music (ECM-SRIG) in 1980 at the MENC national conference. Among its purposes were the dissemination of research to teachers and child care workers, and the development of working relationships with professional organizations that serve the personnel who work with the education of young children.

6. Early Childhood Music Conferences, which provided needed dialogue and communication among early childhood classroom teachers, child care givers, psychologists, and researchers. A major one was the Music in Early Childhood Conference, held at Brigham Young University in 1984. This Conference made important progress in bringing together persons from many areas of preschool education

who share one common interest—quality educational programs for our young children. The proceedings of the Conference were published in a volume, *The Young Child and Music: Contemporary Principles in Child Development and Music Education* (Boswell, 1985).

Today, early childhood music education still suffers from lack of communication between researchers, classroom teachers, and music educators. However, it is evident that progress is being made. Music education for young children will always reflect the interest and importance placed on it by society. Although the present decade's interest among researchers in the musical development of the young child and the interest of parents and teachers in materials and methods for teaching music to young children may seem, at times, to be parallel rather than interactive interests, with but scant relationship to each other, there are signs that some progress toward interaction is occurring.

The questions posed earlier in this chapter, "Where and when did early childhood music begin?" and "Where is it now?" have been explored in this chapter's discussion. "Where is it going?" is the question before us today. We can only answer this question with some conjectures. The commitment to early childhood music education appears strong. One need only count the number of music preschools in our cities, consider the number of youngsters of our acquaintance receiving music training, or study the array of preschool music materials available in music and book stores. Such commitment seems to demonstrate more concern about the future of early childhood music education among today's teachers and parents than in previous generations. Such commitment, along with information, materials, and a continued search for effective instructional techniques, may produce a future population of young people who not only enjoy music but also understand it and, because of that understanding, will continue to include it in their life activities.

QUESTIONS FOR DISCUSSION/SUGGESTED ACTIVITIES

1. Of the reasons given for early childhood music instruction, which seem most important to you? Why?

2. If possible, visit a day-care center, an early childhood center, and a kindergarten. Are musical activities included in all these settings? What kinds of musical activities are provided?

3. The early years are now recognized as influential in the musical development of children. Do you feel that all children can benefit from early instruction? Why or why not?

REFERENCES AND SUGGESTED READINGS

Alper, C. D. (1980). The early childhood song books of Eleanor Smith: their affinity with the philosophy of Friedrich Froebel. *Journal of Research in Music Education, 28*(2), 111–118.

Alper, C. D. (1982). Froebelian implications in texts of early childhood songs published near the turn of the century. *Journal of Research in Music Education, 30*(1), 49–60.

Aries, P. (1962). *Centuries of childhood: A social history of family life* (R. Baldick, Trans.). New York: Alfred A. Knopf.

Bereiter, C., & Engelmann, S. (1966). *Teaching disadvantaged children in the preschool.* Englewood Cliffs, NJ: Prentice-Hall, Inc.

Blow, S. E. (1895a). *The mottos and commentaries of Friedrich Froebel's mother play.* New York: D. Appleton & Co.

Blow, S. E. (1895b). *The songs and music of Friedrich Froebel's mother play.* New York: D. Appleton & Co.

Blow, S. E. (1899). *Letters to a mother on the philosophy of Froebel.* New York: D. Appleton & Co.

Boswell, J. (Ed.). (1985). *The young child and music: Contemporary principles in child development and music education.* Reston, VA: Music Educators National Conference.

Bowen, H. C. (1906). *Froebel and education by self-activity.* London: William Heinemann.

Carabo-Cone, M. (1969). *A sensory-motor approach to music learning: Book 1: Primary concepts.* New York: MCA, Inc.

Choate, R. A. (Ed.). (1968). *Documentary report of the Tanglewood symposium.* Reston, VA: Music Educators National Conference.

Dann, H. (1914). *First year music: Rote songs for kindergarten and first grade.* New York: American Book Co.

Downs, R. E. (1975). *Heinrich Pestalozzi: Father of modern pedagogy.* Boston: Twayne Publications.

Foster, F. P. (1965). The song within: Music and the disadvantaged preschool child. *Young Children, 20,* 373–376.

Froebel, F. (1887). *The education of man* (W. N. Hailmann, Trans.). Atlanta, GA: Milton Bradley Co.

Froebel, F. (1904). *Pedagogies of the kindergarten* (J. Jarvis, Trans.). New York: D. Appleton & Co.

Goals and objectives for music education. (1970). *Music Educators Journal, 57*(4), 24–25.

Grimsley, R. (1973). *The philosophy of Rousseau.* London: Oxford University Press.

Heyge, L. L. (Translator). (1980). *Kindermusik: Music for the very young.* St. Louis: Magnamusic-Baton.

Humphreys, J. (1985). The child-study movement and public school n education. *Journal of Research in Music Education, 33*(2), 79–86.

Hymes, J. (1981). *Teaching the child under six* (3rd ed.). Columbus, OH: Charles E. Merrill.

Keene, J. A. (1982). *A history of music education in the United States.* Hanover and London: University Press of New England.

Laurie, S. S. (1892). *John Amos Comenius, bishop of the Moravians: His life and educational work.* Syracuse, NY: C. W. Bardeen.

Leeper, S. H.; Dales, R.; Skipper, D.; & Witherspoon, R. (1974). *Good schools for young children* (3rd ed.). New York: Macmillan, Inc.

Mark, M. (1986). *Contemporary music education* (2nd ed.). New York: Schirmer Books.

Monroe, W. S. (1900). *Comenius and the beginnings of educational reform.* New York: Charles Scribner's Sons.

Moorhead, G., & Pond, D. (1978). *Music of young children.* Santa Barbara, CA: Pillsbury Foundation for Advancement of Music Education.

Morley, J. (1910). *Rousseau* (Vol. 1). London: Macmillan & Co., Ltd.

Music Educators National Conference. (1974). *The school music program: Description and standards* (1st edition). Reston, VA: MENC.

Music Educators National Conference. (1981). *Documentary report of the Ann Arbor symposium: Applications of psychology to the teaching and learning of music.* Reston, VA: MENC.

Music Educators National Conference. (1983). *Documentary report of the Ann Arbor symposium session III: Applications of psychology to the teaching and learning of music.* Reston, VA: MENC.

Music Educators National Conference. (1986). *The school music program: Description and standards* (2nd edition). Reston, VA: MENC.

Pemberton, C. A. (1985). *Lowell Mason: His life and work.* Ann Arbor, MI: UMI Research Press.

Pestalozzi, J. (1898). *How Gertrude teaches her children* (L. E. Holland, Trans.). Syracuse, NY: C. W. Bardeen.

Rousseau, J. J. (1893). *Emile, or treatise on education* (W. H. Payne, Trans.). New York: D. Appleton & Co.

Sadler, J. E. (1966). *J. A. Comenius and the concept of universal education.* London: George Allen and Unwin, Ltd.

Seashore, C. E. (1939). Music before five (*Child welfare pamphlets,* no. 72). Iowa City, IA: University of Iowa.

Stoddard, G. D. (Ed.). (1932). *The measurement of musical development* (*University of Iowa studies in child welfare,* Vol. 7, no. 1). Iowa City, IA: University of Iowa.

Tolbert, M. (Ed.). (1977). *Music for the preschool child.* Columbus, OH: The Ohio State University.

Tolbert, M. (Ed.). (1980). *Music of young children.* Columbus, OH: The Ohio State University.

Vandewalker, N. C. (1971). *The kindergarten in American education* (reprint ed.). New York: Arno Press and the New York Times. (Original publication, 1908: The Macmillan Co.).

Weiser, M. G. (1982). *Group care and education of infants and toddlers.* St. Louis: C. V. Mosby Co.

Williams, H. M. (1933). Musical guidance of young children (*Child welfare pamphlets,* no. 29). Iowa City, IA: University of Iowa.

Chapter 2

Developmental Learning Theories and Early Childhood Music

Education is life: it must presume first-hand contact with real vital situations.
—William Kilpatrick

AN APPROACH TO THEORIES

Teaching music to young children is both an art and a science. The conscious use of skills and creative imagination in planning and presenting musical experiences makes it an art. However, effective instruction is as much dependent upon the teacher's possession of scientific knowledge of children's musical development as upon skills and imagination. Good teaching takes into account the ways in which children acquire musical information, organize and process it, and use it in musical activities. Such knowledge permits age-appropriate planning, sequencing, and presentation. The twentieth century has seen the appearance of much published music research that has addressed these topics, but, as yet, each teacher must separately synthesize and apply such information, for no fully developed theory of music learning has yet been developed.

However, musical intelligence does not develop independently of other intellectual processes. Musical growth is but one facet of intellectual growth. In this chapter, our interest is in the learning theories of prominent psychologists whose work, though not primarily concerned with musical development, has influenced all aspects of early childhood education. A study of these theories and of their implications for music instruction is, therefore, as relevant to music educators as to classroom teachers.

In the following sections, the developmental theories of Jean Piaget, Jerome Bruner, and Maria Montessori will be discussed. While the work of these psychologists is no doubt familiar to most educators, the applications of their theories to music education may not be so well known. Examination and study of their material from the perspective of a music educator, however, may lend new insights about how children develop musically and may help teachers plan more effective programs of music education.

PIAGET'S DEVELOPMENTAL STAGES

The work of the eminent Swiss psychologist Jean Piaget has perhaps contributed more to our understanding of children's intellectual growth than that of any theorist of the present century. Working with children over a period of fifty years, he has helped us understand how children learn to know and how they organize their thinking. Piaget's theory is a stage-developmental one, which asserts that a child's intellectual functioning is qualitatively different at various stages of development. He has helped us understand how a four-year-old child's reasoning is different from that of an eight-year-old, for example. Piaget has asserted that the stages occur in invariant order and that no stage is skipped. Gifted children may develop more quickly than less gifted ones, but their progression from stage to stage is the same.

Piaget designated four major stages from birth to maturity. They are: (1) sensorimotor (birth to approximately two years), (2) pre-operational (two to approximately seven years), (3) concrete operational (seven to approximately eleven years) and (4) formal operational (eleven to approximately fifteen years). Although the stages are commonly assigned a chronological age range, Piaget was interested not so much in studying age-referenced characteristics as in interpreting developmentally sequenced characteristics. Although there is little in his writings about auditory development (the foundation of musical intelligence), his theories have excited interest among music researchers, and a number of studies have attempted to discover the relevance of the theories to musical development (Serafine, 1980). Each stage is described briefly in the following section, and the implications for music instruction during the preschool years are described.

SENSORIMOTOR DEVELOPMENTAL PERIOD

Beginning from the moment of birth, children use their senses (hearing, vision, taste, smell, touch) and motor activities to understand the world.

An infant's eyes will follow a moving object; he will turn his head in response to a noise, such as a toy rattle. If given the rattle, he will probably explore it by putting it in his mouth! In these ways he is acquiring sensory information. During the sensorimotor period, children progress from egocentric beings, unable to conceptualize their own "separateness," to persons aware both of their self-identity and autonomy. They learn by "acting upon their environment." At the culmination of this period, they are capable of:

1. imitating quite complex actions of persons and objects, whether visibly perceptible or remembered
2. truly pretending or engaging in make-believe
3. remembering and thinking about actions, rather than simply performing them
4. inferring a cause, given only its effect, and foreseeing an effect, given its cause
5. recognizing that an object is a thing (or person) apart, subject to its own laws of displacement and action.

(Weiser, 1982, p. 28)

These characteristics seem to suggest certain experiences that the care giver or teacher can provide throughout the first two years to enhance early musical learning. Figure 2.1 presents these suggestions.

---

1. Engage in musical action songs and games, with appropriate actions associated with the words of the song or game.
2. Initiate sound-imitation games. Imitate infants' sounds; they will try to repeat your imitations of their sounds.
3. Develop a repertoire of songs with associated actions, which are sung often to the children; allow them to initiate the action when they can.
4. Plan sound-discovery experiences in which the sources of sounds are investigated and discovered (both environmental and musical sounds).
5. Personalize songs; invent new words to fit a situation.
6. Provide a sensory-rich environment, which includes music-listening, rhythmic movement, and vocal experiences.

Figure 2.1. Sensorimotor developmental stage: suggested music activities.

PREOPERATIONAL DEVELOPMENTAL PERIOD

The period of preoperational thought is characterized by the rapid development of language and perception. Children learn to substitute symbols—mental images and language—for the sensorimotor activities of infancy (Pulaski, 1971, p. 25). The progress in achieving these competencies, however, is gradual, and preoperational children are limited in their ability to "manipulate mentally" experiences or objects. Some characteristics of the younger preoperational child (two to four years) that limit completely logical thinking are the following (adapted from Weiser, 1982; Andress, 1980):

1. difficulty in assuming any point of view from their own and difficulty in understanding how a thing or an object would be (or look) from another point of view (egocentrism).
2. tendency to concentrate on one perceptual feature of an experience, usually the variable that stands out visually (centration).
3. difficulty in integrating a series of events from beginning to end, which often results in their focusing on separate aspects of the event, rather than how they transform from one state to the next (transformation).
4. difficulty in "reversing" their thinking back to the beginning of an event or idea (reversibility).
5. difficulty in perceiving the commonalities among objects or experiences when irrelevant changes are imposed upon the object (conservation).

The applicability of Piaget's theories to musical experiencing is still being debated (Serafine, 1980). Some implications for music instruction have been derived, however, and they are presented in Figure 2.2.

Preoperational children become increasingly able to discriminate, categorize, and classify, and at the end of this period they have overcome many of the perceptual limitations described above. Awareness of the stages, however, helps us match experiences to the child's level of development and avoid a frustrated learner.

CONCRETE OPERATIONAL DEVELOPMENTAL PERIOD

The period of concrete operational thought spans the elementary school years. It sees increasing stabilization and systemizing of mental operations. Concrete operational children are adept at classifying and seriating tasks. They understand relationships between objects and events within the realm of their experiences. Zimmerman (1971) has empha-

1. Ritualized musical games, such as "Mulberry Bush," "Farmer in the Dell," "Looby Loo," "Hokey Pokey," "In and Out the Window," and finger plays, such as "Two Little Blackbirds," are more appropriate for three- and four-year olds than are competitive games (Kamii and DeVries, 1980, p. 207). These games encourage group action and sharing oneself.

2. There are many musical games that can encourage decentering. Hiding games fit in this category. Consider the example below:

"Cuckoo"

Cuck - oo, Where are you?   Answer: Cuck - oo

One child is the mother cuckoo. She hides her eyes while a number of children hide. She searches for the hidden birds. When she sings, "Cuckoo, where are you?" the birds must answer "Cuckoo". The last bird found becomes the new mother (or father) cuckoo. (This game is adapted from Kamii and DeVries, 1980, p. 49.)

"Cuckoo" would not be very interesting for older children, for whom the clues are too obvious. "For younger children, however, these clues do not make the game silly. When three-year-olds hide themselves or an object, they want it found immediately" (Kamii and DeVries, 1980, p. 52). Such games help the child who is looking for the object or person adjust actions to the clues given; furthermore, the child can call for additional clues when more information is needed and can practice singing skills as well.

3. Mentally "reversing" operations is difficult for preoperational children. Often we ask children to play a rhythm pattern over and over to form an "ostinato" accompaniment for a song, e.g., "♩ ♫ ♩♩." Many young children are unable to do this, for it requires reasoning back to where the pattern started each time it is repeated. They may have mentally cut this pattern in two parts: ♩ ♫ and ♩♩.

Figure 2.2 Preoperational stage: applications of Piagetian theories to music instruction.   (continued)

> They can think about the whole, but not when they are thinking about the parts. In order to compare the whole with a part, the child has to do two opposite mental actions at the same time: cut the whole into two parts and put the parts back together into a whole. This, according to Piaget, is precisely what four-year-olds cannot do. (Kamii and De Vries, 1980, p. 233)
>
> Before this type of activity is introduced, children ought to have much experience attending to the "whole"; for example, clapping the rhythm of the words of a song rather than producing a patterned accompaniment.
>
> 4. In music research, conservation has been defined as the ability to maintain mentally some aspect of a musical stimulus in the face of changes. For example, recognizing the invariance of "steady beats" (or clicks) when rhythm patterns are superimposed may be very difficult for preoperational children. Serafine (1980), when testing four-, five-, seven-, and nine-year-olds' ability to determine whether clicks became faster, slower, or stayed the same when rhythm patterns were added, found that children who were conservers in Piaget's space, number, and substance tasks were more likely to recognize the sameness of the clicks through altered presentations (pp. 12-13). Preoperational children need many experiences that provide visual, tactile, and kinesthetic images of fast/slow, same/different to develop the necessary perceptual processes for a task like this.

Figure 2.2. (continued)

sized the need for "hands-on" activities during these years. "Doing music" rather than talking about music should be the guiding principle for music teachers of elementary school children.

FORMAL OPERATIONAL DEVELOPMENTAL PERIOD

The preteen and teenaged child can "think about thought," can consider hypotheses and test them mentally.

BRUNER'S THEORY OF INSTRUCTION

Jerome Bruner, professor of psychology and director of the Center for Cognitive Studies at Harvard University, has made extensive contributions to our understanding of how children learn and how they can be helped to learn. To Bruner, intellectual growth is characterized by progressive ability to free one's responses from the immediate stimulus, to "store information mentally, to put into language what one has done or what one will do, and to deal with several alternatives at once" (Bruner, 1968, pp. 5, 6). Such growth is dependent upon "systematic and contingent interaction between a tutor and a learner" and is "vastly facilitated by the medium of language" (p. 6).

Bruner has proposed three ways in which children process information and turn it into a "model of the world" (1968, p. 10). The first is through action—"enactive representation." The second is through "iconic representation" whereby an image or a graphic may stand for a concept without fully defining it. The third is through words, language, or the symbols of a language—"symbolic representation." Bruner says, "What is abidingly interesting about the nature of intellectual development is that it seems to run the course of these three systems of representation until the human being is able to command all three" (p. 12). Preschool children are at the enactive level; however, four- and five-year-olds may be ready for iconic representations of experiences and objects.

What implications for music teaching may this model contain? The authors of *The Music Book: Early Childhood* (Boardman and Andress, 1981) have described some musical behaviors that young children at the various levels of intellectual functioning may exhibit. These are presented in Table 2.1 (extracted from Boardman and Andress, 1981, p. viii).

In his book *Toward a Theory of Instruction* (1968, pp. 40–42), Bruner outlined several features of effective instruction:

1. It should specify the experiences which predispose the child toward learning. . . . For example, what sorts of relationships with people and things in the preschool environment will tend to make the child willing and able to learn when he enters school?
2. It must specify the ways in which knowledge should be structured so that it can be most readily grasped by the learner.
3. It should specify the most effective sequences for presentation of material.
4. It should specify the nature and pacing of rewards and punishments. . . . Rewards should shift away from extrinsic rewards, such as teacher's praise, toward intrinsic rewards inherent in solving a . . . problem for oneself.

This theory of instruction has several implications for music teaching. The first has to do with motivation. Music should be fun for chil-

Table 2.1. Musical Behaviors: Enactive, Ikonic, Symbolic Levels

Level	Musical Behaviors
Enactive: At this level of development, children will be:	1. Demonstrating understanding through active physical involvement. 2. Performing music by imitating what they hear. 3. Describing what they hear with gestures or dance movements. 4. Organizing their own musical ideas by improvising on instruments and verbally.
Ikonic*: At this level of development, children will be:	1. Growing in ability to retain a mental image and to associate that image with visual images ("ikons") that "look like the music sounds." (Example: ⟋ might represent "sounds getting higher"; I I I I might represent "steady beats.") 2. Performing music by interpreting what they see (the "ikon"). 3. Organizing their own musical ideas and communicating them through ikons of their own invention. 4. Describing what they hear by choosing appropriate ikons, developing their own, or by using their own verbal images.
Symbolic: At this level of development, children will be:	1. Growing in . . . ability to associate their aural concepts of music with traditional symbols (words or notation). 2. Describing music by turning sound into symbols, or by using musical terms. 3. Performing music by turning symbols into sound (reading notation). 4. Organizing their own musical ideas and recording them with traditional notation.

*Two spellings of this word are found in the literature: in Bruner's text, *icon*; in *The Music Book*, *ikon*.

dren. Fun means play, and because children learn through play, music lessons should contain many playful activities.

The second has to do with presentation of material. How can a young child best be led to understand the concept of, for example, "steady beat"? Surely enactive representation should be included. Would icons be appropriate?

What type of terminology should be used?

The third feature addresses the teacher's knowledge of the developmental sequence of musical understanding. Such knowledge enables teachers to plan experiences that lead from a known concept to a new idea, with enough of the known and enough of the new to motivate learning.

Bruner's final recommendation underscores the importance of choosing age-appropriate experiences. Music learning should be success-laden. Most children learn nothing from failure except how to fail. "Intrinsic rewards" are the result of self-satisfying, successful experiences.

Bruner's theories challenge us to take a "new and innocent look" (Bruner, 1966, p. 171) at what music education for young children should be.

MONTESSORI'S PREPARED ENVIRONMENT

Maria Montessori (1870–1952) was an Italian physician and educator who began to formulate her educational theories while working with retarded children in the slums of Rome. Subsequently, she became interested in the education of normal children and in 1907 opened a "Casa dei Bambini" (Children's House), the first of her schools for children from two-and-a-half to seven years of age.

She believed that the best education was one that put the child in control of his or her own learning. According to Montessori, each child possesses an internal pattern for intellectual growth. So that this pattern may be followed, two conditions are necessary: an integral relationship with the environment, including both people and objects, and freedom (Lillard, 1973, p. 30). Several of her principles of "psychic growth" (adapted from pp. 30–49) further interpret this theory:

1. A child is impelled to learn. Learning is a child's work, and if it is self-chosen and self-directed, it is more intense and self-fulfilling. Children work (learn) for the sake of working (learning), rather than to achieve an end result.

2. Self-chosen and self-directed learning develop self-discipline, for the will to complete a task necessitates compliance with the requirements of the task.

3. Intellectual development involves receiving impressions and then mentally organizing them. Teachers' tasks are to help the child develop order from these impressions.

4. Creativity is developed when children are given freedom to select materials to work with, to relate to them without interruption for as long as they like, to discover various solutions and select one, and to share their discoveries with others if they wish to.

5. Children undergo identifiable stages in mental development, progressing from unconscious growth and absorption (birth to three years) to a period when "the knowledge of the unconscious" is brought to a conscious level (three to six years of age).

6. Learning develops from experiences with real life tasks.

To Montessori, "things" were the best teachers. Her approach to education, therefore, was to prepare an environment containing materials that were self-teaching and could be self-administered and self-corrected. She developed hundreds of educational toys, each serving several purposes, but each leading a child from sensory learning to symbolic understanding:

> buttoning frames; lacing frames; series of pegs with corresponding pieces to develop the concept of numbers; weights to be fitted into progressively deeper or wider holes; map puzzles with small knobs, to develop the kind of dexterity required for writing; . . . the famous sandpaper letters which a child could trace with his fingers until the movements of forming each letter became permanently engraved in his memory. (Pines, 1967, pp. 105–106)

Figure 2.3. The Montessori bells.

In games of localizing sound, the participant is blindfolded. Another person moves away from the first person while quietly ringing a small bell. The blindfolded person indicates the direction in which the sounds of the bell moved. When this has become too easy and a new point of interest is needed, the person with the bell may walk quietly to a place in the room and then ring the bell once softly. This may be close to, far from, in front of, next to, behind or directly above the blindfolded person. The latter is the most difficult to distinguish. (Miller, 1981, p. 85)

Figure 2.4. A Montessorian sound discrimination exercise.

The child mixes one set of eight bells (consisting of the pitches C, D, E, F, G, A, B, C) randomly on a table. The task is to find "do" (the lowest pitch of the eight), the "re" and so on through the octave, one note after the other, placing the bells in order in their proper places. (Miller, 1981, p. 149)

Figure 2.5. A Montessorian bell exercise.

With her teaching colleague, Anna Maria Maccheroni, she planned a music curriculum through which both individual and group experiences would lead to an understanding of the structure of music. Her music curriculum is discussed in some detail in Chapter 7; at this point, some of her self-teaching musical materials will be described.

Categorization and ordering of objects and events are important aspects of Montessori's learning program. For the ordering of sounds, she developed various sound cylinders containing materials such as flour, salt, and pebbles, which could be matched or ordered from loud to soft. For pitched sounds, she invented a series of small, mushroom-shaped bells (Figure 2.3). Two series of bells were provided; each series sounded the notes of the chromatic scale. Children matched the like tones, ordered the tones from low to high, and formed scales and melodic patterns. Dummy keyboards and staff boards with discs representing notes helped them translate pitched sounds into note symbols. Wooden rods of relative length gave similar sound-to-symbol experiences with rhythm, with longer rods representing "long" sounds and shorter ones "short" (or faster) sounds.

Activities involving these musical materials could be self-directed, and they required minimal teacher help. Figures 2.4 and 2.5 present two exercises from a Montessori music curriculum. Figure 2.4 deals with the exploration of unpitched sounds and illustrates the teacher's role of helping the children to "order their impressions." Figure 2.5 describes an individualized bell activity with pitched sounds.

AN APPROACH TO GOALS

Perhaps there are still teachers who feel that "enough music" for preschool children happens in the traditional singing circle where one song after another is sung. Even a cursory examination of the child development information contained in the learning theories of Piaget, Bruner, and Montessori shows us the inhibitions to musical development that such a limited program would impose. Rather, effective music programs for young learners should have certain characteristics.

First of all, effective music programs assist the child in acquiring musical information in ways that are compatible with age and stage of development. Moreover, effective music programs lead outward—they proceed in the direction of more learning.

Second, effective music programs provide opportunities for young children to learn many patterns and modes of response to music. Singing, moving, playing instruments, discussing, describing, and representing—all these are ways to help children react and respond to musical sounds. Some are more appropriate for one age group than another. As children become skilled in a response mode (such as physical movement), their understanding of sound is enhanced. Then other response modes should be explored.

Third, effective music programs help children develop attitudes and emotional responses to music. The pervading ambiance of a learning experience is often remembered longer than the information acquired and may influence subsequent learning. Young children's musical experiences should be enveloped in pleasure, for from such pleasure comes the motivation to learn more.

Finally, effective music programs provide many opportunities for children both to explore music individually and to interact with other children and adults. They help them to develop the social skills necessary for participatory musical encounters. For most persons, peak musical experiences occur when engaged in music-making with other people—choirs, bands, orchestras. Preschool children only gradually acquire these skills, to be sure, but experiences that accommodate their social stages of development help them acquire the skills of group music-making.

QUESTIONS FOR DISCUSSION/SUGGESTED ACTIVITIES

1. Of the Piagetian characteristics of the preoperational child listed in this chapter, which seem to you most important to music learning?

2. Choose a number of early childhood action songs or finger-plays. Analyze the accompanying movements to discover whether they provide "enactive" representation of the musical elements of the song—rhythm, melody, form, etc.

3. What aspects of the Montessori music curriculum could account for the fact that it is not carried out in many Montessorian schools?

REFERENCES AND SUGGESTED READINGS

Andress, B. (1980). *Music experiences in early childhood.* New York: Holt, Rinehart & Winston.

Boardman, E., & Andress, B. (1981). *The music book: Teacher's reference book, Grade K.* New York: Holt, Rinehart & Winston.

Bruner, J. (1968). *Toward a theory of instruction.* New York: W. W. Norton & Co., Inc.

Kamii, C., & DeVries, R. (1980). *Group games in early education: Implications of Piaget's theory.* Washington, DC: The National Association for the Education of Young Children.

Lillard, P. P. (1973). *Montessori: a modern approach.* New York: Schocken Books.

Miller, J. K. (1981). The Montessori music curriculum for children up to six years of age. *Dissertations Abstracts International,* 1981, 41, 4638A-4639A. (University Microfilms no. 81 09 598)

Pines, M. (1967). *Revolution in learning: The years from birth to six.* New York: Harper & Row.

Pulaski, M. A. (1971). *Understanding Piaget: An introduction to children's cognitive development.* New York: Harper & Row.

Serafine, M. L. (1980). Piagetian research in music. *Council for Research in Music Education, 62,* 1–21.

Weiser, M. G. (1982). *Group care and education of infants and toddlers.* St. Louis, MO: The C. V. Mosby Co.

Zimmerman, M. P. (1971). *Musical characteristics of children.* Reston, VA: Music Educators National Conference.

Chapter 3

Early Musical Development: The Research Base

Early musical development during the first years of life in the home and in the nursery school, and the musical education in schools built on such foundations, are the Alpha and Omega of our musical culture.

—Michel, 1973, p. 19

The intellectual developmental theories of Montessori, Piaget, and Bruner have had much influence on the way we plan, organize, and carry out educational programs for children. These theories have provided guidelines for teaching by making us aware that children are not miniature adults; consequently, their methods of acquiring, processing, and using information are often different from those of adults or even older children. Today's teachers know that preparing the kind of environment from which information may be derived, employing instructional strategies appropriate to the stage of the learner, and providing opportunities for applying information in a variety of situations are vital considerations to effective early education. Understanding the theories of cognitive development helps in all these tasks.

For the music educator, however, perhaps these theories raise a whole new set of questions, particularly in regard to preschool music education. For example, when does a child begin to acquire *musical* information? What constitutes musical information? What is appropriate musical knowledge for an infant, a toddler, or a prekindergarten child? Furthermore, how is it acquired? And how is it used?

To answer questions of this type, we may look to the body of research concerning the musical development of children. Such research reveals that musical growth does not exist in a vacuum, apart from other child development processes. Rather, it is rooted firmly in the context of physiological, psychological, and socioemotional development.

Music research fleshes out the information base provided by general learning theory. It provides us with answers to specific questions that are relevant to one aspect of cognitive development—musical growth. Although we still do not know a lot about how a child becomes "musical," we have an accumulating body of information that permits us to formulate some principles of musical development.

In this chapter such research will be synthesized, and certain principles will be formulated. Like all principles and theories, the ones presented throughout this chapter are generalizations. Generalizations cannot describe absolute conditions of learning. However, they are applicable to the music learning process of young children as we understand it at the present time. As such they can provide guidelines for nurturing children's musical growth during the preschool years.

The body of research concerning musical development perhaps is not so well known to early childhood educators as that in other areas of child development. Many volumes of research on the growth and development of the young child contain no discussions whatsoever of musical development. On the other hand, textbooks for students and teachers in the field of early education and child care invariably include chapters on the arts and music. Obviously, music is regarded as an important curricular component in early childhood programs.

We might assume from this situation that music developmental research is nonexistent and that music curricular decisions must be based on tradition, experience, and assumption. Such is not the case. Although music research studies are few, when numerical comparisons with studies in other areas of development are made, Simons (1984) identified 169 noteworthy early childhood music studies published between the years 1960 and 1982. Listed by years, the numbers indicate the increasing interest in early childhood music from 1960 on; from 1960 to 1962, only seven were published, while in 1981 twenty-four such studies appeared. Figure 3.1 shows the rather sporadic but progressive increase in the publication of early childhood music studies.

In the broad sense, most research in early childhood music has attempted to provide information about one basic question: "How do people become musical?" More specifically, it has sought to determine which factors significantly influence the development of musical ability, what musical behaviors are typical of certain ages or stages of development, and what instructional strategies may be effective in teaching our youngest learners. All of these are important considerations, for observation and experience tell us that many lifelong attitudes and understandings about music are formed during the preschool years. Teachers' awareness of the existing literature, therefore, can be a useful part of their professional knowledge. Child psychologists tell us that a child learns more during the first half-dozen years than at any other time

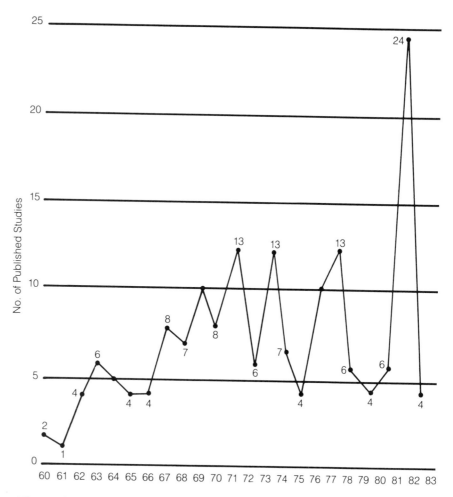

Figure 3.1. Number of early childhood music research reports published 1960 to 1982.

and that deprivation during these years can inhibit intellectual growth. Gordon (1986), a prominent music researcher, calls these years the period of "developmental music aptitude" and states that "music aptitude is a product of both nature and nurture." Moreover, "a child born with a high degree of music aptitude who does not receive appropriate early environmental influences will lose his potential" (pp. 18–19).

We, the teachers and caregivers, can help to provide the "nurture." Research can suggest guidelines. Let us begin our exploration of music developmental research with the "nature-nurture" issue.

HEREDITY AND ENVIRONMENT

There still lingers in the attitudes of many parents and teachers the assumption that "musicians are born, not made." While heredity does set upper levels to achievement in music, as in any human endeavor, such an assumption carelessly made is apt to influence seriously our actions and attitudes when planning music curricula. An elementary school music specialist related an incident, not unusual, that demonstrates such influence. In a parent-teacher conference, a parent was discussing plans for engaging a tutor to help her child overcome some math deficiencies. When the subject of the child's achievement in music came up, the parent laughed and said, "Oh, well, her father can't carry a tune, either!"

While the nature-nurture issue is not as controversial as it once was, it does persist. In comparatively recent times, Seashore (1938) and Schoen (1940) emphasized the influence of heredity on musical talent. Schoen wrote: "All that training can do is develop that which already exists potentially" (p. 161). The problem with this statement is not with its truth, for any education can only develop what potentially exists. Rather, we might ask ourselves, as music educators: "But have we discovered and helped to develop what *does* exist?"

Evidence is mounting that musical environment does have great effect upon a young child's musical development. Not only has it been shown that musical children come from homes where the family listens to, is interested in, and participates in musical activities, thereby providing much informal, incidental music "instruction" for youngsters (Kirkpatrick, 1962; Moore, 1973; Hill, 1968), but that preschool children from musically disadvantaged homes can develop neglected musical skills through planned instruction and intervention (Young, 1974). "What a child brings into the world sets an upper limit to the achievement [in any area] that he can attain. However, it provides no guarantee whatsoever of reaching any level of achievement" (White, 1975, p. 252).

The predominant opinion in recent years is that heredity and environment are interactive influences in musical development (Lundin, 1967; Ginsburg and Opper, 1969; Shuter-Dyson and Gabriel, 1981). Radocy and Boyle's statement summarizes the current view:

> Musical ability is not influenced significantly by hearing, genetics, and physical features, provided minimal perception and physical capabilities are present. Sex and race are irrelevant psychologically, although not necessarily sociologically. . . . Although the major determinants of musical ability are not understood, it probably results from audition, physical coordination, intelligence and experience. (1979, p. 272)

Thus, research provides our first principle of musical development:

> Heredity and environment are interactive; musicality is a product of both nature and nurture, and one does not operate without the other.

BEGINNING BEHAVIORS

We seldom think of an infant as a musically sensitive person. Despite the increasing interest among researchers in studying infants' responses to their environment, the past twenty years have produced only a small number of infant music studies. However, a newborn arrives in this world ready to learn. Weiser (1982) has listed the three essential tools they bring with them: "the five historic senses, the ability to move, and an innate curiosity" (p. 130). Particularly important to music educators is their curiosity about, and attentiveness to, musical sounds (both tonal and rhythmic). Although hearing ability is not fully developed at birth, newborns can hear moderately well, can discriminate sounds, and tend to seek their source. In short, they arrive as attentive music listeners (Figure 3.2).

Spiegler (1967) reported the attention of infants not yet two days old to the fluctuations in rhythmic beats produced by tape recordings of heartbeat sounds and rhythmic clicks. Michel (1973) observed that children as young as two months will stop moving and give fixed attention to the sound of singing or a musical instrument, and that "at five months this attention may last for half an hour" (p. 15). This researcher also described the progress in infants' ability to discriminate individual musical pitches:

> The differentiation of two notes of similar timbre, differing in pitch by barely two octaves, occurs at (about) 3 to 3.5 months; . . . tones of an interval of a fifth (e.g., C up to G) can be distinguished in the 4th or 6th month. In the 6th to 7th month, the child can differentiate between two notes separated by 1.5 steps (e.g., E up to G) or less. (p. 15)

Such information may appear to have little relevance to the day-to-day activities of a teacher or care giver in the crib room of a day-care or early childhood center. On the other hand, it may give new importance to "Pat-a-Cake," "Ride-a-Cock-Horse," and other song-games we play

Figure 3.2. We begin with a listening child. Attentiveness to music is an almost innate characteristic.

with babies, or the lullabies and nursery tunes we sing for them. At the very least, it makes us aware that even the first year of life can be an important beginning in "learning to be musical." Young (1982), in a review of early musical development, cited a study by Stephens and Evans (1973) that presented a theory of "stimulus hunger" arising "in a critical period during the first year and a half of life, when the child is particularly responsive to various kinds of stimulation. The learning which takes place during this time is referred to as exposure learning and is passive" (p. 9).

According to this theory, a child will be especially sensitive to the kind of stimuli that predominated during this critical period. A similar view, placed in a musical context, was expressed by Noy (1968), who described music as an "auditory channel" and suggested that if music were a primary mode of communication between mother and child during infancy, it would continue to be important in the child's emotional exchange with the world.

Children do not remain passive receivers of music for long, however. Between five and eight months of age, they initiate rhythmic-movement responses to music (although they do not "keep time"!) and soon many are trying to join in the singing game (Moog, 1976; Leach, 1983). One study (Kucenski, 1977) suggests that, before the age of one year, children can learn to distinguish individual songs sung often over a period of months and relate the tune to the activities that accompanied their presentations. Does the acquisition of a song "repertoire" begin even before babies learn to sing? Such a tentative conclusion might be drawn. Another study found that when adults purposefully engaged in "pitch-matching" activities with infants, they matched the tones sung to them more often than not (Wendrich, 1981).

Perhaps the "early singers" we encounter in preschools are not those children who have inherited some special gift, but are those who have heard much singing, have been sung to, and have "conceptualized" what pitch-matching and pitch imitation (important skills in learning songs) are all about. A second principle of musical development, therefore, is concerned with the role of the teacher, parent and caregiver.

> Musical development is enhanced when children are provided many opportunities to participate in enjoyable musical experiences with adults.

SKILL DEVELOPMENT

Musicality in all persons is commonly linked to demonstration of certain overt skills: the ability to listen perceptively and describe how the music is structured, to sing tunefully and accurately, to move rhythmically and with "beat competency," and to improvise and create music. Possession of these skills has generally singled out a person as "musical." How these skills are developed, and to what extent they may be developed in the early years, have been topics for many music studies. What information these studies have provided is presented in the following sections.

LISTENING SKILLS

Music is an aural art; it follows that perceptive listening is the essence of musical intelligence. We have found that young children are "natural" music listeners. As teachers, we want to know how to help them to become perceptive music listeners.

What musical information does a typical children's song contain? Many musical elements are present. It has a tune (melody), a rhythmic scheme, and a structure (form). It may have an accompaniment (texture or harmony). It is produced by a human voice or instrument with identifiable tonal characteristics (timbre). It may be loud or soft (dynamics). Piagetian theory has suggested that young children tend to center or fixate on one attribute of an object or event, and that this tendency may interfere with their attention to the whole. Similarly, studies of the listening behaviors of young children show that certain elements of music may be distinguished and understood earlier than others. From such studies has emerged a tentative sequence of music-listening perception.

It appears that response to and discrimination of dynamics and timbre develop early. Understanding of pitch (melody) and rhythm develops later, and that of harmony appears to develop last (Greenberg, 1976; Moog, 1976; Zimmerman, 1978). Information from these studies also reveals some surprisingly sophisticated musical skills among young children. For example, the studies of young children's attentiveness to timbre are particularly interesting. At least two researchers have reported success in teaching four- and five-year-olds to identify traditional orchestral instruments and categories of instruments (for example, wind, electronic, string, or percussion) by sound (Fullard, 1967; Loucks, 1974). Moreover, children's preference for one type of sound ("timbral preference") does not appear to interfere with their ability to classify musical pitches (Scott, 1977). In many music series texts, studies of instrument identification are presented at the third- and fourth-grade levels, which seems very late in light of these studies.

Through studying the taped performances of songs for accuracy of melodic contour (shape), interval, and rhythmic reproduction and by equating accuracy of performance with evidence of perception, researchers have found that three- to five-year-old children possess concepts of melodic shape (contour), rhythm, and some aspects of interval ("steps and skips" in a melody) (Ramsey, 1983; Davidson, 1985), even though they lack the vocabulary to verbalize their understandings. The terms "up," "loud," and "high" and their opposites are traditionally confused. Kindergarten and first grade children, however, are often able to show their understanding by demonstration on small keyboard instruments (Van Zee, 1976) or bells (Hair, 1977), even though they may not be able to link terminology with their perceptions.

In the area of listening skill development, the issue of musical terminology is a particularly troublesome one. Studies that have attempted to discover ways of helping children link the "labels" of common music terminology to musical sounds are described in Chapter 5.

Although Moog (1976) flatly stated that the young child is "deaf to harmony" until at least age six, Hair (1973) found that 83 percent of the first grade children she studied were able to identify pairs of chords as "same" or "different."

The discovery of a stage-development pattern in the comprehension of musical elements leads to a third principle of development:

> Musical perception develops in a sequential manner, dependent upon the age and experiences of the learner.

SINGING

Children who can "carry a tune" at an early age have always delighted their parents and teachers, and this skill has often been regarded as evidence of a special musical talent. Yet, according to Michel (1973), it is very much dependent upon informal instruction:

> "first attempts at . . . singing/speaking, and the pace of . . . further development depend vitally on the extent to which people immediately concerned with the child occupy themselves with him, sing and speak to him" (p. 16).

As with the development of listening skills, learning to sing follows sequential stages, somewhat dependent upon age. Table 3.1 shows this sequence. We should remember that the "age" column designates the average age for emergence of the characteristics described. Averages tell us what we may expect of 50 percent of the children; many young singers who are not at all abnormal may be behind or ahead of these norms. The information in Table 3.1 was taken from a study of the singing development of nine firstborn, middleclass children over a period of five years. The characteristics described here have been confirmed in other studies.

In the singing of songs for children, the pitch range chosen by teachers is important. It does little good to teach a song in a key too high or too low for a preschooler to reproduce. Finding the most comfortable singing range of young children has been the thrust of much research. Table 3.2 synthesizes the existing information about vocal ranges of children from two to six years of age. Although differences, particularly in the lowest and highest pitches, have been found relative to age and individual differences, a range common to all age groups is from middle C or D up to G or A five tones above. It is likely that songs pitched so that they fit in this range can be reproduced by most preschool children.

Table 3.1. Age-Referenced Singing Characteristics

Age	Characteristics
12–18 months	Vocal play, experimentation with sound.
19 months	Melodic and rhythmic patterns appearing in vocalizations.
19–24 months	Free experimentation with songs; short spontaneous songs, often consisting of a small melodic interval with a flexible rhythm pattern.
2 years	Use of melodic patterns from learned songs in spontaneous singing. Ability to sing parts of songs.
2½–3 years	Imitation of songs, though rarely with total accuracy.
4 years	Sequence followed in learning songs: words, rhythm, phrases, melodic "contour."
5–5½ years	Sense of "key" stabilized; can sing most songs when learned fairly accurately.

Adapted from Davidson, McKernon, and Gardner, 1981.

Table 3.2. Major Research Findings Related to Vocal Range

Researchers	Range Findings	Range Spans
Williams (1932)	Natural range of the young child's voice (4 and 5 years) lies between c′ and c″.	c′-------------c″
Hattwick (1933)	Vocal range of preschool children (4½ to 6 years) extends from b to g′.	b--------g′
Jersild and Bienstock (1934)	Range of tones increases progressively from 2 years through 5 years.	d′ 2 yrs. a′ c′---- 3 yrs. ----a′ b------ 4 yrs. ----c″ a------ 5 yrs. ----d″
Updegraff, Heiliger, and Learned (1937)	Half of the 3-year-old subjects had a range from g to c″; half of the 5-year-olds, from a to c″.	g----- 3 yrs. ----c″ a------ 5 yrs. ----c″

Table 3.2. (continued)

Researchers	Range Findings	Range Spans
Drexler (1938)	Majority of 3- to 6-year-olds sang within the range from c′ to d#″.	c′----------------d#″
Spencer (1958)	The ability to match pitch within the range c′ to a′ is independent of chronological age.	c′---------a′
Kirkpatrick (1962)	Most frequently used range was from g to b$^{b′}$ with 78 percent of the sung tones ranging between b and g#′.	g---------------b$^{b′}$
Alford (1966)	A total vocal range from a^{b} to d″ was used by preschool subjects.	a^{b}-----------------d″
Smith (1968)	Four developmental stages occur in range expansion with 3-year-olds exhibiting more of a limited range than older children.	c#′--------a′ older b-------------b′
Young (1971)	Four stages in development of vocal range; a to f#′ is the range most common to all stages.	a--------f#′
Klanderman (1979)	Young children's (3 to 5 years) vocal range extends from c′ to a′.	c′---------a′

Ramsey (1981, p. 158).

RHYTHM AND MOVEMENT

Movement is a natural response to music. Children as young as six months show movement responses to music and often pause to listen attentively before starting to move (Moog, 1976). Moog provided the following age-related sequence of rhythmic responses to music:

1. six months: whole body movements not synchronized with the music but, rather, a generalized response.
2. two years: arm and leg movements used; temporary synchronization with the beat from about 10 percent of this age group: a chance occurrence.
3. three to five years: variety of movements declined; a period of practicing and exploring known movements.
4. four to six years: as physical coordination improved, increasing ability to keep time occurred.
5. six years: hand-clapping, rarely seen before the sixth year, was the most common rhythmic response.

Young children's rhythms are likely to be quite fast. In one study, the rhythmic "beats" produced by preschool children in their play activities were reported to average 170 beats per minute (Simons, 1964).

The ability to keep time, or attain "beat competency," depends on physical maturation, which brings better coordination, as well as on rhythmic perception. The years up to age six should be regarded as developmental in the most literal sense: Failure to "keep time" should not be equated with poor perception during these formative years.

This interrelationship between chronological age and the development of singing and rhythmic skills leads to a fourth principle:

> The development of singing and rhythmic skills is dependent upon physical maturation and coordination; these skills increase with age and experience.

AFFECTIVE DEVELOPMENT

Historically, music was accorded an identifiable place in early childhood education because of its perceived power to influence feelings and emotions. Although it also was perceived as influential in the development of moral character, citizenship, and good behavior—attributes that elude scientific investigation—music has always belonged to the affective domain of human behavior. And, because affect cannot be separated from learning, researchers have regarded the values and preferences of children toward music as important educational considerations. Infants have shown affective reactions to music (Tims, 1979; Michel, 1973; Moog, 1976) and even preferences (Moog reported six-month-old children's preference for "sensuously beautiful music"). However, music educators want to present not only the types of music that children like and casually respond to, but also that which may extend the musical horizons of their students. All young children seem to be attracted to strongly rhythmic music, such as current rock tunes; can they be led to value symphonic music also?

Although studies regarding musical preferences are few in number, there is some evidence that, among four- to six-year-old children, preferences are already formed and not easily changed (Schuckert and McDonald, 1968). However, nursery school children can be encouraged to listen to symphonic music (rather than rock or "white noise") by listening with an adult who shows approval (Greer, Dorow, and Hanser, 1973). The importance of the physical presence of adults interacting with children and music was also found in a study of first grade children who were taught by two instructional modes: televised lessons and lessons taught by a teacher. The televised lessons did not change the children's preferences: the lessons taught by a teacher brought about significant differences (Brown, 1978).

In our fifth principle of musical development, the role of the teacher or care giver is again emphasized:

> The values that young children assign to music are influenced by interactive experiences among teachers, children, and music.

CREATIVITY

Creativity has been described as "a quality possessed in some measure by all individuals. [It] is expressed when an individual relates things in his experience which were previously unrelated, and . . . produces something that is new and satisfying to him" (Cox, 1966, p. 13). When we think of creating music, often the ability to compose it comes to mind. Creative musical behaviors manifest themselves long before children can read or write music, however. If judged by the definition provided above, the earliest babbling songs of children are "musical creations," and the preschool years are marked by creative music-making activities.

The most extensive research about the development of creative musical behaviors is found in the reports of the Pillsbury Foundation School, described in Chapter 1. The main function of the school's program was to identify and describe every indication of children's natural musical inventiveness. To encourage musical activity, the students, aged three to six years, had access to a variety of good-quality instruments, including some rather unusual Oriental ones. The children were permitted to play the instruments whenever and wherever they wished. They also initiated many spontaneous singing and dancing activities. Certain characteristics of creative behavior were reported:

1. Creativity often occurs through the excitement generated by discovering, testing, and comparing instrumental sounds.
2. Creative singing often takes the form of chants, which occur extensively in spontaneous play activities.
3. The key to developing innate musicality is improvisation. (Moorhead and Pond, 1978)

More than thirty years after the Pillsbury School closed, Shelley (1981), seeking to confirm the observations of the Pillsbury School's directors and to study the musical creations of three- to five-year-old children, found that today's children exhibit the same creative musical behaviors as those at the Pillsbury School. She listed several factors that, she believed, encourage creativity:

1. Musical instruments that produce beautiful sounds.
2. Supportive physical and emotional environment.
3. Freedom of choice within structural limits.
4. Teachers, who, at various times, are participators, observers, or fellow musicians!

The development of creativity is the most elusive of all the musical processes. Study of the character of children's improvisatory creations on instruments has provided some information about the nature of the process. Flohr's study (1984) of improvisations, created on xylophones by two- to five-year-old children (Figure 3.3), identified some age-related characteristics. These are presented in Table 3.3. The study shows that children as young as three years start to impose a structure on their improvisations by repeating selected patterns. In addition, they are able, at quite a young age, to fit together quite diverse rhythm patterns. Moorhead and Pond, similarly, had observed among the Pillsbury School students an "innate" sense of the function of form (repetition and contrast); Flohr's study seems to reinforce this observation.

Figure 3.3. Flohr studied improvisations created on xylophones by two- to five-year-old children.

Table 3.3. Flohr's Summary of Children's Exploratory Improvisations

	Two-Year-Olds	Three-Year-Olds	Four-Year-Olds	Five-Year-Olds
Rhythm	moderate, even, inaccurate— motor energy	moderate, even, some triple, matched bordun rhythm pattern	moderate, even, fairly accurate, some triple	moderate, even, some triple, matched bordun rhythm, accurate steady beat
Form	not evident	some repetition	some repetition and ostinato	rhythmic repetition common, also melodic repetition

Definitions:

Bordun: a recurring "drone" often produced by playing the first and fifth tones of a scale (e.g., C and G) together. Often borduns are used as accompaniments to songs.

Triple: the organization of beats into patterns of threes: e.g., the first beat of the three is performed more strongly than the other beats. Example: "BEAT, beat, beat."

Repetition: a melodic or rhythmic pattern is repeated; such repetition tends to give structure to a series of patterns and suggests a "composition" rather than random sounds.

Ostinato: a recurring melodic or rhythmic pattern that is often used to accompany songs.

Torrance (Gowan, Demos, and Torrance, 1967) stated that "the weight of present evidence indicates that, fundamentally, man *prefers* to learn in creative ways—by exploring, manipulating, questioning, experimenting, . . . testing, and modifying ideas" (p. 57). In creative activities, children show us their uniqueness and their individuality. Using the tools that they have acquired through informal exploration and planned encounters with musical ideas, they show us not so much how they are alike, but how they are different. Insights about the uniqueness of each child are cherished by sensitive teachers. Our final principle of musical development is an important reminder:

In musical development, as in all growth processes, each child is unique, and each child's musical growth pattern must be understood and respected.

QUESTIONS FOR DISCUSSION/SUGGESTED ACTIVITIES

1. Think of one of your acquaintances who is a "musical" person. Did this person grow up in a "musical" home? What about an "unmusical" friend?
2. Ask a young child to sing his or her favorite song for you. Have a set of song bells available to determine the note(s) the child chooses for starting and singing the song. Do they fit in the "comfortable" limited range identified in this chapter?
3. Have your musical preferences changed since you were in elementary school? If they have, to what influences do you credit the changes?
4. Considering the research on creative behavior reviewed in this chapter, formulate a list of suggestions for experiences, equipment, and teaching strategies that might encourage musical creative behavior among preschool children.

REFERENCES AND SUGGESTED READINGS

Alford, D. L. (1966). Emergence and development of music responses in preschool twins and singletons: A comparative study. (Doctoral dissertation, Florida State University, 1966.) *Dissertation Abstracts, 27,* 220-A.

Brown, A. (1978). Effects of televised instruction on student music selection, music skills, and attitudes. *Journal of Research in Music Education, 26* (4), 445–455.

Cox, E. M. (1966). A functional approach to creative experiences in music in the elementary school (Doctoral dissertation, Columbia University, 1966). *Dissertation Abstracts International, 27,* 4277A.

Davidson, L. (1985). Preschool children's tonal knowledge: Antecedents of scale. In J. Boswell (Ed.), *The young child and music: Contemporary principles in child development and music education: Proceedings of the Music in Early Childhood Conference.* Reston, VA: Music Educators National Conference.

Davidson, L., McKernon, P., and Gardner, H. (1981). The acquisition of song: A developmental approach. *Documentary Report of the Ann Arbor Symposium: National Symposium on the Applications of Psychology to the Teaching and Learning of Music.* Reston, VA: Music Educators National Conference.

Drexler, E. N. (1938). A study of the development of the ability to carry a melody at the preschool level. *Child Development, 9,* 319–332.

Flohr, J. W. (1984). *Young children's improvisations.* Research paper presented at Music Educators National Conference, Chicago, IL.

Fullard, W. G., Jr. (1967). Operant training of aural musical discriminations with preschool children. *Journal of Research in Music Education, 15* (3), 201–209.

Gardner, H.; Davidson, L.; and McKernon, P. (1979). The acquisition of song: A developmental approach (*National symposium on the applications of psychology to the teaching and learning of music*). Reston, VA: Music Educators National Conference.

Ginsberg, H., & Opper, S. (1969). *Piaget's theory of intellectual development.* Englewood Cliffs, NJ: Prentice-Hall, Inc.

Gordon, E. (1986). A factor analysis of the Music Aptitude Profile, the Primary Measures of Music Audiation, and the Intermediate Measures of Music Audiation. *Council for Research in Music Education, 87,* 17–25.

Gowan, J. C.; Demos, G. D.; & Torrance, E. P. (Eds.). (1967). *Creativity: Its educational implications.* New York: John Wiley & Sons, Inc.

Greenberg, M. (1979). *Your children need music.* Englewood Cliffs, NJ: Prentice-Hall, Inc.

Greer, R. D.; Dorow, L.; & Hanser, S. (1973). Music discrimination training and the music selection behavior of nursery and primary level children. *Council for Research in Music Education, 35,* 30–43.

Hair, H. I. (1973). The effect of training on the harmonic discrimination of first-grade children. *Journal of Research in Music Education, 21* (1), 85–90.

Hair, H. I. (1977). Discrimination of tonal direction on verbal and nonverbal tasks by first-grade children. *Journal of Research in Music Education, 25* (3), 197–210.

Hattwick, M. S. (1935). A genetic study of differential pitch sensitivity. In *The Measurement of Musical Development II,* G. B. Stoddard, ed. (University of Iowa Studies in Child Welfare, Vol. 11, no. 2). Iowa City, IA: University of Iowa.

Hill, J. D. (1968). A study of the musical achievement of culturally deprived children and culturally advantaged children at the elementary school level (Doctoral dissertation, University of Kansas, 1968). *Dissertation Abstracts International, 29,* 2738A.

Jersild, A. T. and Bienstock, S. F. (1935). *Development of rhythm in young children.* New York: Columbia University Press.

Kirkpatrick, W., Jr. (1962). Relationships between the singing ability of prekindergarten children and their home environments (Doctoral dissertation, University of Southern California, 1962). *Dissertation Abstracts International, 23,* 886A.

Klanderman, N. Z. (1979). The development of auditory discrimination and performance of pitch, rhythm, and melody in preschool children. (Doctoral dissertation, Northwestern University, 1979). *Dissertation Abstracts International, 40,* 3177-A.

Kucenski, D. (1977). Implication and empirical study of a sequential musical sensory learning program on the infant learner (Doctoral dissertation, Northwestern University, 1977). *Dissertation Abstracts International, 38,* 4646A.

Leach, P. (1983). *Your baby and child from birth to age five.* New York: Alfred A. Knopf.

Loucks, D. G. (1974). The development of an instrument to measure instrumental timbre concepts of four-year-old and five-year-old children: A feasibility study (Doctoral dissertation, The Ohio State University, 1974). *Dissertation Abstracts International, 35,* 5446A.

Lundin, R. (1967). *An objective psychology of music* (2nd ed.). New York: Ronald Press.

McDonald, D. T. (1979). *Music in our lives: The early years.* Washington, DC: National Association for the Education of Young Children.

Michel, P. (1973). The optimum development of musical abilities in the first years of life. *Psychology of Music, 1*(2), 14–20.

Moog, H. (1976). The development of musical experience in children of preschool age. *Psychology of Music, 4*(2), 38–45.

Moore, D. L. (1973). A study of pitch and rhythm responses of five-year-old children in relation to their early music training (Doctoral dissertation, Florida State University, 1973). *Dissertation Abstracts International, 34,* 6689A–6690A.

Moorhead, G. E., & Pond, D. (1978). *Music of young children.* Santa Barbara, CA: Pillsbury Foundation for Advancement of Music Education.

Noy, P. (1968). The development of music ability. *The psychoanalytic study of the child, 23,* 332–347.

Radocy, R., & Boyle, D. (1979). *Psychological foundations of musical behavior.* Springfield, IL: Thomas Publishing Co.

Ramsey, J. H. (1981). The effects of age, singing ability and instrumental experiences on the melodic perception of preschool children (Doctoral dissertation, University of Iowa, 1981). *Dissertation Abstracts International, 42,* 3053A.

Ramsey, J. H. (1983). The effects of age, singing ability and instrumental experiences on preschool children's melodic perception. *Journal of Research in Music Education, 31* (2), 133–145.

Schoen, M. (1940). *The psychology of music.* New York: Ronald Press.

Schuckert, R. F., & McDonald, R. L. (1968). An attempt to modify the musical preferences of preschool children. *Journal of Research in Music Education, 16* (1), 39–44.

Scott, C. R. (1977). Pitch concept formation in preschool children (Doctoral dissertation, University of Washington, 1977). *Dissertation Abstracts International, 38,* 3133A.

Seashore, C. (1938). *Psychology of music.* New York: McGraw-Hill, Inc.

Shelley, S. (1981). Investigating the musical capabilities of young children. *Council for Research in Music Education, 68,* 26–34.

Shuter-Dyson, R., & Gabriel, C. (1981). *Psychology of musical abilities* (2nd ed.). London: Methuen.

Simons, G. M. (1964). Comparisons in incipient music responses among very young twins and singletons. *Journal of Research in Music Education, 12* (3), 212–226.

Simons, G. M. (1984). Modes and areas of research in early childhood music. *Canadian Music Educator, 26* (1), 31–36.

Smith, R. B. (1963). The effect of group vocal training on the singing ability of nursery school children. *Journal of Research in Music Education, 11* (2), 137–141.

Spencer, E. M. (1958). An investigation of the maturation of various factors of auditory perception in pre-school children. (Doctoral dissertation, Northwestern University, 1958). *Dissertation Abstracts International, 19,* 2690.

Spiegler, D. (1967). Factors involved in the development of prenatal rhythmic sensitivity (Doctoral dissertation, West Virginia University, 1967). *Dissertation Abstracts International, 28,* 3886B.

Stephens, J., & Evans, E. (1973). *Development and classroom learning.* New York: Holt, Rinehart & Winston.

Tims, F. C. (1979). Contrasting music conditions, visual attending behavior, and state in eight-week-old infants (Doctoral dissertation, University of Kansas, 1978). *Dissertation Abstracts International, 39,* 4111A–4112A.

Updegraff, R.; Heiliger, L.; and Learned, J. (1937). The effect of training upon the singing ability and musical interest of three-, four-, and five-year-old children. *Studies in Preschool Education I,* G. B. Stoddard, ed. (University of Iowa Studies in Child Welfare, Vol. 14). Iowa City, IA: University of Iowa.

Van Zee, N. (1976). Responses of kindergarten children to musical stimuli and terminology. *Journal of Research in Music Education, 24* (1), 14–21.

Weiser, M. G. (1982). *Group care and education of infants and toddlers.* St. Louis: C. V. Mosby Co.

Wendrich, K. A. (1981). Pitch imitation in infancy and early childhood: Observations and implications (Doctoral dissertation, University of Connecticut, 1981). *Dissertation Abstracts International, 41,* 5019A.

Williams, H. M. (1932). Studies of vocal control of pitch of preschool children. *The Measurement of Musical Development,* G. B. Stoddard, ed. (University of Iowa Studies in Child Welfare, Vol. 7, no. 1). Iowa City, IA: University of Iowa.

Young, L. (1982). An investigation of young children's music concept development using non-verbal and manipulative techniques (Doctoral dissertation, The Ohio State University, 1982). *Dissertation Abstracts International, 43,* 1345A.

Young, W. T. (1971). *An investigation of the singing abilities of kindergarten and first grade children in east Texas.* Bethesda, MD: ERIC Document Reproduction Services, ED069, 431.

Young, W. T. (1974). Musical development in preschool disadvantaged children. *Journal of Research in Music Education, 22*(3), 155–169.

Zimmerman, M. P. (1971). *Musical characteristics of children.* Reston, VA: Music Educators National Conference.

Chapter 4

Planning the Environment

Theory that does not someway affect life has no value.

—*Terman*

THE LEARNING ENVIRONMENT

The discussion in the preceding chapters has been somewhat theoretical—how this or that theory or principle of development affects our planning a music program for young children. The content of this chapter attempts to bridge some of the gaps between theory and practice. Theoretical information may have little or no effect on how we teach our students if it is not "practical"—that is, applicable in the actual planning of a music program.

Planning and organizing the learning environment for a preschool or kindergarten is perhaps the most demanding and challenging of the many tasks of an early childhood educator. It involves selecting and formulating instructional goals, arranging the physical setting, preparing equipment and materials, planning a flexible schedule, and generally setting the stage for learning. All of these tasks involve decisions that are critical to the success or failure of our programs. In this chapter, we will consider the various aspects of a music learning environment and their effect on the music learning of our preschool and kindergarten students. For no other age group are growth and development so intertwined with the physical and social environment of the classroom and with the interactions between adults and children.

BEGINNING CONSIDERATIONS

Prior to any planning of a program, it is well to consider the music education philosophy held by the administrators, teachers, and staff of a school. Why should music experiences be planned as part of the curriculum? Of what value are they to the students? If a philosophy can be defined as a set of beliefs about what we do or do not value, then the music education philosophy of a school may well determine whom we teach, what we teach, and how we teach.

The question of whom we teach becomes apparent when we consider the age of our students. Many young children are not ready for group instruction. Providing a music program for the youngest learners necessitates planning individual experiences as well as group encounters. Some of these experiences may occur spontaneously; some may be prearranged. Some will occur in the individual music centers, which have been prepared with materials and equipment. But they need to be planned. Whether or not all the children will receive music instruction is a reflection of the music education philosophy of a school.

The philosophy held by the school is also reflected in the kind of music that is taught and how it is taught. If music experiences are deemed important, then the music chosen for singing and listening will be of good quality and will represent the best of musical literature for children. It will be taught in ways that will help the children derive understanding and find pleasure in learning. Instructional techniques appropriate for the ages of the children will be employed.

Discussion of the place of music in young children's school experiences and formulation of a music education philosophy may be two of the more important first steps in planning an environment that promotes musical learning. A school that values music and provides musical experiences for all of its children is expressing its philosophy to its students and their parents.

SETTING PROGRAM GOALS

Emanating from a philosophy and based on principles of growth and development, program goals for music are generally determined and formulated in discussions among teachers, administrators, curriculum directors, and parents. Program goals give direction and focus to an ongoing course of instruction. They remind us of what we are working for over the long range. The history of early childhood music education has witnessed a variety of approaches to program goals. In the early nineteenth century, instruction was focused on development of singing and music-reading skills. This relatively narrow focus was replaced in the twentieth century by broader musical goals, in part because of the accumulating body of research and inquiry about children's musical development.

A synthesis of research was presented in Chapter 3. The research was categorized under the headings of musical skills—listening, singing, and rhythmic movement—and affective development—creativity and preferences. These categories may be used to describe long-range program goals for an early childhood music curriculum. They are listed below:

1. **Learning to listen.** In our sound-laden environment, young children often learn how not to, rather than how to, listen to music or any other sound. However, research has shown that, insofar as musical sounds are concerned, we begin with a listening child. Attentiveness to music is an almost innate characteristic. The nurturing of this skill is an important program goal.

2. **Learning to sing tunefully.** Perhaps the ability to "carry a tune" at an early age identifies, to most of us, a "musical child." The fact that singing, like other vocal skills, is a learned behavior makes teachers' understanding of its development, and ways to enhance that development, especially important.

3. **Learning to move expressively and rhythmically.** The research reported in Chapter 3 reveals that, for most young children, listening to music means moving to music. The development of rhythmic competency not only enables children to enjoy music, but also helps them to understand it more fully.

4. **Learning to play classroom instruments.** One of children's deepest and first interests in music is in timbre—the tonal characteristics of instruments. Learning about instruments gives experience with tone, melody, rhythm, and form. It has been shown to help in the development of singing skills as well.

Many of the listening studies reviewed in Chapter 3 were concerned with children's development of musical concepts. From the concepts that children form comes their understanding about how the elements of music interact to form an expressive whole. As a result of these understandings, preferences are formed, and creative behaviors emerge. Therefore, the final three program goals that we present embrace understanding and affect:

5. Developing age-appropriate musical concepts.
6. **Creating self-satisfying music.** The ability to create music evolves in no small part from the understandings that children gain from singing, movement, and instrumental instruction.
7. Respecting and valuing music as a part of everyday life.

These program goals represent the skills, understandings, and attitudes about music that we hope our young students will achieve as a result of having spent their preschool years with us and music. Formulating goals is a task that should precede all other aspects of curricular planning. As one teacher commented, "You can't just go into a classroom and try to pull things out of the sky. You do have to have an idea of what you're going to teach and its significance to the child" (Newman, 1984, p. 175). Lack of goals leads to inefficiency: "Without goals a program goes willy-nilly like a rudderless boat. It may contain all kinds of wonderful opportunities for learning, but without preconceived direction, the time and energy expended by both the adults and children will have less than optimal results" (Weiser, 1982, p. 154).

General goals, such as have been stated in the preceding paragraphs, may be made more specific by designating the types of experiences appropriate for a specific age group. This approach has been used in a publication of the Music Educators National Conference, *The School Music Program: Description and Standards* (Music Educators National Conference, 1986). This book was prepared "to serve as a resource for school administrators, music educators, and interested parents and citizens who are concerned about quality music programs" (p. 9). It describes the types of music experiences appropriate for the years from infancy through high school. Of special interest to early childhood educators is the description of a quality music program for children from infancy through kindergarten.

A reprint of the early childhood music program in the above publication is presented in Figure 4.1. The types of experiences are stated in the headings: Performing/Reading, Creating, Listening/Describing, and Valuing. The experiences are categorized according to a specific age group. The authors state that such experiences should be an integral part of the whole program, should occur every day, and should constitute at least 7 percent of the contact time with the children (p. 20).

These categories and experiences served as the organizational format for the songs and activities given in Chapter 9 of this text.

Figure 4.1. A program in early childhood music.

MUSIC EXPERIENCES FOR INFANTS

Infants and very young children experience music by hearing and feeling it. Children should experience music daily while receiving caring physical contact. Adults can encourage the musical development of infants by:

- singing and chanting to them;
- imitating the sounds infants make;
- exposing them to a wide variety of vocal, body, instrumental, and environmental sounds;
- providing exposure to selected recorded music;
- rocking, patting, touching, and moving with the children to the beat, rhythm patterns, and melodic direction of music heard; and
- providing safe toys that make musical sounds that the children can control.

Figure 4.1. (continued)

MUSIC EXPERIENCES FOR TWO- AND THREE-YEAR-OLD CHILDREN

Two- and three-year-old children need an environment that includes a variety of sound sources, selected recorded music, and opportunities for free improvised singing and the building of a repertoire of songs. An exploratory approach, using a wide range of appropriate materials, provides a rich base from which conceptual understanding may evolve in later years. A variety of individual musical experiences is important for children of this age, with little emphasis on musical activities that require children to perform together as a unit.

AGES 2–3. BY FOUR YEARS OF AGE, CHILDREN ARE ABLE TO:

Performing/Reading

Sing in a freely improvised style as they play

Sing folk and composed songs, although not always on pitch or in time with others

Play simple rhythm instruments freely and explore sounds of rhythm instruments and environmental sources

Walk, run, jump, gallop, clap, and "freeze" while an adult responds to the child's movements with sound on a percussion instrument

Recognize printed music and label it as music

Creating

Explore the expressive possibilities of their own voices

Improvise songs as they play

Create sounds on instruments and from other sound sources in their environment

Listening/Describing

Listen attentively to a selected repertoire of music

Move spontaneously to music of many types

Recognize the difference between singing and speaking

Demonstrate awareness of sound and silence through movement and "freezing"

Improvise movements that indicate awareness of beat, tempo, and pitch

Valuing

By four years of age, children:
Enjoy listening to music and other sounds in their environment
Like being sung to
Enjoy singing as they play
Enjoy making sounds with environmental, body, and instrumental sound sources

MUSIC EXPERIENCES FOR FOUR- AND FIVE-YEAR-OLD CHILDREN

Four- and five-year-old children are becoming socially conscious. Appropriate music-making experiences include group activities such as singing and playing song games and playing classroom instruments. Many opportunities for individual exploration of voice, body, nature, and instrument

(continued)

Figure 4.1. (continued)

sounds should also be included. Movement is the most effective means for children of this age to describe their musical experiences. They enjoy playing with ideas, movements, language, and sounds. Music activities that allow opportunities for free exploration provide the most positive foundation for creative musical growth later.

AGES 4-5. BY THE COMPLETION OF KINDERGARTEN CHILDREN ARE ABLE TO:

Performing/Reading

Utilize the singing voice, as distinct from the speaking voice

Match pitches and sing in tune within their own ranges most of the time

Show an awareness of beat, tempo (e.g., fast-slow), dynamics (e.g., loud-soft), pitch (e.g., high-low), and similar and different phrases through movement and through playing classroom instruments

Enjoy singing nonsense songs, folk songs, and song games

Utilize pictures, geometric shapes, and other symbols to represent pitch, durational patterns, and simple forms

Creating

Explore sound patterns on classroom instruments

Improvise songs spontaneously during many classroom and playtime activities

Complete "answers" to unfinished melodic phrases by singing or playing instruments

Express ideas or moods using instruments and environmental or body sounds

Listening/Describing

Give attention to short musical selections

Listen attentively to an expanded repertoire of music

Respond to musical elements (e.g., pitch, duration, loudness) and musical styles (e.g., march, lullaby) through movement or through playing classroom instruments

Describe with movement or language similarities and differences in music such as loud-soft, fast-slow, up-down-same, smooth-jumpy, short-long, and similar-contrasting

Classify classroom instruments and some traditional instruments by shape, size, pitch, and tone quality

Use a simple vocabulary of music terms to describe sounds

Valuing

By the completion of kindergarten, children:
Demonstrate an awareness of music as a part of everyday life
Enjoy singing, moving to music, and playing instruments alone and with others
Respect music and musicians

INSTRUCTIONAL OBJECTIVES

While the program described in Figure 4.1 offers many suggestions about the types of experiences that should be provided in a preschool music program, it is necessary to translate these experiences into specific activities with defined purposes if they are to have more than limited use for teachers. This task involves formulating instructional objectives. Instructional objectives tell us what is to be learned—the musical content—and what behaviors—musical skills—will be involved. Musical content refers to the "elements" of music, while musical behaviors describe what the learner will be able to do (sing, move, play instruments, describe) as a result of instruction. Instructional objectives replace the vague statements, such as "learn to enjoy music," which have sometimes served as lesson objectives.

Instructional objectives are especially useful when (1) they are specific, (2) they describe a behavior that is observable, and (3) they are expressed from the learner's point of view. That is, they are stated in terms of what the child will be able to do or describe as a result of instruction. If formulated in this way, they may also serve as criteria for the teacher to evaluate whether or not learning has taken place.

Teachers generally do not ask *how* to write instructional objectives, but, rather, *why*. There are many reasons. Activities based on defined objectives have focus. They provide a sort of road map leading to a program goal. They enable teachers to plan a "course" of instruction rather than a meandering journey. They help us relate one day's lesson to prior and subsequent lessons. They keep us "on track." In addition, interrelated, sequenced lessons enable even very young children to "begin to perceive the leaf as being part of the tree that is part of the forest" (Newman, 1984, p. 178).

Well-designed instructional objectives are the heart of most successful music lessons. Figures 4.2, 4.4, and 4.5 present examples of music activities based on instructional objectives for infants, three-year-olds, and five-year-olds. They all deal with rhythmic learning and are related to the program goal "learning to move rhythmically." The "type of experience" statement is taken from *The School Music Program: Description and Standards.* The instructional objective describes a specific activity, appropriate for the age of the learner.

All of these minilessons involved recognition of rhythmic beats. The difference in the chronological ages of the children necessitated

Program Goal: Learning to move expressively and rhythmically.

Type of Experience: Rocking, patting, touching, and moving with the children to the beat of music heard.

Instructional Objective: The infant will experience the concept of rhythmic beat by rocking back and forth to the steady pulse of the song "See-Saw, Margery Daw" sung by the teacher.

The Activity: The teacher sits with the baby perching on the teacher's knees, the infant's feet resting against the teacher's body (Figure 4.3). Rock the baby forward and back, either with arms around it to give support or holding it by the arms. Rock in time to the song "See-Saw, Margery Daw."

Figure 4.2. A musical experience for infants.

formulating different objectives, planning different activities, and using different approaches. However, in each lesson, the instructional objective determined the focus of the activity and provided an observable behavior that would serve as a criterion for judging the effectiveness of the activity in realizing the objective and contributing to the program goal.

LESSON PLANS

Figures 4.2, 4.4, and 4.5 might easily be called lesson plans. The only additional information that a teacher might want to include are a

Figure 4.3. A young child may experience the concept of rhythmic beat by rocking back and forth to the steady pulse of a song.

Program Goal: Learning to move expressively and rhythmically.

Type of Experience: Improvise movements that indicate awareness of tempo.

Instructional Objective: Children will demonstrate their understanding of the terms "fast" and "slow" in music by improvising fast or slow hopping movements suggested by the tempo of the song "Old Molly Hare."

The Activity: Improvise a story about a rabbit name Molly Hare who lives near a cotton patch. Introduce the musical concepts of fast and slow through the story. For example: "When I first saw Molly, she didn't know who I was. I called to her, and she called back. It sounded like this." (Sing at a very quick tempo.)

Figure 4.4. A musical experience for three-year-old children.

(continued)

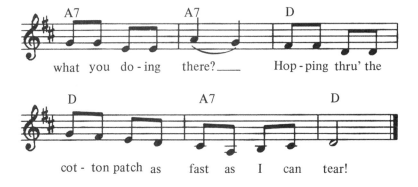

what you do-ing there?____ Hop-ping thru' the

cot-ton patch as fast as I can tear!

"Can someone show us how she hopped? How does the music tell
us how to hop?" As a child demonstrates, try to match the speed
of the child's movements by patting thighs and saying, "Hop, hop,
hop," etc. Encourage children to join.

Continue story. "When Molly and I got to be friends, we met often and
talked with each other. Then our song sometimes sounded like
this." (Sing song at a very slow, easy tempo.)

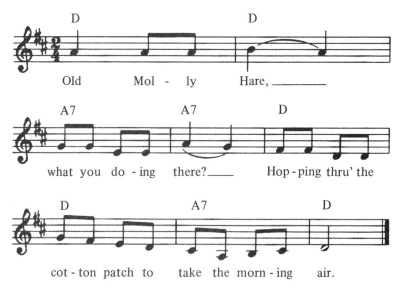

Old Mol - ly Hare, _____

what you do - ing there?____ Hop-ping thru' the

cot-ton patch to take the morn-ing air.

"Can someone show us how she hopped this time? How does the music now tell us how to hop?" As a child demonstrates, again match
the speed of the movements with thigh-slapping and chanting,
"hop, hop, hop," etc. Discuss with the children the differences in
the way the song was sung, and label the musical movement as
fast or slow.

Figure 4.4. (continued)

66

Program Goal: Learning to move expressively and rhythmically.

Type of Experience: Utilize symbols to represent durational patterns.

Instructional Objective: Children will demonstrate their understanding of the musical symbol representing a quarter note by walking when quarter notes are played on a drum and "freezing" when faster or slower notes are played.

The Activity: Prepare a poster showing quarter notes: ♩♩. Demonstrate how quarter notes sound when played on a drum. Ask children to pat thighs and say "beat, beat, beat, beat" as you play quarter-note beats on a drum. Then, with children standing in randomly spaced formation, introduce a "Simon Says" game:

1. "When I say 'Simon says,' and I play quarter notes, everyone walk with the drum."

2. "When I say 'Simon says,' but I play faster or slower sounds, you 'freeze.' Let's begin. Don't let Simon fool you!"

Discuss with the children how they identified the quarter-note sounds.

Figure 4.5. A musical experience for five-year-old children.

listing of materials and equipment needed and comments regarding possible alterations, extensions, or revisions needed. Figure 4.6 presents a suggested format for a lesson plan.

Date:_____   Age Group_____

Large Group Activity_____; Small-Group Activity_____; Individual
    Activity_____
    Program Goal:
    Instructional Objective:
    Materials and Equipment:
    The Activity:
    Evaluation:
    Comments:

Figure 4.6. Suggested lesson plan format.

Preparing lesson plans helps us organize our ideas and activities so that what our children experience on one day may be related to what they learn and do on the next. Lesson plans may be prepared for a week or a month or longer. Although a plan is seldom carried out exactly as it appears on paper, it helps guard against music periods that are merely a series of isolated, unrelated activities. Very few teachers, even experienced ones, can improvise effective lessons for very long. Rather, good teachers are good planners.

THE PHYSICAL ENVIRONMENT

Planning an environment that nurtures musical growth involves more than goal-setting and instructional planning, important as these are. Music activities need space in which to happen and equipment to enhance interest and learning. If you have visited the music room of an elementary school, you are aware of the various types of instruments, listening equipment, records, and music books that are available for teaching. You might have observed the furniture arrangement; often chairs and equipment are arranged so that large-group, small-group, and individual activities may be carried out.

Space, materials, and equipment are just as important in the preschool or kindergarten. The authors of *The School Music Program* provide two recommendations for the physical facilities for an early childhood program. The first is "an area designated as a music corner in which children have easy access to music materials"; the second is "an area large enough for movement activities" (Music Educators, 1986, p. 20). Organizing classroom space so that both large-group and individualized activities may occur may be more important to the success of an early childhood program than most teachers realize, according to Kritchevsky and Prescott (1982).

SPACE: ITS IMPORTANCE

"Space communicates with people—in a very real sense it tells us how to act and how not to act" (Krivchevsky and Prescott, 1982, p. 9). Movement activities with a large group of children may turn into chaos if they take place in a space that is too small or, also, too large. Individualized, self-directed experiences may never occur if the space planned for these encounters is in a poorly chosen area. In short, organization of space may have a significant effect on the realization of musical program goals.

Kritchevsky and Prescott analyzed the "intimate relationship between the goals of any group and its use of space" in early childhood centers (p. 6). While their analysis is concerned with planning general play units in a day-care or center setting, some of their recommendations are applicable to the planning of space for music activities.

These investigators identified factors that "might be predictive of differences in program quality" (p. 5). They found that one of the most significant predictors of program quality was physical space. High-quality space produced friendly and sensitive teachers who encouraged children in their self-chosen activities. Where spatial quality was low, children were less likely to be involved and interested and teachers more likely to be neutral or insensitive in manner (p. 6).

LARGE-GROUP UNITS

What characterizes "high-quality" space? First of all, enough space, and space that is clearly defined. Space units for group singing, movement activities, or playing instruments should be large enough to allow children to interact without bumping into each other, or the tables, shelves, or play units that abut the areas. Providing tangible boundaries to cordon off the area (perhaps shelves, edges of a rug, or the like) defines the space and encourages children to interact with one another and to stay in the area. Neither should large-group space units occupy what are natural pathways to other learning units, as there will be continuous problems with children's seeing, moving to, and/or staying in the unit. Teachers need to analyze the areas selected for large-group activities using these criteria.

When children are engaged in large-group activities, they should not have to sit in "classroom formation." Some children prefer to sit facing others, some in front and center, some at the rear. Group music-making events are comfortable and informal experiences where teachers, children, and music interact. Instruments and other equipment should be stored close at hand.

Large-group music activity units also exist out-of-doors. A grassy spot under a tree in the play yard can become a most satisfactory music classroom. Its boundaries, too, should be defined, and it should be separated from other distracting units.

INDIVIDUAL LEARNING UNITS

In addition to large-group space units, a classroom should contain a number of smaller units for individual and small-group activities. In many preschools and kindergartens, music-learning centers fill this need. These centers enable young children to explore musical instruments, listen to music, and create or explore sound at their own level of interest and ability (Figure 4.7). The Montessori music program is built around the concept of individual music-making.

Such centers may simply be large tables on which sound-producing objects or musical instruments—autoharp, xylophone, resonator bells, or percussion instruments—have been placed. The equip-

Figure 4.7. Music centers enable children to explore musical instruments at their own level of interest.

ment in the centers should be changed frequently. Some units may contain equipment for private listening to music, and this privacy will be assured if a number of headsets are kept on hand. If a teacher does not wish to have children handle a destructible record player, a cassette player can be managed easily by most children. Some of the tapes available for private listening should be those made by the teacher of the children's own singing.

An upright piano with the front panel removed is also a music-learning unit. Most children are interested in discovering how sounds are produced on a keyboard instrument, and through the process of such exploration they form concepts about "same/different," "high/low," and "fast/slow."

A "sound box" may also be constructed for a music-learning unit. Andress (1980, p. 13) described such a unit: "It consists of a plywood or cardboard box with a removable panel, the sound wall. [It] has a lid, floor and four sides each approximately four feet square. Crawl-in holes in the sides and openings in the lid for light . . . may be cut in free-form design" (p. 13). The sound wall (the removable panel) may contain metal tubes hung from the top of the sound box for children to strike with dowel sticks, a set of song bells attached vertically (from lower tones to higher) to the sound wall, or other sound-producing objects. In such a private spot, a child can explore and create music that is uniquely satisfying.

GENERAL CONSIDERATIONS

Individual music-learning units, like all play units, need space around them. "The space surrounding a table where children shift their chairs or stand just watching, all belong to the respective play-units" and if teachers do not organize these units to provide for the needed surrounding space, "there will quite naturally be conflicts and interruptions of play" (Kritchevsky and Prescott, 1982, p. 11).

Units planned for individual and small-group activities should be analyzed for their "complexity." Complexity refers to the extent that such units contain potential for active manipulation and variation of equipment (Kritchevsky and Prescott, 1982, p. 11). If learning centers are to hold the interest of young children for more than a short time, they should contain materials that can be improvised. A learning center where the teacher must handle all the materials and "guard the contents" is not apt to interest young children for long. Neither is the piano about which the children are constantly warned to "be careful." If centers do not provide for active exploratory or organizing activities, "teachers probably will need to compensate, through their own active participation, for the failure of the setting to provide enough ideas" (p. 12).

Music-learning centers must invite the children to them. They may be well equipped but rarely used if they are not clearly visible or if they are difficult to reach. A clear "path" leading to the unit invites children to go and initiate activity. The same warning applies that was given earlier regarding large-group units. If the unit occupies space that is a path to another unit, there will be constant interruptions and distraction of attention.

A physical environment that promotes musical learning is in part the result of space analysis and planning. The planning evolves from a thorough understanding of the program goals and objectives, as Kritchevsky and Prescott (1982) remind us:

> If program goals are so clear that they can be stated in behavioral terms, it is much easier to see how space can be developed to support these goals. Conversely, an understanding of the ways in which space can shape program goals almost inevitably leads to clarification of these goals. (p. 7)

MUSICAL EQUIPMENT

Music learning can occur with no equipment except the teacher's and children's voices. However, good-quality instruments provide a whole new dimension to children's understanding of sound. Playing instruments provides the sensory information from which musical concepts are formed. They help children develop eye-hand coordination and fine motor skills. They are a medium for self-expression. But, above all, they provide pleasure. A well-chosen assortment of musical instruments is almost an essential component of a well-planned music curriculum.

Classroom instruments may be categorized as nonpitched percussive, pitched percussive and melodic, and chordal accompanying instruments. *The School Music Program* lists those recommended for preschool and kindergarten music programs, and brief descriptions of these are provided below.

NONPITCHED PERCUSSIVE INSTRUMENTS

Rhythm instruments may be purchased in sets for a specific number of children. Although this method of purchase may imply that they be used to form a rhythm band, this is not their best use in a preschool or kindergarten. Young children enjoy learning about the sound possibilities of individual instruments; Moorhead and Pond (1978) stated that a child's "deepest interest" is in timbre, or tone color. Mass use does little to accommodate this interest.

A list of rhythm instruments includes the following:

- Rhythm drums of various sizes. Drums may consist of only a circular frame with plastic or skin stretched over one side. These are easy for children to hold and use. Large conga drums, sets of bongo drums, and tom-toms may be added to the drum ensemble.
- Rhythm sticks. Some sticks are smooth and some are serrated. They are played by holding one still and striking it with the other. If one smooth and one serrated stick are paired, interesting variations of sound may be produced by rubbing the smooth one along the serrated one, in a motion away from the body. One pair should be available for each child.
- Sandblocks. These are rectangular pieces of wood with one side covered with sandpaper. They produce a swishing sound when rubbed together.
- Woodblocks. Tone blocks, or woodblocks, are hollowed-out wooden blocks that are struck with a small mallet or wooden beater. Some are in the shape of a rectangle; others have a cylindrical shape with a handle for easier playing. They make interesting "clip-clop" sounds.
- Tambourines. Many teachers regard these as the most versatile of the rhythm instruments, as so many types of sounds can be produced.

They can be tapped with fingers or knuckles or shaken so that the jingles, which are attached to the circular frame, sound.

- Claves. Claves are often heard in orchestral music to represent the sound of horses' hooves. They are similar to rhythm sticks but are fatter and produce a more resonant sound. One should be held in the cupped palm of the hand; it is struck with the other.
- Maracas. These are hollow gourds containing seeds which sound when the instrument is shaken.
- Guiros. These are elongated hollow gourds. They are authentic Mexican folk instruments and are played by scraping a stick the length of the ridged body of the instrument.
- Finger cymbals. About two inches in diameter, these small concave metal disks can be managed by young children if one is held horizontally and struck on the edge with the other one. The sound is delicate and lasts for quite a long time.
- Gongs. A large gong produces a deep ringing sound which lasts a very long time! They are struck with a felt beater.
- Jingle bells. These small bells are attached to a strap (which can be secured around a child's ankles or wrists) and produce jingling sounds when the child moves.
- Cowbell. The cowbell is played by holding it in one hand with the open end facing toward the playing hand. It is struck with a stick.

PITCHED INSTRUMENTS

Having a number of good-quality pitched instruments greatly enhances a music program. *The School Music Program* recommends these:

- Resonator bells or tone bars. These pitched metal bars, mounted on rectangular wooden or plastic blocks of varying length, come in sets, but individual bars may be removed from the set as needed. They are played with small mallets.
- Xylophones. These instruments come in various sizes, ranging from small soprano to large deep-sounding bass. The pitched bars are made of wood; individual bars may be removed when only a limited number of pitches are needed for a song or accompaniment. They are played with soft mallets.
- Metallophones. Like xylophones, metallophones range from soprano to bass sizes. A metallophone's removable pitched bars are made of metal, producing a more ringing tone than the xylophones.
- Glockenspiels. Small pitched bars, glockenspiels are found in soprano and alto sizes. The individual bars are removable.

- Recorders. Although very young children cannot usually play these small, flutelike instruments very successfully, a teacher who has developed some proficiency can play the songs the children have learned, or improvise tunes to "fit" with xylophone- or metallophone-produced borduns.

HARMONY INSTRUMENTS

Children enjoy singing songs with accompaniments provided by the teacher. Easily produced accompaniments may be played on:

- Autoharps. These instruments remain the most functional accompanying instrument available. Teachers with little musical background can produce satisfying accompaniments with little or no training. (See Appendix A for tips on playing the autoharp.) Children should also have the experience of accompanying songs. The teacher may press the chord bars while the child strums.
- Guitar. Guitars produce lovely accompaniments for children's singing. Learning a few chords and playing them well is worth the effort for any classroom music teacher.

LISTENING EQUIPMENT

Each school needs a record player, a cassette recorder, and at least two sets of headphones in a "listening center." Cassettes that can be used by the children to record their "musical events" may also be available. Tapes or records of music representing a wide variety of styles and music texts with accompanying recordings enable even the most "nonmusical" teachers to present interesting and attractive musical activities for their students.

THE SOCIAL ENVIRONMENT: THE TEACHER

Of the many components that contribute to the effectiveness of early childhood music programs, the last to be discussed, but the most important, is the teacher. What makes a good music teacher? Musical skills are necessary. Ability to sing tunefully and easily is a skill that can be acquired by most teachers. Instrumental skills, such as playing the piano, guitar, or autoharp, add to the effectiveness of music instruction. Teachers who like to dance or move to music and do it comfortably and with pleasure bring this security and pleasure to their students. An understanding of musical concepts and the ability to discern the appropriate "teachable" element in a child's song, rhyme, or recorded composition make for effective teaching.

Given all these skills, however, the really effective early childhood music educator is the one who understands children as well as music. A listing of some of the desired personal attributes of successful teachers will conclude our discussion of a quality "musical environment," for it is the teacher who ultimately creates that environment.

1. Effective teachers are willing to invest time and effort in getting to know their children. They involve themselves with the children's interests, needs, and desires, and they respect their students as individuals.

2. Effective teachers model the behaviors, both social and musical, that they want to teach.

3. Effective teachers have a sense of humor; they smile, laugh, play with, and enjoy the children.

4. Effective teachers plan musical experiences that are of interest to the children and that channel and give direction to emerging skills and understandings.

5. Effective teachers provide children with time and opportunity for individual musical experiences.

6. Effective teachers are aware of children's developmental musical, social, physical, and cognitive stages of development. They realize that children will not learn skills or develop concepts that are inappropriate for their stages of development.

7. Effective teachers realize the importance of creating a music learning environment that is success-laden. They plan experiences from which the children learn how to succeed, rather than how *not* to succeed.

8. Effective teachers realize that children learn at their own rates in their own unique ways. They remember that musical *process* is more important than the musical product. Praising the process is as important as praising the product.

9. Effective teachers evaluate their planning, their lessons, and their attitudes. They make necessary changes, adjust to children's needs, and constantly strive to become more effective human beings.

Musical children are the products of musical environments that promote learning, offer wide and varied experiences, and engender feelings of security and well-being. Musical children are the real goals of a musical environment.

QUESTIONS FOR DISCUSSION/SUGGESTED ACTIVITIES

1. Think of your school music teachers. Choose one who was particularly successful. Analyze his or her philosophy of music education as manifested in attitudes toward the children, instructional strategies, and musical materials used in teaching.

2. Choose several songs from a current early childhood or kindergarten text. Plan an accompanying activity for each. Place each song/activity in the appropriate "category" and "type of experience" as described in *The School Music Program*.

3. List the criteria that should be followed in organizing large-group activity units and individual music-learning centers.

4. List the musical skills and personal attributes that distinguish a successful early childhood music educator. Evaluate yourself. Which are your strong areas? Which need improvement?

REFERENCES AND SUGGESTED READINGS

Andress, B. (1980). *Music experiences in early childhood.* New York: Holt, Rinehart and Winston.

Cherry, C. (1976). *Creative play for the developing child: Early lifehood education through play.* Belmont, CA: Fearon Pitman Publishers, Inc.

Gary, C. L. (Ed.). (1967). *The study of music in the elementary school—a conceptual approach.* Reston, VA: Music Educators National Conference.

Kritchevsky, D., & Prescott, E. (1982). *Planning environments for young children: Physical space.* Washington, DC: National Association for the Education of Young Children.

Moorhead, G. E., & Pond, D. (1978). *Music of young children.* Santa Barbara, CA: Pillsbury Foundation for Advancement of Music Education.

Newman, G. (1984). *Teaching children music: Fundamentals of music and method.* Dubuque, IA: Wm. C. Brown Co.

Nye, V. (1983). *Music for young children* (3rd ed.). Dubuque, IA: Wm. C. Brown Co.

Music Educators National Conference. (1986). *The school music program: Description and standards.* Reston, VA: MENC.

Weiser, M. G. (1982). *Group care and education of infants and toddlers.* St. Louis: C. V. Mosby Co.

Chapter 5

Teaching Music: The Research Base

The whole art of teaching is only the art of awakening the natural curiosity of young minds for the purpose of satisfying it afterwards.

—*Anatole France*

Most young children acquire some musical skills and understandings whether or not they have experienced a planned program of instruction. Given a minimal exposure to singing, the majority of our students learn to sing more or less tunefully by the time they leave elementary school. Because television and radio music has surrounded so many of their activities, they have formed some preferences for the kind of music they like to listen to and have learned to distinguish many songs even before they enter primary school.

However, few of us would choose this type of "instructional program" if provided an alternative. We have seen the striking differences, not only in performance skills, but also in sensitivity to music, between those children who have experienced good teaching and those who have received poor—or no—instruction.

What constitutes good teaching for young children? Are there basic instructional principles that can help us plan lessons and guide learning? The purpose of this chapter is to explore music instructional research literature to discover basic guidelines for teaching music to young children.

We may begin by studying the following statements. All of them are related, directly or indirectly, to instructional considerations and strategies. Are they true or false?

1. While infants enjoy listening to music, they are capable of making few discriminations about musical sounds.

2. Learning to talk about music, for example, to verbalize understandings, has little effect on preschoolers' music-listening skills.

3. Children's musical tastes are formed early and cannot be changed through instruction.

4. The ability to sing tunefully is related to the ability to control speech inflections.

5. Children's comfortable singing ranges are much higher in pitch than those of adults.

6. Activities involving large-muscle movements, such as marching, are good beginning experiences to help children acquire rhythmic accuracy.

7. Forming a rhythm band is a good way to introduce children to classroom instruments.

8. Creativity in music-making cannot be taught; it is a product of heredity.

9. Age five or six, when children enter public school, is the best time to commence music instruction.

How did you rate these statements? Perhaps the information in earlier chapters helped you answer some of them. The answers that music instruction research has provided will be reviewed in the following sections.

APPROACHES TO INSTRUCTION

Before we begin our exploration of the research that has provided some answers to our true-false statements, a word of caution about the definition of "music teaching," as it applies to young children, is warranted. For most of us, the term calls up memories of group instruction in a traditional classroom setting where, at a predetermined time, songs are sung and rhythmic exercises are performed "in concert." While this type of instruction is sometimes appropriate, it precludes any kind of music experience for children too young to enjoy group instruction or too young to possess the prerequisite vocal and motor skills required for successful participation.

In our discussion, we will use the term "music teaching" to mean selecting and planning appropriate experiences for individual children, for small groups of children, or for large groups of children. The experiences may happen spontaneously or be preplanned. They may occur in the home, in the classroom, or out-of-doors. They take place because teachers have prepared for both planned experiences and for informal encounters with music—those teachable moments that occur often in early childhood centers (Figure 5.1).

It is important to consider music teaching in this context, for the development of musical skills and understandings begins long before children appear in a kindergarten or primary school classroom, where a music specialist sometimes is employed to teach music. Perhaps it begins before they "appear" at all, according to recent studies of fetal responses to musical stimuli. According to Kodaly, "music [education] should start nine months before a baby is born" (Fridman, 1973, p. 63). According to this statement, the last true-false statement at the beginning of this chapter is false. Ages five or six may be very late to give attention (and appropriate instruction) to the musical component of a child's education.

CONCEPTUAL UNDERSTANDINGS

In Chapter 4, goals and instructional objectives for an early childhood music program were presented. They included the development of ba-

Figure 5.1. "Teachable moments" occur often to teachers for whom musical goals have become part of their overall concept of early childhood education.

sic musical skills—perceptive listening, tuneful singing, rhythmic movement, playing instruments, and creating self-satisfying music. Following these goals was one goal that addressed conceptual development. The goal was called "Developing age-appropriate concepts about music; for example, how the elements of music interact."

All music has common properties, or "elements." These include melody, rhythm, timbre, dynamics, harmony, and form. The development of concepts, or understandings, about these elements helps us respond to all music more fully. Concepts make it easier to think about what we have experienced.

Concepts about music cannot be taught; they are acquired through meaningful experiences. Developmental research has shown that some concepts are acquired more easily than others by young children. Instruction involving the ones that have been shown to be understandable to children obviously makes more sense than teaching "above and beyond" a certain age or stage of development.

Table 5.1 lists basic concepts about music that are regarded as appropriate for our youngest learners to acquire. These provide the foundation for learning about music.

Understanding of concepts like these develops more or less sequentially, dependent upon the child's age and experience. The concept formation studies that were reviewed in Chapter 3 revealed a measure of agreement among researchers about the sequential development of these understandings. This sequence was followed in the above listing. You will notice that understanding of timbre and dynamics occurs before conceptualization of rhythm and melody; comprehension of form (dependent on tonal memory) and harmony are the last to develop.

This sequence may indicate a broad framework for instructional planning; for example, for young children, timbral exploration activities,

Table 5.1. Basic Concepts to Be Acquired by Youngest Learners

Concept	Important Characteristics
Timbre	1. The unique qualities of sounds are determined by the type of instrument or voice that produces them.
	2. Musical instruments or voices may be recognized and identified by their characteristic sound.
	3. When instruments or voices are played or used in different ways, the quality of sound (tone color) produced by them may be different.
Dynamics	1. Musical sounds are relatively loud or soft, or they may become gradually or suddenly louder or softer.

Table 5.1. (continued)

Concept	Important Characteristics
	2. The mood of a song or composition is somewhat dependent upon the level and changes in dynamics produced by the performer(s).
Rhythm	1. In most music there is an identifiable underlying pulse—a "steady beat" that may be sounded or sensed.
	2. Regularly recurring beats may be fast or slow, or they may quicken or slow as a musical composition progresses.
	3. Rhythmic beats are usually sensed in groups of twos or threes, defining a metrical organization.
	4. Rhythmic patterns result from combinations of long and short sounds and silences.
Melody	1. Musical sounds may be high or low, or relatively high or low in pitch.
	2. The musical pitches in a melody may move higher or lower or may remain the same for a number of beats.
	3. Musical pitches in a song may move higher or lower by "steps" or "skips."
	4. Many melodies revolve around, and end on, a "tonal center" that may be aurally identified.
	5. Melodic patterns may be repeated in a song or composition; such repetition may be recognized and identified.
Form	1. A recognizable musical idea or thought in a song or instrumental composition is called a phrase; phrases may be combined to form sections.
	2. Musical phrases or sections may be alike, nearly alike, or different; the structure of most musical compositions is determined by the combination of like and unlike phrases or sections.
Texture and Harmony	1. Two or more musical sounds produced simultaneously produce harmony.
	2. Harmony may occur in accompaniments to melodies—either as chords, as ostinati (repeated rhythmic or melodic patterns) or as borduns (a "drone" produced by sounding the first and fifth tones of a scale simultaneously), for example.

experiences with dynamic contrasts in music and melodic and rhythmic games are more appropriate than those involving harmony and form.

Within this framework, let us begin by considering the first of our true-false statements: "While infants enjoy listening to music, they are capable of forming few discriminations about it." True or false?

LISTENING SKILL INSTRUCTION

THE BEGINNINGS OF PERCEPTIVE LISTENING

We are aware that infants are "born listeners." They are attentive to many sounds; however, they seem to prefer human sounds to all others (Weiser, 1982, p. 139). Therefore, "live" music is especially important. Beginning instruction in listening means singing to the child—nursery songs, rhythmic chants, lullabies, improvised tunes about the day's events. All of these provide music instruction for our very young children. Babies try to match pitches of our songs or chants long before they understand the words. We should, in turn, imitate their sounds; this type of activity provides "instructional feedback."

However, one researcher found that infants can benefit from instruction that goes further (Kucenski, 1977). In this study, a music-learning program for children, three to nine months of age, was designed to determine whether or not the children could learn to recognize and distinguish selected songs presented over periods of three to six months. The investigator used a multisensory approach and developed four modes of presenting the songs. A film was presented concurrently with one song; during another song, a puppet activity was carried out. A large beach ball, with which the children played (assisted by their parents), provided a rhythmic movement experience. For another song, a game-choice activity was introduced. The children heard the songs while engaged in these activities; the songs were also recorded on cassette tapes and sent home with the parents, who were instructed to play them during feeding times. The songs were traditional tunes with newly created words that included the names of the children and described the activity—the ball song's lyrics named the color of the balls, for example.

Results of the program showed that not only did the infants learn to recognize and distinguish the songs (demonstrated by their rhythmic and attending responses), but also that the children who had undergone the training showed unusual increase in language development. The children who had received the longer training period showed the greatest achievement.

Such results show that multisensory instructional methods, which provide visual, kinesthetic and tactile information, may indeed improve infants' listening skills. Associative techniques, such as puppet play, ball manipulation, and colored film (or pictures) engage visual and kinesthetic senses as well as auditory ones and enhance development of perceptive listening.

Infants' innate curiosity about the sources of sounds also has instructional implications. Mobile toys that make interesting sounds may be suspended over a crib; wind-up music boxes—even our Peek-a-Boo games—all accommodate this curiosity.

Table 5.2 charts an age-related sequence of auditory development through the first year. This material is adapted from Weiser (1982); implications for "music instruction" have been added.

Although research studies regarding infants' discriminatory listening skills are far from numerous, the information we have seems to suggest that the first statement in our true-false test is false. Planned instruction may result in improved auditory discrimination, even among infants.

CONCEPTUAL GROWTH

As children mature, they grow in their ability to make finer distinctions about the musical sounds they hear; consequently, their understanding increases. However, it is often difficult for adults to know how much they understand because of their limited verbal ability and unfamiliarity with music terminology. How do we know what they understand if they cannot tell us what they hear or demonstrate it in some way? Furthermore, how do they know what they know if it has no name?

The research dealing with concept formation has generally been concerned with two questions: (1) what specific aspects of the elements of music can children understand, with or without instruction, and (2) what modes of instruction are most appropriate to enhance understanding?

Studies have focused on quite definitive tasks, including basic questions such as "Does this rhythm pattern get faster or slower?" or "Does this melody move higher or lower?" or even specific questions such as "Of the two tones we heard, which one is higher?" or "What instrument is playing the melody we hear?" Children who acquire these types of understandings early in life have the foundational skills for listening to many kinds of music, for learning to read music, and for creating music.

Research, first of all, has indicated a sequence of conceptual understandings. This sequence is presented in Table 5.1. However, quite

Table 5.2. The Development of Auditory Perception in the First Year

Age	Perceptions	Implications for Music Instruction
3 months	Discriminates between tonal and nontonal sounds, pitches and timbres.	Sing many songs and chants. Provide interesting sound-producing toys.
	Looks for souce of sounds.	Direct infant's attention to source of sound, both musical and nonmusical.
	Soothed by soft, rhythmic sounds.	Sing lullabies, rocking songs, rhythmic chants.
6 months	Differentiates tones of voice and speech sounds. Likes to "talk" to self. Coos and gurgles and engages in vocal play.	Initiate musical conversations during care-giving tasks. Imitate pitches produced by the child. Sing songs of a variety of moods.
9 months	Associates sound with its source (person or object).	Focus attention on source of sound. Provide toys that produce contrasting sounds.
	Enjoys listening to musical sounds. Attempts "conversations."	Listen *with* the child to a variety of music. Initiate pitch-imitation play. Change some of the conversations into songs.
12 months	Imitates adult vocalizations.	Build a repertoire of songs that will become familiar through repetition.
	Responds rhythmically to music.	By tactual demonstration, link movements— rocking, bouncing, moving arms—with music.

Table 5.2. (continued)		
Age	Perceptions	Implications for Music Instruction
	Knows own name and names of other persons.	Personalize songs by inserting child's name and names of persons important to the child. Include action songs in which words give cue for actions.
	Understands more than can verbalize. Tries to comply with verbal requests.	

specific accomplishments at each step have been identified as attainable by preschoolers, and some of these are listed below:

1. Timbre: Aural identification of selected orchestral instruments and instrumental groups (Fullard, 1967; Loucks, 1974).
2. Dynamics: Discrimination of loud/soft sounds (Andress, Heimann, Rinehart, and Talbert, 1973; Piper and Shoemaker, 1973).
3. Rhythm: Identification of steady pulse, fast/slow tempi (Young, 1982; Moog, 1976).
4. Melody: Identification and categorization of high/low sounds (Romanek, 1974; Scott, 1977) and melodic direction (Van Zee, 1975; Hair, 1977; Webster, 1980).
5. Form: Identification of same/different phrases (Piper and Shoemaker, 1973).
6. Texture and Harmony: Recognition of accompanied/unaccompanied melody (Piper and Shoemaker, 1973). First grade children can also discriminate same/different chords (Hair, 1973).

INSTRUCTIONAL STRATEGIES

Through what kinds of experiences may such concepts be acquired? In Chapter 2, the educational theories of Jerome Bruner were discussed. Bruner proposed a model that a learner uses to "store and retrieve" information. The model included three modes: through action (enactive); through something that stands for the concept (iconic); and through language or symbols (symbolic). He stated that intellectual development "runs the course of these three systems of representation until the human being is able to command all three" (1968, p. 12).

Children are helped to acquire musical concepts when we, the instructors, heed this intellectual model of development. Preschoolers acquire and store information through acting upon it (enactive representation) or linking it to some visual representation (iconic). For example, studies have shown that young children are able to demonstrate their understanding of musical ideas by:

1. Enactive representation. Children can illustrate fast/slow, high/low through whole body movement or directional gestures (Young, 1982; Webster, 1980).

2. Iconic representation. Children can illustrate fast/slow, high/low, up/down on classroom instruments (drums, resonator bells, songbells, keyboards) (Webster, 1980; Van Zee, 1975) or by relating the sound to pictures of high/low or fast/slow objects (Young, 1982).

Listening experiences that involve identification of such concepts should be accompanied by many activities using movement, instruments, or visual representations of the sounds.

However, the terms used to describe concepts should not be neglected. This has been a persistent problem. Young (1982) recommended that some sort of consistent terminology should be taught "prior to or as these terms are used in a musical context" (p. 138), so that the concept may be linked with its name.

Some of the terms we use to describe music are more elusive for children to grasp than others. Teachers can anticipate particular difficulty with "high/low" or "higher/lower," due in part to the multiple meanings these terms have in common usage. "Turn that radio down!" does not refer to pitch, we know. "Slow" is often equated with "soft"; "high" with "loud." Many repeated experiences, consistent use of the terms, and instructional strategies that allow for action and manipulation are recommended to establish meaning of the terms.

> Place a set of song bells (with lowest pitches to the left) in front of one child. Ask the other children to close their eyes. Announce (substituting appropriate name): "Arlie is going to play a tune that goes up, or perhaps he will play one that goes down. Let's listen carefully and see whether we can describe which he chooses to play." All children should have a turn. (A group of four-year-old children enjoyed playing this "drill-for-skill" game repeatedly.)

> "How shall we get from here to there? Let's let Mary
> play some drum sounds to see whether we should move
> fast or slow."

> "When the sounds I make on the drum are soft, stroke
> one hand; when they are loud, clap."

Therefore, the answer to our second true-false statement must be qualified. The ability to "talk about music" and use correct terminology results from the understanding of the concepts and the terms derived from effective instruction.

MUSIC APPRECIATION

Because music is an aural art, listening is the "mode" of understanding. Children must listen carefully to learn to sing a song, to move in a rhythmically appropriate way, or to play an instrument. However, learning to listen also means listening to music made by others. This type of listening—attending to unfamiliar, and perhaps more complex music than the child is able to analyze—seems to demand a special approach. Such music might include recorded compositions; music presented by visiting performers, parents, or teachers; classical music available on TV, radio, filmstrips; serious art music; folk and ethnic musics; and contemporary compositions. Too often these kinds of music are not included in early childhood music programs.

When planning for such music in the classroom, teachers should remember the quite significant influence they have on children's preferences and interests. Preschoolers' willingness to listen to music may depend, to a degree, upon teacher approval (Greer, Dorow, and Hanser, 1973). And, although children's preferences are formed early and not easily changed, repetition of certain musical compositions also may lead to acceptance and enjoyment (McDonald and Schuckert, 1968). What is liked by persons important to the child and heard often may become preferred.

However, music listening experiences should also provide for some kind of interaction. Such a program was planned for five-year-olds, and associative techniques were used to encourage the children to listen purposefully to a number of classical compositions (Turnipseed, Thompson and Kennedy, 1974). Each recorded composition was introduced by telling a story related to the work or by initiating appropriate movements to accompany the music. As a result of the program, the children showed gains in ability to follow directions and discriminate sounds. Of special interest was the increase in the group's attention span for listening to music. By midyear, the initial twenty-minute sessions had lengthened to fifty minutes. A music/movement/story approach was also described by Christiansen (1938), who reported the interest of four-year-old children in acting out and dramatizing ideas expressed in the music they heard.

Music that appeals to young children is "interesting in tone color, short and rhythmically dynamic, played by many different instruments—solos and in small instrumental combinations" (Moorhead and Pond, 1978, p. 46); active participation in the musical experience by the children is recommended always (Zimmerman, 1971, p. 20).

Listening experiences help children to become acquainted with, and to respond to, a wide variety of music. Their musical horizons are extended, and their preferences may be widened. The answer to our third statement, "Children's musical tastes are formed early and cannot be changed through instruction," is "false."

SINGING SKILLS

BEGINNING SINGING

As infants are "programmed to learn," they might also be described as "programmed to sing." As the inner process of sorting sounds from the environment progresses, they learn to discriminate their own sounds from those of others. They become increasingly interested in the sounds they can produce and they engage in much vocal play. In about the second half of the first year, however, they are no longer content with "solo" productions:

> The talking game is too good for the baby to let himself be left out for long. Soon he learns to shout for attention. . . . Soon after the shout, many babies learn to sing. . . . The song is not elaborate; four notes up or down the scale is about average. But it is quite definitely musical and usually set off by your singing, by music on the radio or "theme tunes" on television. (Leach, 1983, pp. 262–263)

Ostwald (1973) called this period one of "vocal contagion"—the period when babies become interested in environmental sounds to the extent that they are stimulated to participate. In some cultures, according to this researcher, nurses of very young children are specifically instructed to encourage these infant songs by imitating them. These early attempts at mimicking both speech and song appear to lead to early speech development. They should not only be encouraged by adults, but should arouse some response or "feedback," for it is through the responses of those around them that infants learn to attach meaning to their sounds.

Instruction in singing for all preschoolers means singing to them, with them, and for them. A child who has heard much singing will produce parts of songs by age two; at age three, many children are tuneful singers who possess quite an extensive repertoire of songs. The preschool years are the ones when language skills are developing rapidly; singing skills, another form of language, should develop as well.

SONG ACQUISITION

It is perhaps surprising, considering the "hit or miss" kind of instruction that most young children receive, that most do learn to sing. However, too many do not. The number of nontuneful, inaccurate singers in our public school music classes, a persistent problem in music education, has shown that, for some youngsters, hit-or-miss training is not good enough. Too many children are missed. Yet, if we examine the research that has been accumulating for many years, we find quite specific and practical suggestions for helping children achieve tunefulness. The research concerning singing may be categorized as follows: (1) studies of the sequence of song acquisition, which can help teachers organize song materials for effective instruction; (2) studies of young children's spontaneous singing, which provide criteria for song selection; (3) studies of various instructional practices, which suggest specific techniques to use; and (4) information about the social-emotional development of preschool children, which helps us know when and how to manage individual or group instruction.

The first group of studies, concerning the sequence of song acquisition, reveals that for all children there is a predictable pattern of song acquisition. The sequence is: words; rhythms; phrases; contour. Following an initial period of vocal play and experimentation (twelve to eighteen months), two-year-olds may produce "phrase-songs," which consist only of the rhythmic repetition of a word or phrase, with undulating pitch inflection close to the pitch of speech. As vocal control is gained, children expand their range of usable pitches and are able to produce the shape, or contour, of a melodic line more accurately. Intervallic accuracy and sense of tonality, however, may remain imprecise (Ramsey, 1981; Davidson, 1985).

This research suggests that beginning song instruction should include rhythmic speech play—vocal chants and rhymes—through which children explore the possibilities of their speaking voices. The Orff Method, described in Chapter 7, makes much use of such strategies. Consider the following activity. How could "high/low" and "short/long" be explored?

"Hear the telephone ring!" (Child imitates telephone.)
"Hear the little bird sing!" (Child imitates bird.)
"Hear the water faucet run!" (Child imitates water running.)
"Hear the vacuum sweeper hum!" (Child imitates vacuum sweeper.)
"Hear the siren down the street!" (Child imitates siren.)
"Hear the auto horn go bleep, bleep, bleep!" (Child imitates auto horn.)

Gradually, tonal chants using only two or three sounds, close to speech pitch, are introduced. Many children use this tonal chant instinctively.

For example:

"I   found   a   red   bug!"

Teachers may use this pattern for greeting songs or musical conversations, too.

Speech-to-song instruction also is useful in helping older nontuneful singers achieve pitch accuracy (Gould, 1969; Roberts and Davies, 1976). Gould (1969) outlined this sequence for teachers to follow: first, plan activities that include tone-matching exercises where the teacher first matches tones produced by the children; and then introduce short melodic patterns, pitched in the vocal range of the individual singer. When these patterns are successfully imitated, introduce melodic patterns in a "true singing range" (usually higher). The strategy has produced significant improvement among children who could not match pitches or sing tunefully. "The breakthrough seemed to occur when the children (ages six to eight) realized they could control the pitch fluctuations in their own voices" (Roberts and Davies, 1976, p. 42).

Children need to "conceptualize" singing—to understand the "sustained vocal sounds of singing contrasted with the staccato vocal sounds of speech" (Gould, 1969, p. 20). "Improving pitch, perception and singing voice quality is . . . largely kinesthetic in nature" (Gould, 1969, p. 21); children need to find out how singing "feels" as well as how it sounds, so that they can form a mental image of the behavior.

The earlier vocal instruction is begun, the better. Group instruction can produce significant gains in singing skills even among three-year-olds (Smith, 1963). The early childhood years are the best ones for such instruction. Maturation and experience aid the process of learning to sing, but teaching helps. Thus, the answer to our fourth true-false statement is "true." Singing ability is related to the ability to control speech fluctuations, and speech activities appear to help develop tuneful singing skills.

SONG SELECTION

Most songbooks compiled for use in preschools and kindergartens contain a wide variety of songs, ranging from simple to complex, but provide little information about how and when to teach them. Teachers must do the picking, choosing, and sequencing, with little guidance. The notable exception to this is found in the Kodaly materials, where

Figure 5.2. Parents should participate frequently in natural and pleasant musical expression such as singing.

structured sequence of material is a distinguishing characteristic of the method. (See Chapter 7 for a discussion of the Kodaly Method.) However, teachers may plan their own sequences using available songbooks and guidelines derived from research. These guidelines address (1) the range of pitches used in the songs, (2) the intervallic and structural characteristics of the melodies, and (3) the subject content:

Range. Studies dating as far back as the 1930s have established consensus about the most usable range of young children's singing voices. It appears that the most easily used range of pitches is from approximately A below middle C to the G or A above (summarized in Young, 1982).

Range is a most important consideration when choosing beginning songs for preschoolers. Although some young children use an extensive range of pitches in their spontaneous singing, they maneuver most successfully in a more limited range when words are added to the melodies. Often adults begin a song "from nowhere" with little consideration as to whether the children can comfortably match the pitches they are producing. Most songs in current songbooks are notated in keys that accommodate children's easily produced pitches. Teachers should heed the notated pitches and use a pitch pipe or other instrument for starting songs. If the beginning pitch of a song is unknown, the pitches D, E, or F above middle C may be sounded, as these pitches lie in the middle of most children's initial singing ranges. While some thought must be given to whether the beginning note of the song represents the highest or lowest tones in the melody, such a pitching practice should prevent habitually placing a song in an inappropriate range for children.

Singing ranges expand with age and experience. An early study (Jersild and Bienstock, 1934) showed that the average number of tones sung at each age level increased from age two to nine, with a rapid increase until age six. Therefore, while beginning songs should use the five- or six-note range described above, songs that utilize a greater range of pitches should be introduced when children are secure in singing songs in the limited range.

Intervallic and structural characteristics. Children's songs should contain much repetition of melodic and rhythmic patterns (Smith, 1963). Songs containing descending intervals and few wide skips in the melody are sung more easily (Kirkpatrick, 1962). According to Davidson (1985), children tend to establish "contour schemes" when singing—"tonal territories" characterized by a defined intervallic boundary of pitches—which they "fill in" with leaps and steps. The young child who attempts to reproduce a song with intervals not yet manageable will very likely squeeze or expand the intervals to fit into the contour scheme. Teachers should be aware of this way of processing melodic material so as not to expect intervallic accuracy before contour schemes have become stabilized enough to permit attention to precise interval reproduction. It would appear that choosing songs with limited ranges, small-sized skips, and prevalent descending melodic lines would accommodate this processing procedure.

While such criteria might appear to limit song selection, an examination of the intervallic and structural characteristics of many traditional children's songs shows that they fit these criteria very well. "Go Tell Aunt Rhody," "Twinkle, Twinkle, Little Star," "This Old Man," "Old MacDonald," "Where is Thumbkin?" and "Grandma Grunts" are but a few. Teachers will find many more in American folk song literature. These songs, honed to perfect singability by generations of young performers, provide a wealth of appropriate material for both vocal "instruction" and for informal, spontaneous singing. One is shown in Figure 5.3.

Subject content. Early childhood should be a period for singing about many things. While language development is highly individualistic—some normal two-year-olds use only six words, while others use over two hundred fifty—most children add from five to six hundred words a year to their vocabularies between the ages of two and five (Jenkins and Shacter, 1975, p. 102). Many words are encountered for the first time in songs; music has been called a "language builder" (Bayless and

"Go Tell Aunt Rhody"

Go tell Aunt Rho - dy; go tell Aunt Rho - dy.

Go tell Aunt Rho - dy the old grey goose is dead.

Range: D to A.
Predominant melodic direction: descending.
Predominant melodic interval: sequential steps.
Structure: repetition of words, sequential repetition of melodic pattern.

Figure 5.3. A child's folk song.

Ramsey, 1978). As for what children like to sing about, we should bear
the following in mind:

> [Young children are] learning to know the real world about them.
> [They] enjoy make-believe stories of animals who talk and play like
> children. They never weary of being told stories about themselves
> or their playmates. They listen attentively to the running story
> their parents can make up of what they did. They like stories about
> other children with whom they can identify, who are doing things
> they understand. Some nonsense rhymes and jingles, as well as
> simple poems and songs, appeal to them. (Jenkins and Shacter,
> 1975, p. 103)

These suggestions could serve as guidelines for choosing songs as well
as stories. If some attractive songs are too complex for young children
to learn to sing accurately, teachers should remember that listening to
songs is also a part of "singing instruction." We should at times sing
for our children, not demanding that they join in, but allowing them to
enjoy the rhythmic flow of melody and words.

TEACHING SONGS

Because the development of tuneful singing is so important an objective
of early childhood music instruction, songs should be taught in ways
that help, not hinder, the learning process. Regarding the three topics
named below, research has provided some guidelines for presenting
songs to young children:

1. Accuracy: A song should not change its tune with each rendition.
   What is first learned is longest remembered. Each song should be
   sung consistently and accurately. It may be impossible for a child
   to relearn a song correctly, even after vocal training, if it has been
   learned incorrectly (Roberts and Davies, 1975).

2. Accompaniment: There is much difference of opinion about the
   effect of harmonic accompaniment on the accurate reproduction of
   a song. Some educators believe that accompaniments, such as piano
   chording, may obscure the melody and pitch of songs for young
   children. However, there is little research evidence to confirm this. If
   teachers need the support of a musical instrument to ensure accurate
   singing of the song, they should use it. Autoharps or guitars are
   recommended.

3. Teaching aids: All of the studies reviewed thus far have emphasized
   the use of movement, instruments, and pictures to aid in the development of musical skills. Pictures, songbells, resonator bars, xylophones, and other pitched instruments all provide visual represen-

tation of pitch. Movement also provides physical representation of pitch and melodic direction. Van Zee (1975) found that kindergarten children whose teachers had provided many movement experiences in classroom music were more accurate singers than those who had received no movement training.

INSTRUCTIONAL GROUPING PATTERNS

Most preschool teachers set aside time each day for group singing. While group instruction is appropriate at times, children should hear and learn songs long before they are able to deal with group activities.

Infants and toddlers need one-to-one musical encounters with parents, teachers and caregivers. For example, when working with babies and children up to two-and-a-half or three years of age, adults should take time to sing, move, and listen with a child, and be sensitive to the child's tolerance for movement and sounds (see Table 5.3).

Table 5.3. Musical Encounters between Children and Adults

Age Group	Suggested Encounters
Infants	1. Adults should engage in many face-to-face interactions with infants, including song games such as Peek-a-Boo and Five Little Piggies. All interactions should be characterized by gentle, supportive responses and are done in ways that are sensitive to the child's tolerance for physical movement, louder sounds, and other changes.
	2. Adults should listen and respond to sounds that infants make, imitate them, and respect them as the beginning of communication. They should also sing frequently to the children.
	3. A variety of music should be provided for enjoyment in listening/body movement/singing; in addition, toys that are responsive to the child's actions are needed, e.g., music boxes and bells.
Toddlers	1. Adults should engage in many one-to-one, face-to-face activities; singing with them, doing fingerplays, acting out simple stories and songs.
	2. Toddlers' solitary and parallel play must be respected; many opportunities for active, large-muscle play (rhythmic movement, for example) should be provided.

Adapted from Bredekamp, 1986, pp. 34–46.

Some children are ready for limited small-group activities between three and four years of age. Table 5.4 lists social developmental characteristics for ages three to six, with suggestions for group musical experiences.

By the time children are leaving the primary grades, most can sing fairly well, using a more extended range than that of their preschool

Table 5.4. Social Developmental Characteristics and Implications for Group Music Experiences

Age	Characteristics	Musical Implications
3 years	Cooperative play beginning; sharing, taking turns understood.	Simple noncompetitive games, such as Musical Chairs, Looby Loo.
	Enjoys dramatic play with other children: may have a special friend.	Finger plays, rhythmic movement, songs in which words suggest actions. Some "partner" activities.
	Wants approval of adults.	Encouragement and approval of efforts needed.
4 years	Enjoys playing with other children.	Song games; simple circle and line dances.
	Confident and assured; more able to control emotions.	Opportunities needed to be leader in action songs and games.
	Frequent stormy periods; needs adults as arbitrators.	Encouragement needed, as well as active support of efforts.
5 years	Enjoys other children; wants to be with them. Interested in group activities and group play.	Children ready to learn circle and line dances, group singing games.
	May need help in cooperating with others; wants to please important adults.	Take-a-Turn activities, song games—always with supportive encouragement.
6 years	Friendly, cooperative, generous. Finds frustration difficult to accept; sensitive to real or imagined slights.	Activities needed wherein each child may succeed.
	Desires praise for achievement.	

Adapted from Weiser, 1982; Jenkins and Shacter, 1975.

years. The ability to sing easily and confidently is increased if their teachers have taught them attractive songs that use, first, the limited ranges that accommodate their growing voices, and then those that help them to expand their ranges. It is well to remember that children's voices are not significantly higher in pitch range than those of adults. Therefore, the answer to our fifth true-false statement is "false."

RHYTHMIC MOVEMENT

MOTOR DEVELOPMENT

Preschool children have to involve their bodies as well as their minds in order to understand the world and its experiences: "If he may not engage his body, as well as his mind, he will switch off" (Ambron, 1978, p. 407). Movement is almost synonymous with music for most young children. Dalcroze, whose methods are discussed in Chapter 7, felt that rhythmic movement was the best way to awaken love and appreciation of music and was the response "nearest related to life" (Jaques-Dalcroze, 1921, p. 115). He wrote that children should be trained to respond to music with physical movement as early as the first year of life. He encouraged teachers to help children from infancy on to experiment with movement: "from about the age of ten months the child [should be taught] to imitate movements shown to him and also to link on some idea to each movement" (Jaques-Dalcroze, 1930, p. 98).

Movement instruction for young children should be thought of as "preparation of the instrument." Satisfying expression of music comes about through exploration, experience, and neuromuscular maturation. The preschool years are the ones when fundamental motor patterns and skills are developed. During years up to ages six or seven a child engages in "increasing experimentation with a variety of motor tasks, and a period of gradual and progressive motor development and learning" (Malina, 1982, p. 215). Fundamental motor skills are generally attained by the time children enter the first grade; subsequently, "the quality of performance continues to improve as the fundamental patterns are refined and integrated into more complex movement sequences" (Malina, 1982, p. 215).

Viewed in this context, preschool rhythmic-movement instruction should focus on the *process* rather than the *product*. The importance of selecting age-appropriate movement patterns for musical responses becomes obvious. Table 5.5 lists selected motor developmental objectives for various age levels. Suggestions for linking these objectives with musical activities have been added.

Table 5.5. Motor Developmental Objectives

Age	Objective	Implications for Music Instruction
By age 2	Walks smoothly at various speeds. Hops on either foot. Jumps from still position. Squats and returns to standing position. Claps hands to rhythm, though imprecisely. Walks backward and sideways.	Illustrate the steady beat of walking by playing a drum beat that matches the child's walk, hop, jump, or claps. Illustrate melodic direction with whole body movement.
By age 3	Accomplishes sudden starts, stops, and changes of direction. Walks on tiptoe; learns to gallop. Copies rhythm patterns by clapping or stamping with greater accuracy. Eye-hand coordination developing; enjoys playing mallet and percussion instruments.	Teach simple circle games wherein a change of phrase in the music signals a change of direction. Introduce games in which children echo rhythm patterns of the teacher either by clapping, patting, or playing instruments.
By age 4	Hops, gallops, controls body movements quite well. Jumps forward as well as up and down. Slides, whirls, perhaps begins learning to skip. Eye-hand coordination better; mallet and percussion instruments enjoyed.	Jumping can elicit loud sounds on drum or piano; walking can elicit soft sounds. Teach simple circle and line dances. Provide opportunities for children to play simple accompaniments on drums and barred instruments.
By age 5	Small- and large-muscle control and coordination quite well developed. Learns simple dance steps; shows grace and coordination. Fine motor skills becoming more precise.	Teach circle games and line dances to help refine motor skills. Include echo-clapping and instrumental activities that provide opportunities to refine movement and instrumental skills.

Table 5.5. (continued)

Age	Objective	Implications for Music Instruction
By age 6	Runs, skips, jumps, sways; bounces ball and catches it fairly well. Very energetic; must "move." Skips, runs, jumps; throws and catches gracefully. Moves to music with understanding. Interested in musical games with rules; enjoys structured activities.	Engage in many rhythmic activities, both structured and "creative." Introduce and discuss musical terminology connected with musical movement (fast/slow; loud/soft; high/low). Introduce some simple folk dances.

The grace, consistency, and accuracy of motor movements vary considerably, both within individual children and among a group of young students. Not surprisingly, researchers have found that the ability to perform motor patterns does not mean that the children can synchronize them with a musical beat. This ability is dependent upon maturation, experience, and neuromuscular control. However, a significant factor in most performance achievement is motivation to practice the task. Music can provide that motivation (see Figure 5.4).

Movement activities, when considered in a music-instruction context, fall into two broad categories. The first is creative movement; the second, synchronized movement. A discussion of the existing research about each category follows.

CREATIVE MOVEMENT

Creative movement activities include those that do not necessarily require synchronization with "the beat." During the pre- and primary-school years, children are taught, for example, to respond to fast and slow tempi with whole body movement; to change direction or type of movement in a folk dance at the end of a musical phrase; or to vary intensity and range of movement to express loudness and softness. Such instruction provides the tools they need for creating their own expressive movements to music.

Figure 5.4. Music can provide the motivation for practice in performance of movement activities.

Children need instruction in movement to develop a "creative
movement repertoire." One researcher, studying three- to five-year-old
children's movement responses to music found that, among three-year-
old children, only a small number of movements were used (for half the
observation time, no change in movement was in evidence). This led
her to wonder whether this resulted from "fascination with movement
repetition, or . . . a limited creative movement repertoire which might be
enhanced by modeling or training" (Sims, 1984, p. 18). Perhaps "creative
movement" is possible only when the child has been taught a number
of movement patterns: "Given a particular level of ability, a child needs
more than some chance musical stimulus to help him make forms of
movement other than the instinctive swaying one. To make these new
movements, a child has to learn singing games and round dances"
(Moog, 1976, p. 113).

These studies underscore the importance of teaching many motor
patterns during the early years through action songs, finger plays,
musical games, and circle and line dances—in short, "preparing the
instrument." Normal growth and maturation, aided by experience and
instruction, enable the children to refine these movement patterns,
which they will use "creatively" throughout their life to express and
enjoy music.

SYNCHRONIZED MOVEMENT

How to teach children to "keep time" accurately has always been regarded as an important rhythmic instructional objective. Choksy calls the ability to "correctly identify and perform the beat in music" the most basic of all musical skills (Choksy, 1981, p. 24).

Most of our fine motor skills are learned through imitation. However, the motor patterns that we teach to young children must be compatible with their physical and maturational stages of development. "Keeping the beat" requires a highly controlled muscular response. Some children acquire this ability earlier than others; Moog wrote that "if (a child) can keep time by his fourth birthday, he can maintain it for considerably longer periods by age six" (Moog, 1976, p. 43). For children who need specific instruction and experience to acquire this skill, studies by Rainbow (1981) and Frega (1979) provide information about the kind of movements easiest for young children to synchronize with music. These researchers reported that, for three- and four-year-old children, simple marching or marching while clapping to music was extremely difficult. Chanting speech rhythm syllables was the easiest response, followed by clapping or keeping the beat with rhythm sticks (Figure 5.5). Frega (1979) found that when imitating rhythm patterns,

Figure 5.5. "Keeping the beat" with rhythm sticks helps establish the link between musical pulse and synchronized action.

Step 1: Say the beat. "For example, ask your students to chant 'HEAD, HEAD, HEAD, HEAD' or 'TAP, TAP, TAP, TAP.' . . . No music or movement is used when teaching this step." (p. 18)

Step 2: Say and do. For example, tap top of head while saying "Head." (p. 18)

Step 3: Whisper and do. "The teacher asks the students to repeat Step 2, but to whisper the chant. . . . In Step 3, music is added after the learners have become proficient in the activity." (p. 18)

Step 4: Think and do. "The teacher now asks the students to 'think' the words while responding with music, and while continuing the movement without the music (to internalize the beat)." (p. 19).

Weikart, 1982, pp. 17–19

Figure 5.6. Weikart's sequence for identifying and demonstrating rhythmic pulse.

"the best peformance is reached by chanting, then by using speech patterns, and finally by clapping" (p. 33).

Weikart, who studied methods of developing the ability to identify and "keep the beat" also proposed beginning with speech activities. She stated that "language is a natural bridge to movement" (Weikart, 1982, p. 15). Her four-step sequence for introducing the "beat" is presented in Figure 5.6.

Choksy has also proposed a sequence for achieving rhythmic accuracy. The sequence is: (1) performing the skill within a group situation with a leader, (2) performing the skill within a group, but without a leader, and (3) performing the skill alone. She states that ". . . it is this last step—performing alone—that is most often omitted by teachers, but is the most important step if musical independence is one of the goals of music education" (Choksy, 1981, p. 25).

Most early childhood educators are very adept at initiating and directing movement activities in the classroom. Such activities should be analyzed both for their age- and objective-appropriateness. Both creative and synchronized movement should be included in rhythmic-movement instruction: "The years up to six or seven years of age are among the most important developmentally. Teachers must take advantage of these years" (Choksy, 1981, p. 38).

The answer to the sixth true-false statement should be "false." Although large-muscle movements may be employed in rhythmic activities requiring synchronization, these experiences may need to be preceded by preparatory activities that include chanting and possibly clapping.

PLAYING INSTRUMENTS

EXPLORATION

Musical instruments are of great interest to young children. The last decade has seen acceptance of the idea of quite sophisticated instrumental training for children younger than four years of age, largely through the work of Shinichi Suzuki, who introduced a rote method of teaching stringed instruments to very young children. (The Suzuki Method is discussed in Chapter 7.)

However, the discussion in this chapter is concerned with methods of introducing children to common classroom instruments, such as drums, tambourines, rhythm sticks, tone bars, bells, autoharps and mallet instruments. When such instruments are introduced, young children do not initially use them to produce rhythms or tunes, but to experience sound. Voglar wrote: "At the age of two, the child satisfies his inclination to produce sounds by finding those objects which are sound-producing. Here he is very inventive, making use of everything he gets his hands on; dishes and cutlery, toys, etc." (Voglar, 1977, p. 136). When musical instruments are introduced, a teacher may observe reactions such as these:

> (The children) were simply enraptured by the sounds they produced with these instruments. They did not produce a definite rhythm pattern, but only isolated sounds. . . . Some of them put the instruments to their ears, others would put it against the ear of a friend. . . . In this case, the children were directed solely to sound producing. (Voglar, 1977, p. 136)

Such experiences allow a child to acquire much information about musical sounds. Andress (1980, pp. 88–89) has suggested that the experience of exploring the sound of but a single tone bar—one pitch—can introduce a child to at least three musical concepts:

1. Timbre—a bell has a ringing sound.
2. Duration—it can ring for a *long* or *short* time.
3. Volume—its sound can be *loud* or *soft* and can *gradually change* between the two qualities.

Teachers can find many opportunities during a school day to introduce individuals or small groups of children to instruments. Showing a child how to hold or play a tambourine, helping a child produce a satisfactory tone on a resonator bell or xylophone, or adding a song or a rhythmic chant to a beat produced by a child playing with a drum or pair of rhythm sticks—all of these constitute "instrumental instruction."

SKILL DEVELOPMENT

Perhaps the most complete description of the use of instruments in early childhood education is that given in the Pillsbury Foundation Studies report, *Music of Young Children,* by Moorhead and Pond (1978). In this book are many accounts of the ways children use musical instruments when no structure or instruction is imposed. Summations of their observations can provide guidelines for using instruments in the classroom. These summations, with added implications for teachers, are presented below:

1. Use of musical instruments naturally follows children's interest in all sound-making materials. Children are, first of all, interested in how instruments make sounds and then in their rhythmic and melodic possibilities (p. 46). (This observation suggests that traditional rhythm band activities and similar structured experiences should not be imposed upon children before they have had many opportunities for free exploration of instruments.)

2. "While a child can learn many things about instruments through free exploration, teaching has its place" (p. 48). However, teachers should be careful to heed the child's interest in an instrument, and provide instruction which is needed at the time, rather than "conventional instruction in rhythm or melody" (p. 48). (For example, there are various methods for holding and producing sound on autoharps, xylophones, recorders, and percussion instruments. The child's need for this kind of instruction precedes the need for counting beats or learning a rhythmic ostinato.)

3. Rhythm in music may be expressed in physical movement. When instrumental playing is added, "new resources of tone and rhythm for future musical growth" are provided (p. 116). (Children need to express their musical ideas through physical movement before instruments are introduced.)

4. Experiences with instruments lead to growth in understanding timbre, pitch, vibration, rhythm, tonal relationships and melody (p. 117). (This observation suggests purposeful use of instruments. Instruction should include lessons in how to manage the instrument, how to produce the most satisfactory sound, how to transform physical rhythm into sound, how to produce dynamic contrasts, and how to use instruments to communicate feelings and ideas—in short, how to use musical instruments to nurture creative expression.) "For if technical training is in advance of the child's needs it is unassimilable, and produces (as it does in adult musicians) creative sterility. And if the child has technical needs which are not satisfied his cre-

Figure 5.7. "While a child can learn many things about instruments through free exploration, teaching has its place" (Moorhead and Pond, 1978, p. 48).

ativity is apt to dry up because of his inability to function at his proper level" (p. 48).

The seventh true-false statement, "Forming a rhythm band is a good way to introduce children to classroom instruments," is false. Rather, children should have opportunities for investigating and playing individual instruments so that tone-color as well as dynamic and rhythmic/melodic possibilities may be explored.

CREATING MUSIC

"The child is born with creativity which the teacher fosters by understanding the child and offering him stimulating materials to encourage him to express his own ideas" (Stant, 1972, p. 138).

Singing can be creative. The spontaneous songs of young children are creative compositions. When children change, insert, or add new words to learned songs, they are creating new songs. Children acquire the tools for such creations from the songs we teach them and from the models we present when *we* change words and tunes to personalize, or accommodate their suggestions.

After "Miss Merry Mac" had been learned by a group of four-year-olds, Laura suggested a "coda" (an extended ending). The children thought this addition was fine:

Ne - ver a - gain,   Ne - ver a - gain,   Ne - ver a- gain!

Rhythmic movement can be creative. Children start by learning movements we teach them; later they rearrange and change them to create their own physical expressions of sound. Studies by Sims (1984) and Gilbert (1981) of the movement-to-music responses of young children show that range, scope, and correlation of movement to music improve dramatically during the preschool years. Sims (1984) reported that "The amount of rhythmic movement used by 4 and 5 year olds was . . . over three times as much as that used by the 3-year-olds" (p. 16).

Playing instruments can be creative. One investigator found that improvisations produced by preschool youngsters on xylophones progressed from sheer "motor energy" sounds to those showing musical characteristics, including repetition and synchronization with a rhythmic beat (Flohr, 1984). The ability to create on instruments is largely dependent on the "tools" the child possesses—a sense of musical structure acquired through many and varied music activities.

Much has been written about the loss of creativity among our children as they progress through the elementary school years. Part of this is due to social maturation, when "following the rules" becomes important. Part may be due to the teacher's feeling that there is too much to be taught to allow much time for creative tasks. If the latter is a contributing factor, we need to examine all our planned experiences for their "creative possibilities" and include them in our lessons. In addition, we need to provide time, materials, and a place for individual creative efforts. Every school or center should contain a music interest center where individual children can "make something new to themselves" when the spirit moves.

Choksy (1981) has reminded us, "All the teacher must do is provide opportunity for creativity. He or she will not have to implant ideas; the ideas will evolve from the experiences of the child" (p. 49). But we must learn to listen, respond, and encourage. This is "creative teaching."

(Note: the answer to the eighth true-false statement should be "false." Creativity can be nurtured, if not directly taught.)

SUMMARY

We may conclude this chapter by repeating, for emphasis, the last true-false statement in our "test." It reads, "Age five or six, when children enter public school, is the best time to commence music instruction." The answer, emphatically in the negative, has been provided all through this chapter. Musical skills are developmental in nature, as are intellectual, motor, and social ones. However, the beginnings of all these skills appear in infancy. Therefore, teaching, as we have defined it in this chapter, also should begin in the first year, and continue through the preschool years.

QUESTIONS FOR DISCUSSION/SUGGESTED ACTIVITIES

1. Observe a child at any or all of the following ages: three months, six months, nine months, twelve months. Do the child's behavioral auditory characteristics agree with those stated in Table 5.2?
2. Determine how each of the basic concepts stated in Table 5.1 might be introduced through movement or through pictorial representation.
3. Start a card file of rhythmic chants, rhymes, and poems that could encourage the development of singing skills.
4. Examine a current early childhood songbook. Are most of the songs placed in keys that accommodate the most easily produced singing range of young children? If not, in what direction do they err?
5. Identify several action songs or song games in which various basic motor patterns may be practiced (e.g., skipping, hopping, trotting, galloping).
6. Choose a well-known children's tale, such as "The Three Bears" or "Billy Goats Gruff." Plan how students could provide sound effects using classroom instruments.
7. Learn half-a-dozen songs that may be "personalized" by inserting names of children, or by changing the words to fit various activities.

REFERENCES AND SUGGESTED READINGS

Ambron, S. R. (1978). *Child development.* New York: Holt, Rinehart & Winston.

Andress, B. (1980). *Music experiences in early childhood.* New York: Holt, Rinehart & Winston.

Andress, B. (1985). The practitioner involves young children in music. In J. Boswell (Ed.), *The young child and music: Contemporary principles in child development and music education: Proceedings of the Music in Early Childhood Conference*, pp. 53–63. Reston, VA: Music Educators National Conference.

Andress, B.; Heimann, H.; Rinehart, C.; & Talbert, E. (1973). *Music in early childhood.* Reston, VA: Music Educators National Conference.

Attebury, B. W. (1984). Children's singing voices: A review of selected research. *Council for Research in Music Education, 80,* 51–63.

Bayless, K., & Ramsey, M. (1978). *Music: A way of life for the young child.* St. Louis, MO: The C. V. Mosby Co.

Boswell, J. (Ed.). (1985). *The young child and music: Contemporary principles in child development and music education: Proceedings of the music in early childhood conference.* Reston, VA: Music Educators National Conference.

Bredekamp, S. (Ed.). (1986). *Developmentally appropriate practice.* Washington, DC: National Association for the Education of Young Children.

Bruner, J. (1968). *Toward a theory of instruction.* New York: W. W. Norton & Co., Inc.

Choksy, L. (1981). *The Kodaly context: Creating an environment for musical learning.* Englewood Cliffs, NJ: Prentice-Hall, Inc.

Christiansen, H. (1938). *Bodily movements of young children in relation to rhythm in music.* New York: Columbia University.

Davidson, L. (1985). Preschool children's tonal knowledge: Antecedents of scale. In J. Boswell (Ed.), *The young child and music: Contemporary principles in child development and music education: Proceedings of the music in early childhood conference,* pp. 25–40. Reston, VA: Music Educators National Conference.

Flohr, J. W. (1984). *Young children's improvisations.* Research paper presented at the Music Educators National Conference, Chicago, IL.

Frega, A. L. (1979). Rhythmic tasks with 3-, 4-, and 5-year-old children: A study made in Argentine republic. *Council for Research in Music Education, 45,* 1–20.

Fridman, R. (1973). The first cry of the newborn: Basis for the child's future musical development. *Journal of Research in Music Education, 21* (3), 264–269.

Fullard, W. G., Jr. (1967). Operant training of aural musical discriminations with preschool children. *Journal of Research in Music Education, 15* (3), 201–209.

Gell, H. (1973). *Music, movement and the young child.* Pittsburgh, PA: Volkerin Bros., Inc.

Gilbert, J. P. (1981). Motoric music skill development in young children: A longitudinal investigation. *Psychology of Music, 9* (1), 21–24.

Gould, A. O. (1969). Developing specialized programs for singing. *Council for Research in Music Education, 17,* 9–22.

Greenberg, M. (1976). Research in music in early childhood education: A survey with recommendations. *Council for Research in Music Education, 45,* 1–20.

Greer, R. D.; Dorow, L.; & Hanser, S. (1973). Music discrimination training and the music selection behavior of nursery and primary level children. *Council for Research in Music Education, 35,* 30–43.

Hair, H. I. (1973). The effect of training on the harmonic discrimination of first-grade children. *Journal of Research in Music Education, 21* (1), 85–90.

Hair, H. I. (1977). Discrimination of tonal direction on verbal and nonverbal tasks by first-grade children. *Journal of Research in Music Education, 25* (3), 197–210.

Jaques-Dalcroze, É. (1921). *Rhythm, music, and education.* (L. F. Rubenstein, Trans.). Great Britain: Hazell Watson & Viney Ltd. for the Dalcroze Society.

Jaques-Dalcroze, É. (1930). *Eurhythmics, art, and education.* (F. Rothwell, Trans.; C. Cox, Ed.). New York: A. S. Barnes & Co.

Jenkins, G. G., & Shacter, H. S. (1975). *These are your children* (4th ed.). Glenville, IL: Scott, Foresman & Co.

Jersild, A. T., & Bienstock, S. F. (1935). *Development of rhythm in children.* New York: Columbia University.

Jetter, J. T. (1978). An instructional model for teaching identification and naming of music phenomena to preschool children. *Journal of Research in Music Education, 26* (2), 97–110.

Kirkpatrick, W. C., Jr. (1962). Relationship between the singing ability of prekindergarten children and their home musical environment (Doctoral dissertation, University of Southern California, 1962). *Dissertation Abstracts International, 23,* 886A.

Kucenski, D. (1977). Implementation and empirical testing of a sequential musical sensory learning program on the infant learner (Doctoral dissertation, Northwestern University, 1977). *Dissertation Abstracts International, 38,* 4646A.

Leach, P. (1983). *Your baby and child from birth to age five.* New York: Alfred A. Knopf.

Loucks, D. G. (1974). The development of an instrument to measure instrumental timbre concepts of four-year-old and five-year-old children: A feasibility study (Doctoral dissertation, The Ohio State University, 1974). *Dissertation Abstracts International, 35,* 5446A.

Malina, R. M. (1982). Motor development in the early years. In S. G. Moore & C. R. Cooper (Eds.), *The young child: Reviews of research, Vol. 3* (pp. 211–229). Washington, DC: National Association for the Education of Young Children.

McDonald, R. L., & Schuckert, R. F. (1968). An attempt to modify the musical preferences of preschool children. *Journal of Research in Music Education, 16* (1), 39–44.

Moog, H. (1976). The development of musical experience in children of pre-school age. *Psychology of Music, 4*(2), 38–45.

Moore, S. G., & Cooper, C. R. (Eds.) (1982). *The young child: Reviews of research* (Vol. 3). Washington, DC: National Association for the Education of Young Children.

Moorhead, G. E., & Pond, D. (1978). *Music of young children.* Santa Barbara, CA: Pillsbury Foundation for Advancement of Music Education.

Newman, G. (1979). *Teaching children music: Fundamentals of music and method.* Dubuque, IA: Wm. C. Brown Co.

Noy, P. (1968). The development of music ability. *The Psychoanalytic Study of the Child, 23,* 332–347.

Ostwald, P. F. (1973). Musical behavior in early childhood. *Developmental Medicine and Child Neurology, 15* (1), 367–375.

Piper, R. M., & Shoemaker, D. M. (1973). Formative evaluation of a kindergarten music program based on behavioral objectives. *Journal of Research in Music Education, 21* (2), 145–152.

Rainbow, E. L. (1981). A final report on a three-year investigation of the rhythmic abilities of pre-school aged children. *Council for Research in Music Education: Bulletin, 66/67,* 69–73.

Ramsey, J. H. (1981). An investigation of the effects of age, singing ability, and experience with pitched instruments on preschool children's melodic perception. *Journal of Research in Music Education, 31* (2), 133–145.

Roberts, E., & Davies, A. (1975). Poor pitch singing: Response of monotone singers to a program of remedial training. *Journal of Research in Music Education, 23* (4), 227–239.

Roberts, E., & Davies, A. (1976). A method for extending the vocal range of "monotone" school children. *Psychology of Music, 4* (1), 29–43.

Romanek, M. L. (1974). A self-instructional program for musical concept development in preschool children. *Journal of Research in Music Education, 22* (2), 129–135.

Scott, C. R. (1977). Pitch concept formation in preschool children (Doctoral dissertation, University of Washington, 1977). *Dissertation Abstracts International, 38,* 3133A.

Sims, W. L. (1984). *Young children's creative movement to music: Categories of movement, rhythmic characteristics, and reactions to change.* Research paper presented at the Music Educators National Conference, Chicago, IL.

Smith, R. B. (1963). The effect of group vocal training on the singing ability of nursery school children. *Journal of Research in Music Education, 11* (2), 137–141.

Stant, M. A. (1972). *The young child: His activities and materials.* Englewood Cliffs, NJ: Hall-Prentice, Inc.

Stephens, J., & Evans, E. (1973). *Development and classroom learning.* New York: Holt, Rinehart and Winston.

Tolbert, M. (Ed.). (1980). *Current issues in music education. Vol. 12: Music of young children.* Columbus, OH: The Ohio State University.

Turnipseed, J. P.; Thompson, A.; & Kennedy, N. (1974). *Utilization of a structured classical music listening program in the development of auditory discrimination skills of preschool children.* Research paper presented at the Music Educators National Conference, Atlantic City, NJ.

Van Zee, N. (1975). Verbal-descriptive and performance responses of kindergarten children to selected musical stimuli and terminology (Doctoral dissertation, University of Iowa, 1974). *Dissertation Abstracts International, 35,* 4604A.

Voglar, M. (1977). On musical creativity. *Predskolski Dete, 9,* 129–143.

Webster, P. (1980). Pitch discrimination of tonal direction by preschool children on verbal and non-verbal tasks. In M. Tolbert (Ed.), *Current issues in music education. Vol. 12: Music of young children* (pp. 60–76). Columbus, OH: The Ohio State University.

Weikart, P. S. (1982). *Teaching movement and dance.* Ypsilanti, MI: The High Scope Press.

Weiser, M. G. (1982). *Group care and education of infants and toddlers.* St. Louis: The C. V. Mosby Co.

Young, L. (1982). An investigation of young children's music concept development using non-verbal and manipulative techniques (Doctoral dissertation, The Ohio State University, 1982). *Dissertation Abstracts International, 43,* 1345A.

Zimmerman, M. P. (1971). *Musical characteristics of children.* Reston, VA: Music Educators National Conference.

Chapter 6

Integrating the Handicapped Child into Music Activities

Kate Gfeller

The past decade has seen tremendous changes in the care and education of the young handicapped child. With the passage of Public Law 94-142, The Education for All Handicapped Children, enacted in 1975, there has been a change away from institutionalization of the handicapped and toward inclusion of the exceptional child in the mainstream of educational experiences. Even severely handicapped children now attend public schools with the support of special education services (Alley, 1979; Jellison, 1979; Forsythe and Jellison, 1977).

A second change has been the emphasis on early intervention for handicapped children. Acknowledging the value of early programming and environmental stimulus, the federal government has instituted early childhood programs through Public Law 99-457. This legislation mandates early intervention for the handicapped child from birth. As a result, it is increasingly common to find handicapped children in preschools as well as lower elementary school classes.

In addition to working with children who are diagnosed as handicapped from birth, the early childhood teacher may find another segment of the handicapped population attending preschool programs. This includes children with mild developmental disabilities (borderline and educable mentally retarded) or learning disabled children who have not been formally identified and diagnosed. Such diagnosis may not take place until the first or second grade (Kirk and Gallagher, 1979; Shelton, 1971; Hunter, Schucman, and Friedlander, 1972; Lerner, 1981). Therefore, some children participating in a music program who "appear" normal may deviate somewhat from peers in their level of involvement or proficiency. These children, like their more obviously handicapped peers, can be puzzling to the music teacher unless there exists a basic understanding of such children's capabilities, special needs, and ways of differing from nonhandicapped children.

As Chapter 3 has emphasized, a young child's musical capabilities are shaped by a number of factors: (1) native or inherent capabilities (for the handicapped child, these can include both disabilities resulting from genetic or congenital defects, such as Down's Syndrome, and handicaps acquired in childhood resulting from disease or injury, such as polio or head trauma); (2) developmental factors including both musical skills and skills that influence or interact with musical growth, such as memory and discrimination; and (3) environmental opportunities. These same three factors shape, perhaps more dramatically, the musical capabilities of the preschool child who is handicapped.

These three factors will be examined in this chapter in view of how they affect the skill areas that figure prominently in music activities: cognitive or mental function, listening perception, singing skills, motor/rhythmic competencies, and social skills. While music teachers can do little to change the inherent capabilities of the child, they can structure an environment that will facilitate successful participation of handicapped children in music experiences.

COGNITIVE LIMITATIONS

INHERENT CAPABILITIES

Because mental activity is such an integral part of most musical activities, we often take it for granted. When a music educator works with a child with cognitive difficulties, however, the critical role of cognition becomes painfully clear. Mental activity is the driving force behind such seemingly simple tasks as coming to attention; maintaining attention; following directions; recalling information such as words, melodies, or rhythm; understanding concepts; discriminating; and many creative acts.

Most commonly, the music teacher will encounter difficulties that result from three primary types of cognitive limitations: (1) overall lower mental functioning, as occurs in mental retardation/developmental disabilities; (2) specific learning disabilities, which may result from a variety of causes, including neurological dysfunction; and (3) accompanying attentional problems, which hamper learning (Payne and Patton, 1981; Bruscia, 1981). These disabilities will generally result in a slower rate of learning and/or a higher rate of inaccuracies in many types of musical responses.

While some may entertain the belief that mentally retarded children are naturally gifted in music, research has shown that these children generally earn lower total scores on music aptitude tests than nonretarded children of the same chronological age (Bruscia, 1981; Iancone, 1977; Peters, 1970; McLeish and Higgs, 1967). While there are isolated cases of unusual musical talent among the mentally handicapped (Shuter, 1968), lower musical aptitude is more the norm, and is probably a function of either lower intelligence or lower mental age (Bruscia, 1981; McLeish and Higgs, 1967). While retarded children show capabilities equal to or better than nonretarded peers in tests of simple perception, tests requiring musical memory or discrimination show lower than average proficiency among mentally retarded children when compared with nonretarded peers.

Let us translate these findings into musical skills. The mentally handicapped child may take longer to learn song lyrics or concepts such as size, shape, and color. The child may exhibit more inaccuracies in tasks such as imitation of rhythmic patterns. Responses may be very inconsistent. These problems may be either caused or exacerbated by difficulties in paying attention or attending to the appropriate stimulus (Bruscia, 1981; Shuter, 1968).

DEVELOPMENTAL FACTORS

The role of development is central to understanding the learning patterns of the mentally retarded/developmentally delayed child. Mental retardation results from a defect in intelligence (congenital or due to some damage after birth), which has two major effects: (1) a reduction in the rate at which the different stages of development are reached, and (2) a lower level of attainment within the sequence of stages. In other words, the retarded child will take longer to pass through each stage and will pass through fewer stages than does a normal person (Fotheringham and Morris, 1976). The amount of delay and limitation will depend on the severity of retardation. (See Table 6.1, which provides an overall developmental schedule for mildly, moderately, and severely retarded children.)

For example, an educable mentally retarded child (EMR) develops at a rate that is approximately one-half to three-quarters that of the average child (Kirk and Gallagher, 1979). That means that when an EMR child is about four years old, he may be functioning at about the level of a two- or three-year-old. As a result, a child who is chronologically within the age range of preoperational capabilities may be functioning more closely to a sensorimotor level of development.

In terms of musical development, research with children who have moderate retardation shows these children comparable to mental age peers in musical sensitivity (ability to receive and respond to musi-

Table 6.1. Developmental Rates of Mentally Retarded Children

Degree of Retardation	Preschool Years	Elementary School Years
Mild (Educable) Develops at 1/2 to 3/4 the rate of the average child.	Develops social and communication skills. Minimal sensory or motor deficits that may not be identified until first few years of school.	Reaches academic competencies of a sixth grader by late teens. Can be guided to social conformity.
Moderate (Trainable) Develops at 1/4 to 1/2 the rate of the average child.	Talks, communicates fairly well. Fair motor development. Self-help training can be productive.	Profits from social and occupational training. Works toward 2nd grade academic achievement, although academic tasks are geared toward daily living skills rather than traditional academic tasks.
Severe Develops at a rate of 1/4 or less than that of the average child.	Poor speech and motor development. Profits little from training in self-help.	Can talk or learn to communicate. Can benefit from basic habit training.

Adapted from Kirk and Gallagher, 1979.

cal stimuli) with the exception of lower proficiency in imitation, clapping, and singing. With maturation, these three skills show significant improvement (Peters, 1970). In identifying the acquisition of musical skills, Rider (1977) found that conservation for musical components developed in the following sequence: rhythm first, followed by volume and tempo.

Not only is maturation an important factor for mentally retarded children. It may be an important factor for some children with learning disabilities as well. A learning disabled child has average or higher IQ; yet there are serious learning difficulties that appear in one or more areas of academic functioning. While Reid and Hresko (1981) state that the label "learning disability" is inappropriate for a preschool child since it intimates failure in academic tasks, some of these disabilities surface during the preschool years in activities of a preacademic nature. In some cases, these difficulties can be attributed to maturational lag or an immature neurological system (Lerner, 1981; Reid and Hresko, 1981). If this be the situation, some learning-disabled children may need only additional time to master tasks associated with particular levels of development of their chronological peers. In other instances not attributable to developmental lag, remedial strategies become necessary.

ENVIRONMENTAL FACTORS

While maturation is an important part of readiness for various musical tasks, one cannot underestimate the role of environmental opportunity in mentally handicapped children's development. According to Fotheringham and Morris (1976), experience with the environment produces content of learning, thought, and personality. If the experiences are of inadequate quality, the child's ultimate competence will be adversely affected. In short, while music educators can not change nature, they can provide the type of environment in which the children can reach their potential.

Experiences in the early years are of extreme importance in the mentally retarded child's overall development. According to Fotheringham and Morris (1976), "the 'traditional' middle-class nursery school with its heavy emphasis in general stimulation, . . . self-help skills, socialization, and language is a relevant model for the provision of a good learning environment" (p. 61). While this is not to suggest that the music educator should assume the role of therapist, many of the music activities that are beneficial to the development of the nonhandicapped child can benefit the developmentally delayed child as well. Most important is the opportunity for a wide range of experiences in which the child can practice skills, improve proficiency, and be stimulated toward the next level of skill (Fotheringham and Morris, 1976).

The retarded child goes through the same developmental process as other children and has similar needs for stimulation and affection. Because of the slower rate of learning, however, there will be greater need for highly structured learning, which includes much repetition in order to master each skill (Fotheringham and Morris, 1976; Payne and Patton, 1981; Bruscia, 1981). It is important to keep in mind that repetition refers to the skill being mastered, not the activity. Therefore, a particular skill can be mastered by exposure to a variety of creative and stimulating activities, all of which emphasize the same task. For example, the concepts of "fast and slow" might be reinforced by playing rhythm instruments in various tempi, through movement activities involving various rates of movement, or through listening to contrasting musical examples. In fact, creative and interesting activities will maintain interest and motivation, both important factors in helping the child to learn (Payne and Patton, 1981; Fotheringham and Morris, 1976).

In addition to repetition, several other teaching strategies can be helpful:

1. Select experiences most relevant to the stage of development in which the child can interact, practice skills, and add content to their experiences (Fotheringham and Morris, 1976; Bruscia, 1981). This may mean having the child participate in a music group with peers at the same level of development rather than the same chronological age. With the support of the facility director and family, this can be easily arranged.

2. If possible, have the child incorporated into small-group activities. Because mentally retarded children often have accompanying physical handicaps, they may need additional attention and physical assistance in completing tasks. This attention can be more readily provided in a smaller group or through the help of an aide.

3. Plan the learning environment to reduce the likelihood of distraction by irrelevant stimuli, which can easily interfere with selective attention of the retarded child (Bruscia, 1981).

4. Ritualize verbal and physical cues that signal particular responses such as paying attention, sitting quietly, or listening carefully (Bruscia, 1981).

In addition to these suggestions, the musical task itself might be modified to encourage participation and mastery:

1. Reduce the difficulty of the task by breaking it into smaller sections, using sections of songs with much repetition, adapting the lyrics or melody to include simpler vocabulary or melodic/rhythmic patterns. This should not be misconstrued to mean using bland or uninteresting music. Captivating melodies, rhythm, and harmonies are crucial to maintaining attention (Bruscia, 1981).

2. Provide much repetition, but provide spaced rehearsals rather than long, extensive sessions. Incorporate a nice mixture of familiar and novel approaches to teaching a concept.

3. Select materials that are appropriate for the developmental level of the child. This can include selection of music, instruments, and teaching techniques that may be normally used with a younger child.

4. Try and make instructions short and clear. Give one instruction at a time coupled with a demonstration. Then give adequate time for

response. Bruscia (1981) recommends that verbal instructions be no longer than sixty seconds in length.

5. Break down complex tasks and teach them in a logical sequence. New materials or tasks can be introduced in conjunction with previously mastered skills in order to facilitate assimilation and recall (Bruscia, 1981).

6. Assist the child in selective attention by drawing the focus to the most important part of the stimuli being presented (Bruscia, 1981; Payne and Patton, 1981). For example, if you are focusing on rhythmic skills, initially remove competing musical stimuli such as harmony and melody. Continue to point up the rhythmic qualities as you increase the complexity of the task.

Although learning disabilities have a different etiology from mental retardation (these children have normal intellectual functioning), many of these same recommendations apply. These children, too, require very clear instructions, extra time for response, more repetition, and breaking down of more difficult tasks into smaller parts (Lerner, 1981). However, because learning disabilities tend to affect specific areas of learning (rather than the overall lower functioning found in the mentally retarded), the teacher will find that no single strategy is appropriate for all learning-disabled children. Compensatory or remediation strategies must be individualized. This requires a great deal of patience as well as some trial and error.

LIMITATIONS IN LISTENING SKILLS

INHERENT CAPABILITIES

A child's listening skill is, in part, dependent upon adequate auditory acuity. As any test of musical ability will demonstrate, there is a relatively wide range of recognition and discrimination of sound even among so called "normal" children. For the hearing-impaired child, however, there exist such severe deficits in hearing acuity that some type of amplification will be required in order for the child to access environmental sounds.

Populations who may have poor hearing acuity include the hard-of-hearing or hearing-impaired, as well as other handicapped children (such as mentally retarded or orthopedically handicapped children), who have a hearing loss in addition to their primary disability. A hearing impairment should not be interpreted as total lack of sound. It is quite rare for a hearing-impaired child to have total hearing loss (Darrow, 1985). More often, the child will have some measurable hearing

Figure 6.1. Hearing aids, earphones, cassette players, or similar equipment now enable aural learning for most hard-of-hearing children and help develop residual hearing.

(called residual hearing) in certain frequency and intensity ranges. For example, many children with an inner-ear problem (sensorineural loss) will have very poor or no acuity in upper frequencies, but can hear relatively loud sounds in lower frequencies. Children with conductive hearing losses (which are usually due to a middle ear problem) will have what is known as a "flat" loss, with similar levels of hearing impairment across all frequencies. Children with conductive hearing losses generally benefit to a greater extent from amplification of sounds through a hearing aid than those with sensorineural loss (Buechler, 1982).

In addition to the misconception that deafness involves total lack of sound, many people mistakenly believe that hearing-impaired children cannot hear or enjoy music. Quite the contrary. Research on the musical perception of the hearing impaired shows that hearing impaired children are able to hear or feel many sounds in music—particularly percussive and rhythmic elements (Korduba, 1975; Darrow, 1985; Gfeller, 1986). In fact, when comparing rhythmic perception of normal and hearing-impaired children, Korduba (1975) found that the hearing-impaired children actually performed better in reproducing rhythmic patterns on a drum. She concluded that this was due to the subject's ability to utilize visual and kinesthetic cues. Melodic and harmonic information will probably be less accessible, particularly to the severely hearing-impaired child (Buechler, 1982). In short, while a hearing problem will limit the listening skills in comparison to those of nonhandicapped children, the music teacher can encourage musical enjoyment by making full use of residual hearing (Darrow, 1985).

DEVELOPMENTAL FACTORS

As research has shown, musical listening skills include an array of subskills, including the ability to perceive, discriminate, and recall pitch, melody, rhythm, harmony, and timbre. Chapter 5 pointed up that these subskills develop at different points in a child's normal development. This development is partially dependent on exposure to sound. In the case of the severely hearing-impaired child, there will be little auditory stimulation unless the child is provided with a hearing aid. According to audiologists, the auditory development of such a child begins not at birth, as is the case with normally hearing children, but rather at the time the child is aided (Davis and Hardick, 1981).

Developmental factors are also important in considering the auditory capabilities of the mentally retarded child, with or without hearing loss. Because recognition and discrimination of sounds requires a number of skills such as attending to pertinent stimuli or the ability to recall earlier sounds and make comparisons (McLeish and Higgs, 1967), the listening skills of the retarded child may lag behind those of age group peers (Grant and Share, 1985). Therefore, the music educator may need to adapt the listening environment in order to incorporate successfully the developmentally delayed child. This may include the use of shorter, simpler sound sequences or discrimination tasks that include gross contrasts. As the child progresses, more complex and subtle discriminatory stimuli can be utilized.

ENVIRONMENTAL FACTORS

While Piagetian theory emphasizes the role of maturation in skill attainment, Piaget also emphasized the importance of a rich environment that provides opportunities for assimilation and accommodation. Even for a child with limited auditory capabilities, environmental factors can enhance awareness of and ability to discriminate auditory information (Lowenbraun, Appelman, and Callahan, 1980; Darrow, 1985).

A number of relatively simple strategies can enhance music listening for the hearing impaired child:

1. The music teacher should be familiar with proper use of hearing aids and, whenever possible, place the musical activity in a setting with minimal ambiant noise (these noises are picked up by the hearing aid and compete with desired sounds). A room that is fully enclosed and carpeted is ideal. A wooden surface can be used to "amplify" specific desired sounds.

2. If the hearing-impaired child uses sign language, incorporate signs into singing activities. All of the children can participate in sign as a form of finger play or movement, both a natural part of early childhood music. Exaggerated signing appears much like dance or mime in form and can be aesthetically pleasing to all children.

3. All children benefit from the use of visual aids, but such aids are critical for the hearing-impaired, since the visual system is their primary mode of information. For example, visual cues such as Kodaly pictorial notation can be used in teaching rhythmic patterns (Gfeller, 1986).

4. Hearing-impaired children should be seated in a location where they can see the instructor's face for easy lip reading. They should also be able to watch or "feel" instrumental work on rhythm instruments, since deaf children can often imitate patterns accurately if given adequate visual cues (Korduba, 1975).

5. Sound equipment of good quality should be selected with little distortion and rich bass harmonics (Buechler, 1982). This helps the child use residual hearing more effectively than sound that is distorted or of poor fidelity.

6. Musical instruments should be selected with the child's residual hearing in mind. For example, if the child has greater acuity in low frequencies, select instruments with lower pitches, such as bass xylophones, pianos, and large drums. Instruments with vibrating surfaces, such as guitars, pianos, or drums, allow tactile access to music—even for profoundly deaf children (Buechler, 1982; Darrow, 1985).

7. Emphasize rhythmic and percussive qualities of music (Buechler, 1982; Fahey and Birkenshaw, 1972). They are generally more accessible than melodic or harmonic features. It is interesting to note, however, that some music therapists have had some success in using vocal exercises to improve vocal range and inflection (Darrow and Jones-Starmer, 1986).

LIMITATIONS IN SINGING

INHERENT CAPABILITIES

Communication through speech is a process that seems to occur as if by osmosis for most children (Quigley and Paul, 1984). Infants learn much about language incidentally from hearing speech and song around them. Further, they gather great pleasure from their own babbling as well as the attention they earn from their coos, shrieks, and shouts (Davis and Hardick, 1981). In this early vocal play, the children are learning to control their vocal expression, including the inflections and rhythmic patterns that will soon be part of song.

Unfortunately, this natural language acquisition process is disturbed for some handicapped children. The deaf child will begin to make vocal sounds, but since they are not reinforced by hearing their own miraculous sounds, it is common for this babbling process to stop (Davis and Hardick, 1981). Further, they do not have ready access to vocal models of parents and siblings. There are other handicapped children who can hear the lovely lilt of the mother's lullaby, but because of brain damage or orthopedic handicaps that affect the oral musculature, they have limited or no expressive powers with which to respond (Miller, 1982; Rudenberg, 1982).

Children with severe retardation also may develop singing and language skills at a painfully slow rate, with continual stimulation and reinforcement required to coax even simple utterances. Less severely retarded children may have greater vocal output, but may demonstrate limited vocal range or difficulty in discriminating and matching some pitch and melodic features (Bruscia, 1981; Larson, 1977; Grant, 1977; Dileo, 1976). Other children who suffer from chronic health problems affecting respiratory capacity may have the developmental skills to use longer utterances or wider range but lack the vital capacity to do so (Rudenberg, 1982; Schwankovsky, 1982).

In addition to difficulties with vocal production (pitched inflections, melodic contour), handicapped children may have difficulties with songs that include the use of text. The inability to produce correct vowels or consonant sounds (called articulation disorders) can be a problem for many retarded children, hearing-impaired children, speech-disordered children, and some orthopedically handicapped children (Miller, 1982; Rudenberg, 1982). While stuttering (dysfluency) may momentarily "disappear" (Galloway, 1974) during singing, other speech problems such as articulation or incorrect vocal quality (such as that found in a child with cleft palate) will hamper communication in song lyrics as well as in spoken word (Miller, 1982; Rudenberg, 1982).

DEVELOPMENTAL FACTORS

As in cognitive functioning and listening skills, the subskills required for singing may show some improvement with maturation in children whose difficulty is related to developmental delays. For example, the mildly retarded child who has few physical handicaps may demonstrate very similar singing skills to peers of similar mental age. Carey (1958) found that educably retarded children responded positively to musical activities such as singing, noting that their musical progress was at a similar rate to their progress in other academic areas. Effective teaching methods for singing approximated those used with nonretarded children, although teachers proceeded at a slower pace and included more repetition.

Unfortunately, singing skills among children with some types of neurological and orthopedic dysfunctions do not improve with age. In these situations, the teacher can encourage vocalization of melody and text, but should expect little if any progress as a result of maturation. Consequently, expectations must be realistic in terms of musical objectives.

ENVIRONMENTAL FACTORS

As with the nonhandicapped child, there are a number of instructional decisions that can maximize the handicapped child's ability to sing. These are listed below:

1. The teacher must provide opportunity and encouragement to vocalize and try sounds that approximate singing (Bruscia, 1981). This is particularly helpful for the developmentally delayed child who needs additional time and experience to master a given task. This is also important to hearing-impaired children (Darrow, 1985), who may have little motivation to sing (since they get limited auditory feedback from their own singing) or may even feel embarrassed about their voice if peers have made negative comments.

2. The children need many opportunities to hear good vocal models.

3. Songs should be selected carefully for (a) range, (b) structural characteristics, and (c) lyrics. As Larson's (1977) study on vocal ranges of the mentally retarded indicates, standard music texts for children include many songs outside the optimal vocal range for moderately retarded children. Therefore, songs with lower as well as narrower ranges can be helpful. According to Dileo (1976), the average singing range of the mentally retarded is ten half steps smaller and four half steps lower than nonretarded peers. Such a range proves more comfortable for handicapped voices, and, moreover, Grant and Share (1985) found that pitch perception of mentally retarded children was

significantly better within this range. Therefore, one might anticipate more accuracy in imitation of vocal contour as well.

Structurally, songs that include a great deal of repetition are even more crucial to the developmentally delayed child who has poor short-term recall than for the nonhandicapped child. Further, when presented with very lengthy melodies, the retarded child has a tendency to forget initial segments of the melody. Therefore, melodies should be of reasonable length and include adequate redundancy.

Songs should be selected with concern for their subject matter and vocabulary difficulty. Knowing the mental age of the retarded child should provide guidelines for choice of song topics and appropriate vocabulary. These areas are of concern for hearing-impaired children of normal intelligence as well, for as a result of their hearing loss most deaf children lag several years or more behind age-group peers in language attainment (Davis and Hardick, 1981). Simple vocabulary, meaningful content, and redundant lyrics and melody are all-important to success in singing.

Additional features that can aid acquisition and recall of songs include visual aids and movement activities that "dramatize" the song's content. Visual representation is particularly helpful to the hearing-impaired child who relies so heavily on visual cues for learning.

4. The teacher should provide additional time for mastery by including more repetitions and allowing more time for recall for children with mental deficits (Bruscia, 1981).

5. For children who truly struggle and seem to find no joy in singing, the teacher should consider alternative forms of participation, such as using rhythm instruments or movement.

6. For those children with respiratory limitations, songs should be selected with shorter phrases, which give more opportunity for rest. Some conditions can actually benefit from the exercise of singing; the teacher may allow for gradual increase of vital capacity. But teachers should be aware that some conditions that cause ongoing deterioration (such as cystic fibrosis) will show gradual decline in breath control (Miller, 1982; Rudenberg, 1982).

MOTOR AND RHYTHMIC LIMITATIONS

INHERENT CAPABILITIES

In Chapter 3, movement was described as a natural response to music: Children as young as six months show movement responses to music, starting with whole body, unsynchronized response, with increasing precision as the child matures (Moog, 1976). In music activities, beginning responses will be guided into rhythmic hand-clapping, marching and walking to music, creative movement, imitation of rhythmic patterns, and playing of rhythm instruments. All of these are common activities for the nonhandicapped child but may be labored or impossible for some children with serious motor difficulties.

The primary group of handicapped children with motor difficulties are those who have orthopedic (physical) handicaps (OH). This classification refers to children whose primary disability is some type of motor dysfunction. In addition to OH children, children with other types of handicaps (see Figure 6.2) may also have secondary problems with motor skills.

There can be great variance in the type of motor difficulty or severity of handicap. For example, one child with cerebral palsy may

---

G/F = Difficulty with gross motor movement and flexibility
FM = Difficulty with fine motor coordination
P = Difficulty with motor precision
S/E = Limited strength and endurance

Trainable and severely mentally retarded—G/F, FM, P, and S/E may all accompany this developmental disability. Specific type and severity of motor dysfunction depends on location and extent of accompanying neurological or physical impairments.

Educable mentally retarded—G/F, FM, and P most prevalent but generally to lesser extent than in more severely retarded individuals. Awkwardness, clumsiness, poor precision.

Neurologically impaired—The child may show a variety of motor difficulties of varying degrees depending on location and extent of brain damage.

Orthopedically Handicapped—G/F, FM, P, and S/E will occur in a variety of combinations and a continuum of severity.

Visually impaired—G/F, P the most prevalent due to lack of training or experience in mobility and orientation.

Hearing-impaired—while motor dysfunction is not a primary disability, awkwardness or problems with precision may exist if neurological damage is the cause of the hearing loss.

Figure 6.2. Motor dysfunctions associated with handicapped classifications.

suffer only slight dysfunction in the left extremities, while another child, whose cerebral palsy has resulted in more extensive brain damage, may be confined to a wheelchair and unable to move all four limbs.

There are four major motor requirements needed in rhythmic/movement activities that may be limited as a result of motoric disabilities: (1) fine motor skills, (2) gross motor skills, (3) motor precision, and (4) strength and endurance.

Fine motor skills consist of movement requiring small-muscle control, such as grasping a pick or mallet, playing the keys on a piano, or covering the fingering holes on a tonette. Gross motor skills are those that use large-muscle groups and include activities such as running, walking, hopping, crawling, beating drums, clapping, "patschening" (slapping the thighs), or shaking instruments.

Further classification of these gross motor and fine motor skills includes qualitative and quantitative criteria, such as motor precision, strength, and endurance. In other words, to determine the extent that a child can demonstrate purposeful fine and gross motor movements in a particular sequence and at a desired time is especially important. Strength and endurance refer to continued muscular effort needed to sustain a particular position or movement. For example, holding up a triangle, carrying a drum, holding a horn to one's mouth, or striking a pose in a game, all require strength and endurance. As Figure 6.2 demonstrates, many handicaps will result in limited capacity in one or more of these areas.

Relatively little is known about the motor characteristics of mentally retarded children, particularly as they relate to musical performance (Bruscia, 1981). According to Malpass (1963), retarded children demonstrate less competence in motor tasks requiring precision, quick reaction, and coordination. Grossman (1973), who relates motor competence to mental ability, places moderately retarded children approximately three years behind mildly retarded children in physical development. Similarly, mildly retarded children lag behind nonretarded peers approximately three years.

While motor difficulties will certainly impede a child's ability to imitate and create rhythmic patterns, there are additional factors for the retarded child that may influence rhythmic skills. The inability to maintain attention or recall and organize auditory information may reduce rhythmic accuracy (Bruscia, 1981). According to Peters (1970), the belief that mentally retarded children have a good sense of rhythm is not supported by research data. Moderately retarded children demonstrate rhythmic capabilities below peers of the same chronological age. However, it is worth noting that in listening activities, mentally retarded children appear to prefer rhythmic over less rhythmic music (Cotter and Toombs, 1966). Therefore, rhythmic music may enhance attention and motivation in some types of activities.

DEVELOPMENTAL FACTORS

For those children whose motor difficulties are related to developmental delays or immature neurological dysfunction rather than major brain damage or physical anomalies, physical maturation and additional time to develop skills may be adequate in reducing awkwardness or poor precision. This may be a realistic expectation with some types of minimal brain dysfunctions or learning disabilities as well as for mildly retarded children. These children will not require extensive adaptation—only additional time for mastery of motor skills.

Unfortunately, some orthopedic conditions such as cerebral palsy cannot be cured or reversed by maturation or additional experience. In fact, there are some conditions such as muscular dystrophy that will result in ongoing deterioration as the child grows older. Therefore, for children with serious physical limitations, adaptive methods and materials may be necessary for the child to participate successfully in rhythmic and movement activities with their peers (Rudenberg, 1982).

ENVIRONMENTAL FACTORS

Because motor problems vary so greatly from one child to another, adaptations will vary with each problem and need. Optimally, the music teacher seeks guidance concerning the child's physical limitations, capabilities, and proper positioning and use of orthopedic equipment (such as braces, wheel chairs, and so forth.) The child's parents or the educational staff may be able to provide help. Such information is very important, for the child who is seated in the proper position and has adequate orthopedic support can participate in motor activities to their fullest (Rudenberg, 1982; Bleck and Nagel, 1982); if these adaptations are not included, the child cannot.

While it is best to obtain information relevant to a particular child's specific needs, the following recommendations provide a point of departure for adapting musical equipment and materials for integrating handicapped children in rhythmic activities:

1. Adaptations for fine motor problems. Some motor problems prohibit grasping of picks, mallets, maracas, and other rhythm instruments. For some children, enlarging the handle with a material such as foam rubber is enough. Other children may need to have the instrument attached to the wrist with a velcro strip or similar strap. Many excellent examples of adapted instruments (along with clear instructions

on inexpensive ways to make the adaptations) can be found in Clark and Chadwick's (1979) book, *Clinically Adapted Instruments for the Multiply Handicapped: A Sourcebook.* The teacher can also select instruments that do not require grasping. For example, jingle bells attached to a circular strap can be placed around the wrist.

2. Adaptation for gross motor problems. Movement of large muscles (moving arms or legs, for example) will be maximized (within physiological limits) by using correct seating support (Bleck and Nagel, 1982) and correct placement of the musical instrument (Rudenberg, 1982). For example, some children can play a xylophone more easily if it is placed on a table at chest height.

Unfortunately, most music educators do not have ready knowledge concerning either appropriate positioning and placement or limitations and capabilities of physically handicapped children. Therefore, this is an area best handled through consultation with family or involved professionals. Possessing this information makes a music teacher feel more comfortable about including the child in music activities because there will be less fear of making the child uncomfortable.

Beyond correct positioning of the child, some tasks or instruments may be unrealistic for a child with severe physical limitations. If this is the case, consider alternative forms of participation. For example, a wheelchair-bound child can join movement games if pushed by you or an aide and may even be able to move upper limbs in some fashion. These children will need more time to complete movements or to move in wheelchairs or with walkers from place to place.

3. Adaptations for motor precision. The music teacher should be aware that some physically handicapped or brain damaged children can be helped toward improved motor precision and rhythmicity. For others, attempts at precision may be unrealistic or may result in undesired reflexive movement such as undesirable jerking of the muscles and joints (Bleck and Nagel, 1982). Once again, information from an informed source can help set realistic goals.

In addition to setting realistic goals, the teacher can reduce the level of precision required for successful participation. For example, the motor-handicapped child will strike the surface of a large drum much more easily than that of a very small soprano xylophone bar. If working with Orff instruments, which have removable parts, one should take off all bars that are not needed so as to eliminate possible errors due to poor motor control. In addition to selecting rhythm instruments with larger surfaces or removable parts, the music teacher can select rhythmic patterns for imitation that have limited requirements for quick or precise motor response (such as fast or complex rhythmic patterns).

4. Adaptions for poor strength or endurance. Many times we take for granted the effort required to hold up a tambourine or even to move in a generalized fashion to music. For children with degenerative diseases such as muscular dystrophy, these simple tasks will become more difficult as the child grows older. Other conditions such as cerebral palsy can result in limited strength and easy fatigue—particularly when there has been a series of activities requiring motor activity.

Therefore, for activities involving instruments, it is important to consider (1) the weight of the instrument being held and (2) the prolonged effort needed to play or hold it in proper position. Select instruments of lighter weight and easy playing action, and consider providing stands or frameworks for holding up instruments. For example, you might suspend a triangle from a stand and have the child use the beater without having to hold up the triangle. Or, ask a nonhandicapped child to hold the instrument.

When rhythmic difficulties are related to mental functioning, such as attentional or memory deficits, select only very simple rhythmic responses. In addition, provide adequate time for rehearsal and mastery.

In summary, music for the young child is typically filled with rhythm and motor activities: rhythm bands, action songs, finger plays, dances, and creative movements. Children with poor motor and rhythmic skills need not be entirely excluded from these activities. With some ingenuity and common sense, the teacher can select and adapt appropriate activities, instruments, and musical materials that allow children to participate and realize their potential.

SOCIAL LIMITATIONS

INHERENT CAPABILITIES

While many of a child's social skills blossom with maturation, there are various types of handicaps that will alter the usual pattern of social development to some extent. Probably most apparent are those behaviors related to emotional/behavioral disorders. Socially handicapped children include those who demonstrate aggressive disruptive behaviors as well as those who are unusually withdrawn or have difficulty distinguishing fantasy from reality. Some mentally retarded or brain damaged children also may show unusual social behaviors as a result of neurological dysfunction.

Children with these types of handicaps may have difficulty interacting with peers or following through on an activity. Behaviors that may result often include impulsiveness, physical aggressiveness, contrary behavior, difficulty in completing a task, distractibility, sudden and apparently unprovoked mood swings, overreaction to situations, and unwillingness to play with peers.

As you look at this list, you may say they are all typical of young children at one time or other. That is certainly true. What distinguishes the emotionally or behaviorally disordered child from the nonhandicapped child is that these behaviors tend to occur more frequently, are more intense or severe, and may last for long periods of time (Paul, 1982). In short, these behaviors, which are normal in "small doses," are so prevalent in the handicapped child that they disrupt his social and emotional development.

In addition to children who have been diagnosed as emotionally or behaviorally disordered, there are other children who may lag in social skills. Visually impaired and hearing-impaired children may seem immature in social development because of their sensory limitations. The visually impaired child, for instance, is unable to pick up on the many social cues we learn by watching others' faces and body language. Hearing-impaired children, because of their communication problems, may have limited opportunity to interact verbally with peers. Orthopedically handicapped children, because of their physical limitations, may have fewer opportunities to play and interact with peers. As a result, they may rely more heavily on adult interaction or may stick to interaction with other handicapped peers.

Social and emotional needs of retarded children also may become exacerbated by their common experience with failure. They grow to expect to fail (Cromwell, 1963) and, as a result, lose motivation to participate in activities, particularly new experiences. Failure at an experience never encourages additional efforts to succeed. Children who fail repeatedly often lack basic confidence in their own abilities and judgments; so they look to others for guidance, solutions to problems, and approval (Bruscia, 1981).

Placing a child in a social situation compatible with musical and social capabilities, rather than with chronological age, assures a much greater chance of success and mastery. Praise and encouragement should be given regularly for good efforts and achievements.

DEVELOPMENTAL CHARACTERISTICS

As in all skills areas, social development is greatly affected by maturational factors. Just like their nonhandicapped peers, most exceptional children will, it is hoped, leave behind egocentric behaviors of early childhood as they mature. However, some children, such as the mentally retarded, will pass through stages of social development at a slower pace. Teachers need to be aware that the severely handicapped child may never develop much beyond a mental age of two (Kirk and Gallagher, 1979), an age in which egocentric behaviors are to be expected.

Beyond simple maturation, social development is affected by environmental opportunities. This is where many handicapped children suffer. Too often, peers and adults, through lack of understanding or exposure, may feel uncomfortable interacting with children with handicaps. They see the differences more than the many features that are like those of other children. Handicaps limit the variety and extent of social experiences that are possible. Therefore, unless there is special accommodation by the family or school personnel, handicapped children will lag in social development not only because of their own limitations, but also because of environmental factors.

ENVIRONMENTAL FACTORS

Although the music teacher cannot expect emotional or social difficulties to disappear magically during music time, the social and structured nature of music has some real advantages in integrating a child who has difficulties in social situations. Music is an activity in which children share and cooperate to achieve a unified result. Music activities can be structured so that they provide opportunities for learning to share, take turns, listen, be the center of attention, or make requests—all important social skills. Further, the fascination of musical sounds can generate interest and hold the attention of many children who might normally be more distractible.

These positive factors, however, are greatly dependent on the organizational skills of the music teacher. The manner in which the activity is organized and facilitated can make the difference between an opportunity for social growth and chaos. Several general factors are important to keep in mind when integrating a behaviorally or socially problematic child in an activity:

1. Talk with the child's parents or the program director to determine whether certain strategies for behavioral control are effective. For

example, some children respond to behavioral cues such as "What's your job?" or "Watch me," or "Magic hands, please." All these simple cues remind the child of what behavior is expected (Bruscia, 1981). Or teachers might include a "time out" technique in which children experiencing difficult behavior may leave the circle for a short time, and thus escape the attention of others if their behavior is out of control (Hall, 1974). Such techniques generally work more effectively if facilitated in a consistent way, so utilizing strategies that are employed by other teachers in other situations is preferable to developing your own without consultation.

2. Determine whether children are ready for extensive group work. For example, some preschoolers may still be functioning at a parallel play stage despite a chronological age that suggests they are ready for small-group activity. If this is the case, such a child will be more successful in one-to-one or very small group music experiences with opportunities for a lot of adult attention from the teacher and from other child care workers. The child who shows readiness for group work can be incorporated gradually into small, structured groups.

3. Provide adequate structure and rules for group behavior. While all young children need structure, clear expectations are even more critical for a child with behavioral difficulties. Review rules often, such as how to handle the instruments, how to sit in the group, and how to pay attention (Bruscia, 1981). The rules can be presented in a fun way that encourages the child to comply.

4. Consider shorter sessions for children with attentional problems or overly high levels of activity. Gradually work for a longer attention span (Paul, 1982), but start with short, successful experiences.

5. Provide much positive reinforcement for desired behaviors. While it is not always easy or realistic to ignore negative behaviors, they may decline if they are not given attention. Further, praising positive behaviors (no matter how small) in the child, as well as peers, conveys information on what behavior is expected. Praise should be sincere and informative (Hall, 1974; Reid and Hresko, 1981). Simply saying "Great!" over and over is less effective than a variety of reinforcing statements that are informative, such as: "I like the way Kristin is listening so carefully"; "Jon is holding his mallets so quietly. Good for you!"; "Lisa remembered how we wait in line."

In addition to sensing the integrity of a teacher's compliments and praise, children are experts at sensing how an adult feels about them. Teachers should always look beyond the handicap to find the lovable child. Most handicapped children have a host of "normal" behaviors. Focus on those as much as possible.

In addition to these general concerns, the teacher should plan to provide specific and especially rich social opportunities for children with special needs. For example,

1. Children with visual impairment will need assistance in getting to know other children in the group since they cannot see their peers. This requires specially structured opportunities to interact. They will also need verbal description of visual events in the group, such as pictures that are used or movements of their peers (Codding, 1982). Teachers can readily sensitize themselves and other children to the experiential gaps a visually impaired child faces by doing activities with eyes closed.

2. Hearing-impaired children will miss out on many conversations and instructions because of their hearing loss. Further, their speech may be difficult to understand (Davis and Hardick, 1981). Visual aids can help the child follow the activity more successfully. In addition, if the child uses sign language, the rest of the group might learn some simple signs in songs. Finally, the child with poor speech can be quite successful in experiences involving rhythm instruments and other activities that require minimal verbalization.

3. Children with physical limitations can share in the responsibility for physical tasks with nonhandicapped peers. For example, a child with limited muscle strength might play the triangle, while a stronger peer holds it.

In summary, many of the music activities appropriate for the nonhandicapped child offer valuable opportunities for social, mental, and musical growth of the handicapped child as well. In many instances, the music teacher who looks beyond the handicap will find that these children share more similarities than differences with nonhandicapped children in terms of needs, interests, and development. Often developmental patterns are simply delayed or slightly altered. With a basic understanding of those differences or delays, the music educator, using creativity and common sense, can adapt the musical environment so that handicapped children can be integrated successfully into the world of music.

SELECTED BIBLIOGRAPHY: MUSIC EDUCATION AND THE SPECIAL LEARNER

Birkenshaw, L. (1977). *Music for fun, music for learning.* Toronto: Holt, Rinehart and Winston of Canada, Limited.
This resource includes a collection of musical materials interspersed with ideas for presentation and activity development. The author places

emphasis on learning nonmusical goals, such as auditory perception or motor skills through musical learning.

Bitcon, C. H. (1976). *Alike and different: The clinical and educational use of Orff Schulwerk.* Santa Ana, CA: Rosha Press.
The author of this book is a strong advocate of the Orff technique. Basic background and technique set the stage for later chapters, which provide adaptive techniques for using Orff with a variety of handicaps including MR, VI, and HI.

Bleck, E. E., & Nagel, D. A. (Eds.). (1982). *Physically handicapped children: A medical atlas for teachers* (2nd ed.). New York: Grune & Stratton.
While this text is not a musical resource, it is a valuable collection of articles and visual aids on a wide variety of handicaps and disabilities. It provides basic background and vocabulary that can improve communication with the special education staff.

Cassity, M. D. (1977). Nontraditional guitar techniques for the educable and trainable mentally retarded residents in music therapy activities. *Journal of Music Therapy, 14,* 39–42.
This article provides clear and simple instructions for an adaptive guitar technique appropriate for the MR client with limited grasping or fine motor skills.

Clark, C., & Chadwick, D. (1979). *Clinically adapted instruments for the multiply handicapped: A sourcebook.* Westford, MA: Modulations Company.
The authors describe a large selection of adaptive percussion, string, and wind instruments for a variety of handicaps. This is a very pragmatic book for the teacher who works with the multiply handicapped. Most of the recommendations are inexpensive and easily made.

Darrow, A. A. (1985). Music for the deaf. *Music Educators Journal, 71,* (6), 33–35.
This article provides a theoretical support for the inclusion of music education in deaf education. The author gives examples of adaptations that are appropriate for the hearing-impaired population.

Gfeller, K. E. (1984). Prominent theories in learning disabilities and implications for music therapy methodology. *Music Therapy Perspectives, 2* (1), 9–13.
This article reviews three major theoretical approaches to education for the learning disabled and discusses musical adaptations of each approach.

Gilbert, J. P. (1977). Mainstreaming in your classroom: What to expect. *Music Educators Journal, 63* (6), 64–68.
The author outlines possible difficulties an educator may encounter in working with a mainstreamed child and recommends strategies for a successful learning experience. The article is geared toward the slow or retarded learner.

Hall, R. V. (1974). *Managing behavior. Part 2: Behavior modification—Basic principles; Part 3: Application in school and home.* Lawrence, KS: H & H Enterprises, Inc.
These two short volumes provide a clear and pragmatic view of behav-

ioral management of a variety of academic and behavioral problems. The clear, concise writing style and extensive use of examples make this an excellent starting point for the teacher who is not fully comfortable with behavioral techniques.

Hardesty, K. W. (1979). *Music for special education.* Morristown, NJ: Silver Burdett Company.
The author outlines many of the adaptations necessary for successful music education of the handicapped. Specific chapters are dedicated to the use of instruments, the voice, and the body in making music.

Hoshizaki, M. K. (1983). *Teaching mentally retarded children through music.* Springfield, IL: C. C. Thomas.
This text is actually geared toward the special educator who wishes to use music to teach other concepts to MR students. The recommendations for text and musical selections, along with activity ideas, are also appropriate for the music educator teaching TMR.

Hresko, W. P., & Reid, D. K. (1981). *A cognitive approach to learning disabilities.* New York: McGraw-Hill Book Company.
This is not a music resource. But for the music educator with questions about learning disabilities, it provides an excellent general background.

Krout, R. (1983). *Teaching basic guitar skills to special learners.* St. Louis: Magnamusic Baton.
This resource provides an alternative format to Cassity's adaptive guitar technique. It is geared toward the individual with limited fine motor skills. The book also demonstrates some record-keeping approaches for noting progress toward objectives.

Lathom, W. B., & Eagle, C. T. (Eds.). (1984). *Music therapy for handicapped children.* (Vols. 1, 2, and 3). Lawrence, KS: Meseraull Printing, Inc.
These three volumes provide background information and music therapy techniques appropriate for the following handicaps: Vol. I—VI, HI, deaf-blind; Vol. II—emotionally disturbed, mentally retarded, and speech impaired; Vol. III—other health impaired, multihandicapped, and orthopedically handicapped.

Nash, G. C.; Jones, G. W.; Potter, B. A.; & Smith, P. F. (1977). *The child's way of learning.* Sherman Oaks, CA: Alfred Publishing Co.
This musical resource provides page after page of musical activities geared toward teaching academic concepts. Orff and Kodaly principles are incorporated into the activities.

Nocera, S. (1973). Special education teachers need a special education. In M. Besson (Ed.), *Music in special education.* Reston, VA: Music Educators National Conference.
This article from an MENC collection outlines the primary knowledge base and skills necessary for working successfully with exceptional children in music education.

Nocera, S. (1979). *Reaching the special learner through music.* Morristown, NJ: Silver Burdett Company.

Includes an overview of varying handicaps as well as recommended adaptations for nonmusical goals.

Reichard, C. L., & Blackburn, D. B. (1973). *Music based instruction for the exceptional child.* Denver: Love Publishing Co.

This resource focuses on academic learning using musical activities. The activities are geared toward the TMR population.

Schulberg, C. (1981). *The music therapy sourcebook.* New York: Human Sciences Press, Inc.

This collection of musical activities is generally geared toward music in therapy. However, some of the activities might also be appropriate for special education or music education of the handicapped.

Steele, A. L. (Ed.). (1985). *The Music therapy levels system.* Cleveland, OH: The Cleveland Music School Settlement.

This resource gives examples of behavior modification systems in a variety of settings, including public school settings. Behavioral management examples are available for both emotionally disturbed and mentally retarded populations.

Vernazza, M. (1978). *Music Plus.* Boulder, CO: Pruett Publishing Company.

This collection of songs provides intermittent narrative on lesson planning for the handicapped student.

Zimmer, L. J. (1976). *Music handbook for the child in special education.* Hackensack, NJ: Joseph Boontar, Inc.

This short resource provides teaching approaches to musical concepts for the special learner in K through 3rd grade. A pragmatic, teaching-oriented book.

QUESTIONS FOR DISCUSSION/SUGGESTED ACTIVITIES

1. Give some examples in which handicapped children's needs and capabilities might be described as similar to those of nonhandicapped children.
2. Identify the primary skill areas that may be impeded by the following handicaps: mental retardation, emotional impairment, hearing impairment, learning disabilities, physical handicaps.
3. In order to increase sensitivity to the limitations caused by different handicaps, participate in a music activity while "trying on" a handicap. For example, wear a blindfold to simulate visual impairments, or spend a class using only the left hand.

REFERENCES AND SUGGESTED READINGS

Alley, J. M. (1979). Music in the IEP: Therapy/education. *Journal of Music Therapy, 16* (3), 111–127.

Bleck, E. E., & Nagel, D. A. (Eds.). (1982). *Physically handicapped children: A medical atlas for teachers* (2nd ed.). New York: Grune & Stratton.

Bruscia, K. E. (1981). The musical characteristics of mildly and moderately retarded children. In L. Kearns, M. T. Diston, & B. G. Rochner (Eds.), *Readings: Developing arts programs for handicapped students*. Arts in Special Education Project of Pennsylvania.

Buechler, J. (1982). *Music therapy for handicapped children: Hearing impaired*. Washington, DC: National Association for Music Therapy.

Carey, M. A. (1958). Music for the educable mentally handicapped (Doctoral dissertation, Pennsylvania State University, 1958). *Dissertation Abstracts International, 19,* 2967.

Clark, C., & Chadwick, D. (1979). *Clinically adapted instruments for the multiply handicapped: A sourcebook*. Westford, MA: Modulations Company.

Codding, P. A. (1982). *Music therapy for handicapped children: Visually impaired*. Washington, DC: National Association for Music Therapy.

Cotter, V. W., & Toombs, S. A. (1966). A procedure for determining the music preferences of mental retardates. *Journal of Music Therapy, 3*(2), 57–64.

Cromwell, R. L. (1963). A social learning approach to mental retardation. In N. R. Ellis (Ed.), *Handbook of mental deficiency*. New York: McGraw Hill.

Darrow, A. A. (1985). Music for the deaf. *Music Educators Journal, 71*(6), 33–35.

Darrow, A. A., & Jones-Starmer, G. (1986). The effect of vocal training on the intonation and rate of hearing-impaired children's speech: A pilot study. *Journal of Music Therapy, 23*(4), 194–201.

Davis, J. M., & Hardick, J. (1981). *Rehabilitative audiology for children and adults*. New York: John Wiley & Sons, Inc.

Dileo, C. (1976). The relationship of diagnostic and social factors to the singing ranges of institutionalized mentally retarded persons. *Journal of Music Therapy, 13*(1), 17–28.

Fahey, J., & Birkenshaw, L. (1972). Bypassing the ear: The perception of music by feeling and touch. *Music Educators Journal, 58*(8), 44–49.

Forsythe, J. L., & Jellison, J. A. (1977). It's the law. *Music Educators Journal, 65*(3), 30–35.

Fotheringham, J. B., & Morris, J. (1976). *Understanding the preschool retarded child*. Toronto: University of Toronto.

Galloway, H. F., Jr., (1974). Stuttering and the myth of therapeutic singing. *Journal of Music Therapy, 11*(4), 202–207.

Gfeller, K. E. (1986). Adapting Orff materials for the handicapped child. Part 2: Communication. *Iowa Music Educator, 40*(1), 20–23.

Grant, R. E. (1977). A developmental music therapy curriculum for the mildly mentally retarded, ages 6–12. (Doctoral dissertation, The University of Georgia, 1977) *Dissertation Abstracts International 38/7A,* 4009.

Grant, R. E., & Share, M. R. (1985). Relationship of pitch discrimination skills and vocal ranges of mentally retarded subjects. *Journal of Music Therapy, 22*(2), 99–103.

Grossman, H. J. (Ed.). (1973). *Manual on terminology and classification in mental retardation.* Washington, DC: American Association on Mental Deficiency.

Hall, R. V. (1974). *Managing behavior. Part 2: Behavior modification. Basic principles.* Lawrence, KS: H. & H. Enterprises, Inc.

Hunter, M. H., Schucman, H., & Friedlander, G. (1972). *The retarded child from birth to five.* New York: The John Day Company.

Iancone, R. N. (1977). The measurement of music aptitude for the mentally retarded. *Dissertation Abstracts International, 37*(10-A), 6403.

Jellison, J. A. (1979). The music therapist in the educational setting: Developing and implementing curriculum for the handicapped. *Journal of Music Therapy, 16*(3), 128–137.

Kirk, S. A., & Gallagher, J. J. (1979). *Educating exceptional children* (3rd ed.). Boston: Houghton Mifflin Company.

Korduba, O. M. (1975). Duplicated rhythmic patterns between deaf and normal hearing children. *Journal of Music Therapy, 12*(3), 136–146.

Larson, B. A. (1977). A comparison of singing ranges of mentally retarded and normal children with published songbooks used in singing activities. *Journal of Music Therapy, 14*(3), 139–143.

Lerner, J. (1981). *Children with learning disabilities* (3rd ed.). Boston: Houghton Mifflin Company.

Lowenbraun, S.; Appelman, K.; & Callahan, J. (1980). *Teaching the hearing impaired.* Columbus, OH: Charles E. Merrill Publishing Company.

Malpass, L. (1963). Motor skills in mental deficiency. In N. R. Ellis (Ed.), *Handbook in mental deficiency: Psychological theory and research.* New York: McGraw Hill Book Co.

McLeish, J., & Higgs, G. (1967). An inquiry into the musical capabilities of educationally sub-normal children. *Cambridge Institute of Education. Occasional Research Papers No. 1.*

Meadow, K. P. (1980). *Deafness and child development.* Berkeley, CA: University of California Press.

Miller, S. G. (1982). *Music therapy for handicapped children: Communication disorders.* Washington, DC: National Association for Music Therapy.

Moog, H. (1976). The development of musical experience in children of preschool age. *Psychology of Music, 4*(2), 38–45.

Paul, D. W. (1982). *Music therapy for handicapped children: Emotionally impaired.* Washington, DC: National Association for Music Therapy.

Payne, S., & Patton, J. R. (1981). *Mental retardation.* Columbus, OH: Charles E. Merrill Publishing Company.

Peters, M. D. (1970). A comparison of the musical sensitivity of mongoloid and normal children. *Journal of Music Therapy, 7*(4), 113–123.

Quigley, S. P., & Paul, P. V. (1984). *Language and deafness.* San Diego, CA: College-Hill Press, Inc.

Reid, D. K., & Hresko, W. P. (1981). *A cognitive approach to learning disabilities.* New York: McGraw Hill Book Co.

Rider, M. S. (1977). The relationship between auditory and visual perception of tasks employing Piaget's concept of conservation. *Journal of Music Therapy, 14*(3), 126–138.

Rudenberg, M. T. (1982). *Music therapy for handicapped children: Orthopedically handicapped.* Washington, DC: National Association for Music Therapy.

Schwankovsky, L. (1982). *Music therapy for handicapped children: Other health impaired.* Washington, DC: National Association for Music Therapy.

Shelton, B. O. (1971). *Teaching and guiding the slow learner.* West Nyack, NY: Parker Publishing Company, Inc.

Shuter, R. (1968). *The psychology of musical ability.* London: Methuen & Co. Ltd.

Swaiko, N. (1974). The role and value of a eurhythmics program in a curriculum for deaf children. *American Annals of the Deaf, 119*(3), 321–324.

Chapter 7

Musical Approaches and Methods for Young Children

"Would you tell me, please, which way I ought to walk from here?"
"That depends a good deal on where you want to go," said the Cat.

—*Lewis Carroll*

Teachers throughout history, in every discipline, have been concerned with how to teach their subject. Music educators, in particular, have always been interested in trying out new methods of instruction and, at times, have been criticized for what has seemed to be a preoccupation with "how" rather than "what" to teach. Allen Britton has stated that we "are still a little more concerned with methodologies than we probably should be, but this is a common and venial sin of teachers as a class" (1982, p. 43). The first public school music instruction in America, according to Lowell Mason, was a "new" method, based on Mason's interpretation of the methods of Pestalozzi.

Nor has the interest in methodologies declined, for today's teachers are still seeking the most effective ways of teaching their students. Some of the music methods receiving attention today are of fairly recent vintage; some date back to the turn of the century and are receiving renewed attention. The purpose of this chapter is to present a brief overview of music methods that give particular attention to the general music education of young children. In addition, the research that has been conducted concerning a particular system will be discussed. In our pluralistic society, teachers need to be aware of current educational trends, to evaluate all "new" methods of instruction, and to put into practice what they deem sound and appropriate for realizing overall goals of learning for their students.

The methods discussed in this chapter are all quite comprehensive in scope. That is, they include all the curricular components of a good music program for children—listening, singing, rhythmic movement, playing instruments, and creating music. Yet they are different. Special emphasis is given to self-directed learning in the Montessorian curriculum; rhythmic movement is the heart of Dalcroze instruction. The Orff approach emphasizes creativity and improvisation; the Kodály Method focuses upon the development of reading, writing, and listening skills. The Manhattanville Music Program grows from exploratory experiences in a laboratory-type classroom; Suzuki Talent Education stresses perceptive listening and rote learning.

Are these many and varied approaches to instruction merely a manifestation of our confusion about how to teach music? Probably not. Rather, they tend to emphasize that children can learn about music in many ways. The best method? That is surely for the teacher to decide. Good music teaching results when teachers are sure of their program goals, knowledgeable about the techniques and strategies to achieve desired objectives, consistent in their approach, and comfortable with the teaching style required to teach well using a particular method.

As you read the brief overviews of the various systems described in this chapter, you may become curious to learn more about a particular method, and motivated to seek out information and training. The information presented in this chapter may serve as introductions to these methods.

MONTESSORI AND THE PREPARED ENVIRONMENT

Montessori's theories of educational development and their implications for music teaching were discussed in Chapter 2. Therefore, only brief discussion, directed toward selected aspects of her music curriculum, will be presented in this chapter.

The Montessori Method emphasizes self-directed learning through experiences with prepared, "didactic" materials. With her colleague, Maccheroni, Montessori developed musical materials and exercises for a balanced music program, integrated within her total educational scheme. The program included listening, playing instruments, singing, and rhythmic movement. Examples of some of the self-learning activities and materials used in her method will be described briefly.

LISTENING

Preparation for listening was carefully planned. Montessori regarded preparation as one of the most important aspects of instruction; she described how she prepared her students for careful listening: "I say 'St!

St!' in a series of modulations. . . . The children, little by little, become fascinated by this. . . . Then I say, still in a small whisper, 'Now I can hear the clock, now I can hear the whisper of the trees in the garden' " (Montessori, 1964, p. 205).

Subsequent activities required her students to distinguish "sounds" from "noise" and to formulate these distinctions. This kind of preparation led the children to explore as individuals and to use the materials for self-directed auditory training that were placed in the classroom. The activities included matching and ordering sounds by working with sound cylinders (described in Chapter 2) containing substances that produced same/different and louder/softer sounds. Figure 7.1 is an example of a sound exploratory activity of the type found in the Montessori materials.

Sound exploration exercises also involved matching and ordering of musical sounds. For these, the mushroom bells, invented by Maccheroni, were used. There were two sets of bells—a control set and a working set, each producing the tones of a scale. An exercise might require a child to strike, in turn, each bell of the control set, arranged in scalar order on a board painted to represent a piano keyboard, to find its match from the second set mixed together on a table, and place the two together. Subsequent activities included placing the movable bells in scale sequence, guided only by the sound, and creating melodic patterns and tunes.

SINGING

Although group singing was included in the curriculum, some singing experiences were individual, self-directed activities. Some occurred during the bell-exploration activities. Montessori described how the children, arranging the bells in order, would soon begin to accompany their actions with singing the scale (1965, p. 109). This kind of activity, wrote Montessori, seemed to produce "interest . . . of a higher order than that shown by children in singing songs" (1917, p. 324), especially for beginning singers, for whom songs, with their "capricious intervals, calling

Figure 7.1. A sound exploration activity.

Materials:	Six small boxes or plastic, egg-shaped containers. Fill two with equal amounts of flour, two with sand, two with beans.
The Activity:	Match each pair of similar sounds. Place them together.
Variations:	Increase number of paired cylinders. Or work with one set of the pairs. Order the sounds from loudest to softest.

for pronunciation of words, musical expression, differences in time, etc."
(p. 324), proved too complex.

RHYTHMIC MOVEMENT

Descriptions of Montessori's approach to rhythmic movement are
found as part of the "muscular education" component of the curriculum. Movement to music began as "line-walking" exercises; the choice
to participate in the activity was the child's.

The exercises called for the children to follow a line drawn on the
floor. The objective was erect carriage, freedom of movement, and good
balance. They became rhythmic movement activities when Maccheroni
began to accompany the walking with piano music, matching the tempo
of her playing to the children's steps. Gradually, the children began
to respond to other aspects of the music; for example, "hanging in
position with the long note" or showing, by movement, their awareness
of musical cadences, dynamics, or mood (Montessori, 1917, p. 358).
The line-walking exercises occurred spontaneously during the day,
announced only by the music.

These exercises developed not only the children's rhythmic sense
but also their singing skills. Barnet, who compiled a collection of piano
pieces for the line-walking activities, wrote of the children's singing as
they walked and described how her students learned to sing more than
a hundred pieces "without having been taught" (Barnet, 1973, p. viii).

WHERE IT IS TODAY

While many Montessori preschools exist throughout the country, it
cannot be taken for granted that children attending these schools will
receive Montessori music instruction. The combination of trained musician and trained Montessorian is rare. Montessori herself admitted this
problem. Most school music educators are trained to provide group instruction; in the readied environment of a Montessori school, music
experiences are often individual experiences, elected by the children.
With the prepared materials carrying the burden of instruction, the
teacher's role is one of facilitator—introducing the materials or exercises, diagnosing each child's level of interest and understanding, and
providing guidance.

Given this set of circumstances, it is not surprising that little research exists about the effect of this method on the development of
musicality among children. One researcher attempted such an investigation, but her study did not include enough individualized activities for it to be representative of Montessorian principles (Fitzmaurice,

1971). Miller completed in 1981 a descriptive study of the program, entitled *The Montessorian Music Curriculum for Children Up to Six Years of Age.* This author traced the method's historical development, described its philosophy and goals, and outlined a program providing American folk and children's songs for use in Montessorian programs. Another investigator, Rubin, reported finding thirty-five unpublished booklets about the music program, which "considerably extend the brief portions devoted to music in Montessori's publications" (Rubin, 1983, p. 215).

However sparse the research about the method, the basic tenet of Montessori's philosophy—helping children "learn how to learn"—can be seen in many instructional techniques used by today's music teachers. Exploratory activities, individualized experiences, and "learning by doing" are not new notions. However, today's teachers do have an important legacy from this educator—the conviction that aesthetic sensitivity and understanding of music result from rich sensory experiences begun early in life.

THE DALCROZE METHOD

During the years when Montessori was gaining recognition for her comprehensive early childhood method, a Swiss musician, Émile Jaques-Dalcroze (1865–1950), was also formulating an educational method for children. His approach, like Montessori's, was unique for the time; he also believed that the early years of a child's life are especially important for developing basic skills and perceptions. However, Dalcroze was concerned with but one component of a curriculum—music.

Dalcroze began his career as a professor of harmony at the Geneva Conservatory of Music. Finding that his students were "trained," but not "educated" musically, he developed a system of instruction based on the theory that the human body is the first musical instrument on which we express our perceptions. Therefore, instruction using this instrument should precede all other. He began developing and testing his methods with his own students and in 1905 presented the system to the public at a musical festival. American music educators became interested; in 1915, the New York School of Dalcroze Eurhythmics was founded. During the 1920s and 1930s there was much discussion of the method and its place in American general music education.

EURHYTHMICS

Dalcroze wrote: "There are many more musical children in the world than parents believe. . . . One of the functions of education should be to develop the musical instinct of children. But how is this to be awakened at an early age? And what are its external signs? (Jaques-Dalcroze, 1921, p. 95).

These were rhetorical questions for this educator, for he provided his answers. The "awakening" came about through physical movement. Although his method includes studies in solfége (sight-singing with sol-fa syllables), theory, and improvisation, it begins with rhythmic movement. Called "eurhythmics," this aspect of the method has received the most attention and has been of special interest to early childhood educators.

"Eurhythmics" is defined typically as "harmonious and expressive movement." The objective of eurhythmic training is to enable children to perceive, express, and develop understanding of all the elements of music—melody, rhythm, dynamics, harmony, form, and style—through physical movement. Eurhythmic education involves the interaction of mind and muscle—the training of the body to demonstrate the concept that the mind has formulated. The vocabulary of movements used in eurhythmic training include in-place movements, such as clapping, swinging, turning, conducting, bending, swaying, speaking, and singing, and in-space movements, such as walking, running, crawling, leaping, sliding, galloping, and skipping (Choksy, Abramson, Gillespie, and Woods, 1986, p. 37).

Instruction for children begins with the rhythms and movements of ordinary life activities. Exercises using these movements "prepare the instrument" (the body) and may be taught without music. Figure 7.2 presents some preparatory exercises developed for young children by a Dalcroze teacher.

Subsequent exercises lead children to associate specific movements with specific musical sounds. For example, the sound of played quarter notes may elicit walking movements; eighth notes, running steps. Responding to music improvised by the teacher on a piano (percussion instruments or speech sounds may also be used), students recognize and learn to express these relative durations, and progress to more complex musical events, such as "crescendo," "accent," or "end of a phrase." These musical phenomena are all explored in the context of singing games, finger plays, percussion play, or stories with musical accompaniment (Choksy et al., 1986, p. 154).

Early in the instructional sequence, the visual symbols of music—the printed notation—are introduced. Flash cards, on which notation of rhythm patterns are printed, lead the children to associate printed music with movement. Cards may be joined together, and a sequence of rhythmic patterns may be performed in movement.

Passive relaxation exercises:
  "Let us all lie down and be kittens asleep."
  "Float on water—it is cool, deep water."
Active relaxation exercises:
  "A very loose rag doll can be made to dance, than to fall. Child imitates."
  "Kneel on four legs and be a seat—teacher claps hands or plays a chord and the seat collapses."
Contraction versus relaxation exercises:
  "Strong sounds: clap above the head."
  "Soft sounds: sit and stroke one hand."
Music-with-movement exercise:
  "Stand as straight and hard as a candle. As the music grows softer, the candle burns down and down, until it is only a soft spot of grease on the floor."

Gell, 1973, pp. 3–9.

Figure 7.2. Eurhythmic exercises: Preparation.

More than a basic accurate response is expected of the children, however. The "grace of movement" is of concern to Dalcroze teachers:

> It is well to stress the point that unless teachers do take some trouble in improving the movements, so much will be lost in musical experience. . . . The teacher who waits for everything to come naturally, without suggestion, is going to fail in her purpose. (Gell, 1973, p. 28)

It is easy to see why eurhythmics training is often part of the education of dancers. Bach fugues, Gluck's *Orfeo,* and other classical works have been "realized" by advanced Dalcroze students, and the principles of eurhythmics have been applied in theatrical and operatic productions (Blom, 1959, p. 594).

Dalcroze, however, intended the method to teach music, not dance. Early training was meant to provide a solid foundation of understanding of the elements of music. Typical exercises shown in Figure 7.3, selected from two texts by Dalcroze educators, show how understanding is developed.

Very little printed music is used by Dalcroze teachers. Often, the music for the exercises is improvised on the piano. This aspect of the method implies a combination of teacher skills—keyboard training and improvisational ability. However, teachers may accompany the

Dynamics: Skip to the moon; but when the music becomes quiet, make
      a "picture" of soft music at the end of the room. (Gell, 1973, p. 37)
Duration: Divide the class into two groups, one representing the walking
      rhythm (quarter notes), the other, the running rhythm (eighth notes).
      Each responds to the rhythm of the music played. (Findlay, 1971,
      p. 21)
Meter: The children walk and, at command, clap or stamp vigorously on
      the first beat of a pattern in twos, threes, fours, or fives. (Findlay,
      1971, p. 31)
Phrase: The children move freely about the room, changing direction at
      the resting points in the music and kneeling at the final cadence.
      Findlay, 1971, p. 46)
Melody: The children, sitting close to the piano, move their arms up-
      ward when the melody ascends and downward when the melody
      descends. (Findlay, 1971, p. 51)
Harmony: Single notes—walk alone. Two notes together—walk in pairs.

Gell, 1973, p. 101.

Figure 7.3. Eurhythmic exercises: The elements of music.

exercises with singing (or the children's singing, also), drums, song
bells, or other instruments. In this context, see the chapter in Gell's
study entitled "Movement Minus Music and Movement to the Spoken
Word" (1973, p. 148).

Mentally prepared physical responses are expected even from
preschool children who have received eurhythmics training. The effect
of the training on musical development of preschool children has not
been researched; however, the Gell text includes an interesting set of
statistics showing the achievement of very young children in realizing
selected objectives. This chart is shown in Table 7.1. The "desired response" is identified, and the percentage of children in three age groups
able to "make an adequate response" after one year of eurhythmics instruction is shown.

The study of this chart reveals not only the effects of eurhythmics training but also a sort of "sequence" of development of musical
concepts.

SINGING: SONGS AND SOLFÉGE

Dalcroze valued singing experiences for young children and recommended that singing be included every day—"if only for a quarter of
an hour" (Jaques-Dalcroze, 1921, p. 109). Singing instruction, however,

Table 7.1. Eurhythmic Achievement: Percentages of Children
Demonstrating Adequate Responses

	Just 3 years (%)	3 plus (%)	4 plus (%)
Walk	80	90	90
Run	100	100	100
Gallop	60	80	90
Skip	20	50	80
Sway	60	60	90
Relaxation	90	80	90
Control	80	70	100
Creativity	50	60	70
Participation	100	80	100
Dynamics	80	80	90
Pulse	80	80 (accel.)	80
Bar Time	——	——	90
Note Values	——	——	100
Phrasing	——	——	80
Form (ABA)	——	——	100
Changes of Key	——	——	90
Appreciation	——	——	80

Gell, 1973, pp. 226–227.

also involved (1) eurhythmic activities through which students demonstrated aural and visual recognition of tones and tone-groupings in scales, (2) application of sol-fa syllables to staff notation, (3) exercises to develop absolute pitch recognition, and (4) vocal improvisation.

An activity involving aural and visual recognition of individual tones of a scale is described by Landis and Carder (1972): "The younger students listen to scale tones played at the piano and identify them by standing (or moving to) cards, one through eight, that are placed in a row on the floor" (p. 24).

Sol-fa reading begins with notes placed on a one- or two-line staff. The other lines are added as needed for melodies containing more tones. Children's songs, folk tunes, and singing games constitute the song materials. Gell (1973) recommended those "which are built on only one, two or three sounds, with simple leaps and varied rhythmic patterns" for beginning instruction (p. 206). The song, "Hot Cross Buns" might look like this:

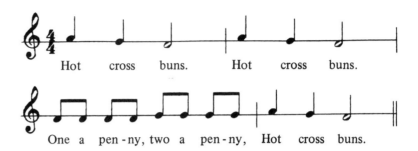

PLAYING INSTRUMENTS: PIANO IMPROVISATION

Early instruction in eurhythmics and solfége leads to the study of the piano, where, unlike traditional methods, improvisation is stressed. Students may begin their acquaintance with the instrument through creative exploratory activities, such as improvising a rhythmic pattern on a single tone while the teacher plays a chordal accompaniment (Landis and Carder , 1972, p. 27).

Piano lessons should not be started until "the child has become capable of experiencing musical sensations, when he feels the desire to express them, and when he has learned to analyze sensations and coordinate them logically" (Jaques-Dalcroze, 1931, p. 121).

CONCLUSION

A small number of research studies have been conducted using the Dalcroze Method (Boyle, 1970; Henke, 1984; Douglas, 1977), but they did not involve young children. Gell's informal study, shown in Table 7.1, provides some imformation about the effect of the Dalcroze Method on selected musical goals. However, it is difficult to imagine teaching young children about music without using movement as an instructional tool. Music *is* movement, not the mathematical division of printed symbols. Dalcroze presented this concept perhaps more clearly than any other music educator of his time.

THE ORFF APPROACH

Dalcroze's belief that "the most potent element in music and the nearest related to life is rhythmic movement" (Jaques-Dalcroze, 1921, p. 115) influenced many music educators and methodologists. Among those who were particularly attracted to his theories was Carl Orff (1895–1982), a German composer, educator, and musicologist. In 1925, he and a colleague founded a school of music and gymnastics. He taught in this school until 1936, following the principles of Dalcroze. The purpose of the school was to teach "creative musicianship" to all the students, very few of whom were musicians. It was from this experience that he developed his method for teaching children.

Orff's approach emphasizes creativity and improvisation: "The primary purpose of music education . . . is the development of a child's creative faculty which manifests itself in the ability to improvise" (Hall and Walter, 1955, p. vi.) The method is distinguished by its emphasis on process rather than product. Creativity, developed through many improvisational experiences, is emphasized in every stage of instruction.

To nurture creativity, a somewhat structured musical environment is created. There is a selected inventory of musical tones with which the children work in beginning instruction; rhythmic movement and speech play an important role; special instruments, invented for the system, are used. Various aspects of this environment are described in the following sections, and can provide an introduction to the method.

RHYTHM

According to Orff, singing evolves from rhythmic speech and chant. In an Orff program, children are led to discover rhythmic patterns in familiar words—their own names, names of flowers, birds, for example—and in nursery rhymes and familiar sayings. Children chant these speech pieces, varying the effect by dynamic contrast (louder/softer, higher/lower, faster/slower, or accents). A simple nursery rhyme can become a dramatic choric-speech event.

BODY PERCUSSION

Rhythmic body-percussion accompaniments are created for both speech pieces and songs. Four basic in-place body rhythms, or "sound gestures" are emphasized: stamping, "patching" (slapping one's thighs), clapping, and finger-snapping. These gestures may be used singly or in combination to create a suitable accompaniment for songs and chants.

DRAMATIC ACTION

Dramatic movement, dance, and "acting-out" experiences are created by the children for speech pieces and songs.

MELODY

Tunes are created for many of the chants. The first tune to which the children fit words consists of two tones—the "cuckoo" interval, "sol-mi" in solfège. Singing games, greeting songs, musical conversations, and echo games establish this interval as the "germ-cell" of song. As instruction progresses, other tones are added. "La," the tone one step above "sol," is added first; when these three tones are used efficiently, "re" and "do" are added. These five tones constitute the children's beginning inventory of pitches used in their improvisations.

These five tones make up what is called a pentatonic scale. Orff believed that this tonal sequence represented the elemental tonality of children. Confining songs and their harmonic accompaniments to these five tones means that musically satisfactory "harmony" can be created by the youngest and most inexperienced musicians, for any combination of these pitches can be played or sung simultaneously without producing dissonance. Pentatonic melodies serve, in the Orff approach, as "plastic material, rather, a basis for improvisation, a starting-point for music-making" (Walter and Hall, 1955). The children create songs using these tones; in addition, they are taught a repertoire of composed pentatonic songs.

PERCUSSION INSTRUMENTS

Children explore, consider, and invent various accompaniments to songs and chants with percussion instruments. The percussion accompaniments may provide a rhythmic background for songs or they may add "color" and dynamic effect to words, phrases, or sections of a piece.

PITCHED INSTRUMENTS

The Orff instrumental ensemble is perhaps the best-known feature of the method. These instruments, developed especially for the system, include not only various percussion instruments but also pitched, barred instruments. There are soprano, alto, and bass xylophones; soprano and alto glockenspiels; and soprano, alto, and bass metallophones (Figure 7.4). All of them have removable bars, so that the instrument can be set up to include only the pitches needed for a particular song or accompaniment. The instruments are of fine musical quality and produce beautiful sounds.

These instruments are used in various ways. The teacher may accompany songs and chants by playing borduns (the "do" and "sol" pitches of a song sounded simultaneously). Children also use the instru-

Figure 7.4. Studio 49 Orff instruments, preschool set. Photo courtesy of MMB Music, Inc., St. Louis 63132, U.S. agents.

ments to play melodic patterns, to create ostinati accompaniments (that is, repeated patterns), or to add dramatic effect to songs and chants.

TEXTURE AND FORM

Depending on the age, experiences, and ability of the students, introductions and codas are created by the children for songs and chants. The songs and chants may be performed as canons (like a round) or alternatively in rondo fashion.

There is more than a little of the dramatic in an Orff piece. When all of the above components are combined, the effect can be quite striking:

"Magic" is a word often used to describe the finished product of an Orff workshop or student demonstration. [In it] an illusion is created in which the musical experience appears to have taken place effortlessly and instantly. Participants realize that without much technique or theoretical background they are making music; they are experiencing an ensemble feeling of a kind normally reserved for professional musicians. (Choksy et al., 1986, p. 137)

AN ORFF ACTIVITY

Each separate stage of instruction, as described in the preceding paragraphs, can constitute a complete musical experience. A single lesson might consist, for example, of creating a rhythmic chant from the names of the children. Or the lesson might be spent in creating a dramatization of a nursery rhyme or song. To illustrate the many treatments that may be applied to a speech chant and to show how it may evolve into a full-scale musical composition, examine Figure 7.5. First a C pentatonic scale is shown. This constitutes the melodic material used in the activity. The greeting, "Hello, what's your name?" is first chanted to discover its natural rhythmic scheme, then is given the "sol-mi" tune. For purposes of illustration, three-tone and five-tone melodies, extensions of the "germ-cell" song, are presented. All of the tunes in Figure 7.5 may be sung simultaneously, or some may be sung and others played on an instrument (as illustrated in Figure 7.6). A possible body-percussion accompaniment and an accompanying bordun to be played on an instrument are also shown.

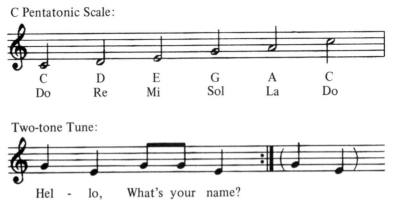

Figure 7.5. Pentatonic Musical Activities

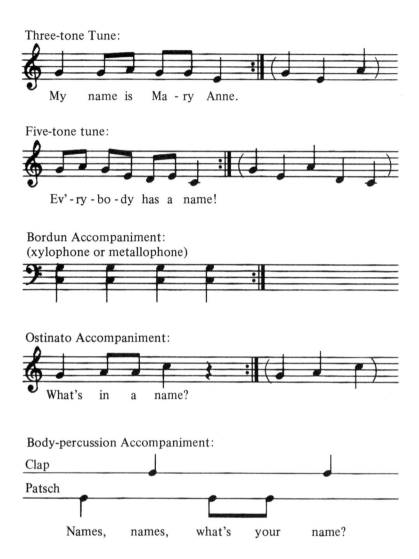

Figure 7.5. (continued)

The tunes in Figure 7.5 may be sung separately or simultaneously. Because they are all in the pentatonic mode, they will harmonize. You might wish to try any or all possible combinations of the melodic patterns to see how the resulting "piece" sounds.

Such a complex activity—the simultaneous production of all of the musical ideas in Figure 7.5—is not realistic for preschool children.

Figure 7.6. At first songs are clapped, sung, and finally accompanied on the barred instruments.

However, students in the primary grades may be able to combine one or two of the tunes with the body-percussion accompaniment. For the youngest children in Orff programs, rhythmic chanting, action games, limited-range songs, and dramatic action are emphasized.

Songs in the Orff method are not confined to those created by the children. Pentatonic folk songs are used extensively, and these are amenable to the same musical treatments shown in Figure 7.5. Many collections of both pentatonic and nonpentatonic songs, with suggestions for "Orff activities," are listed in the references at the end of this chapter and in Appendix B.

CONCLUSION

The Orff Method is followed in many public and private schools throughout the country. Some early childhood music schools feature the method. Research studies of its effect on the musical development of very young children are few. It has been shown to produce more positive attitudes toward music among upper-grade elementary school children than a "traditional" method (Siemens, 1969), but little evidence exists as to its superiority in realizing traditional goals of music instruction. However, the approach, as envisioned by Orff, reminds us that children are creative and can learn about music by producing and creating it themselves, as well as through traditional ways.

THE KODALY METHOD

Perhaps no method of music instruction has received more attention in American elementary schools during the last decade than that of Zoltán Kodály (1882–1967), a Hungarian composer, ethnomusicologist, and educator. In the early years of his career, Kodály became involved in collecting, analyzing, and classifying the folk music of Hungary, and in 1906 published a collection of these songs. Kodály continued his interest in the collection and preservation of folk music throughout his life, and under his leadership the Folk Song Research Group, a division of the Hungarian Academy of Sciences, has published a number of volumes of Hungarian folk songs (Choksy, 1974, p. 8).

With this deep interest in the musical folk culture of his country, it is not surprising that Kodály became interested in how this musical heritage was being passed on to the young. As a teacher, he became increasingly dismayed at the low level of musical literacy he found among the students entering the highest music school in Hungary. The students' lack of fundamental skills in reading and writing music, plus their ignorance of their own musical culture, inspired him to try to remedy the situation. He felt that the place to start was in the education of teachers:

> It is much more important who is the music teacher in Kosvarda than who is the director of the opera house in Budapest . . . for a poor director fails once, but a poor teacher keeps on failing for 30 years, killing the love of music in 30 batches of children. (Choksy, 1974, pp. 7–8)

The objective of the Kódaly Method is the development of music literacy: the ability to read, write, and think music. Kodály regarded this as a right of every human being. He believed that instruction should begin early:

> The years between three and seven are educationally much more important than the later ones. What is spoiled or omitted at this age cannot be put right later on. In these years man's future is decided practically for his whole lifetime. (Choksy, 1981, p. 7)

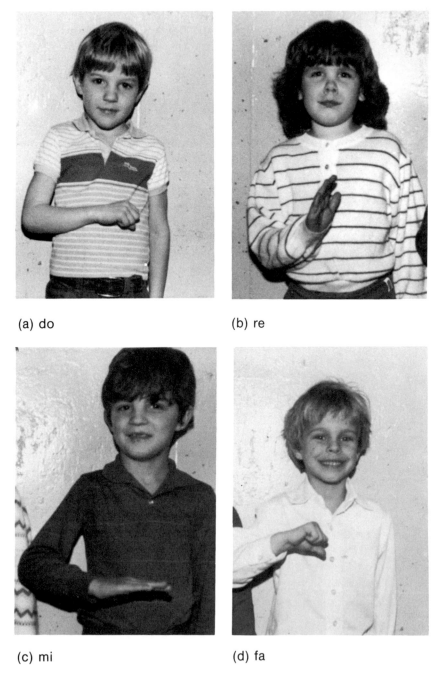

(a) do

(b) re

(c) mi

(d) fa

Figure 7.7. Kodály hand positions representing steps in a scale.

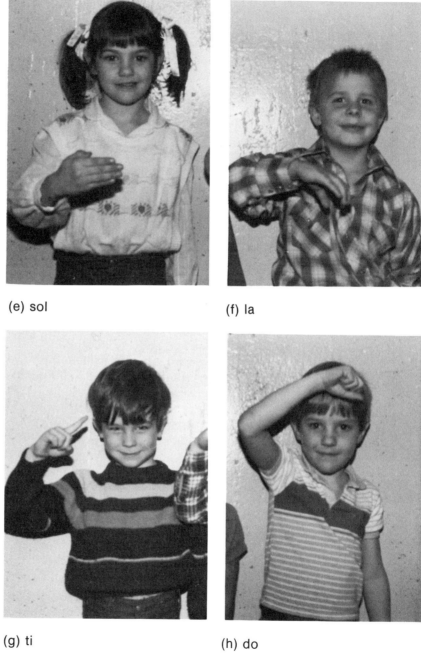

(e) sol

(f) la

(g) ti

(h) do

Figure 7.7. (continued)

INSTRUCTIONAL TOOLS

The instructional techniques of the method were developed by Kodály's teaching colleagues, working under his leadership. Kodály had travelled throughout the world studying music instruction methods. Impressed by the singing of English school children's choirs, he adopted their sol-fa system for teaching melodic reading. He added a series of hand signs—a different hand position to represent each step in a scale (Figure 7.7). These were adapted from those originated by John Curwen, founder of the tonic sol-fa system.

For rhythmic instruction, he devised a series of speech syllables, with a different syllable for each note value. The syllable "ta" is assigned to quarter notes; "ti" to eighth notes. In notation, the notes are shown with stems only, for example, " | ⊓ || " (called "stick notation").

INSTRUCTIONAL SEQUENCE

Perhaps the most notable feature of the method is its attention to the sequential presentation of material. Songs selected for singing instruction and melodic study are sequenced for presentation according to the pitches they contain. The sequence is that used in the Orff method: Beginning songs contain only two tones—the "sol" and "mi". "La" comes next, then "re" and "do". Both Orff and Kodály chose pentatonic literature for beginning instruction, but for different reasons. For Orff, the songs served as "plastic material" for improvisation; for Kodály, they are substantive material for developing accurate singing and music reading skills. Kodály believed that most children do not sing half-step intervals accurately; pentatonic melodies contain no half-steps. Only when "sol-mi" songs are sung correctly are those containing other tones added; "if a child cannot sing three notes in tune there is little point to performing music with an octave range" (Choksy, 1981, p. 20).

Rhythm patterns are also presented sequentially. At first, songs containing only quarter notes (♩), eighth notes (♫), and rests (𝄽) are taught; these serve as the instructional material to teach beat, accent, and rhythm patterns.

THE EARLY CHILDHOOD PROGRAM

Kodály's early childhood program covers six areas of skill and concept instruction. They have been summarized by Choksy and include the following (adapted from Choksy, 1981, p. 17):

1. *Unaccompanied singing.* Songs have limited ranges, and a limited number of tones are taught. All singing is unaccompanied, and accurate interval reproduction is stressed.

2. *Movement.* The sequence moves from free expressive movement to singing games and dances and hence to responding correctly to the rhythmic beat.

3. *Refinement of rhythmic skills.* Accurate identification and demonstration of beat, accent, and rhythm patterns receive emphasis; in addition, children invent their own rhythm patterns and clap or play rhythmic ostinati to familiar songs.

4. *Concept development.* Distinguishing "the comparatives." The children learn to discriminate faster/slower, softer/louder and higher/lower, and they study the timbres of various instruments and voices.

5. *Ear-training and musical memory.* Children develop a repertoire of songs and learn to "think" music in their minds.

6. *Listening.* Children listen critically to their own voices, to those of classmates and teachers, and to the instruments played by the teacher, students, or visiting performers.

Figure 7.8 illustrates some of the ways in which these areas of instruction may be addressed in the teaching of the simple song "Rain, Rain, Go Away."

Some American music educators feel that selecting music that fits the Kodály sequence inadequately represents our body of American folk song literature, and they believe that the exclusive use of these songs for beginning instruction is restrictive. Kodály himself believed that any instructional sequence should be based on the folk material indigenous to the children's culture. Nonetheless, American teachers have identified a whole body of American folk songs in the pentatonic mode and have assembled many collections for the Kodály Method. Happily, the assemblage of these songs has brought to American school children many little-known folk songs of excellent quality. Selected collections of these songs are listed at the end of this chapter.

STUDIES OF THE METHOD

Although the goal of Kodály instruction is the development of music literacy, teachers have claimed that it has positive effects on nonmusical skills, including math, reading, and certain peceptual-motor skills. Kokas (1969), a Hungarian music teacher, reported that kindergarten children who had received Kodály-based instruction demonstrated superior observational ability to those who had not had such instruction. She also noted superior rhythm skill development and better coordination among three- to six-year-old children than among six-year-olds in a control group. An American music educator, Harper (Harper, Flick, Taylor, and Waldo, 1973), found that a kindergarten group who had re-

"Rain, Rain, Go Away"

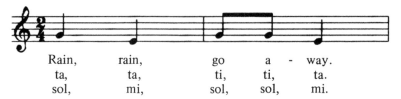

Rain, rain, go a - way.
ta, ta, ti, ti, ta.
sol, mi, sol, sol, mi.

Come a - gain an - oth - er day.
ti, ti, ti, ti, ti, ti, ta.
sol, sol, mi, mi, sol, sol, mi.

1. Learn the song by imitating the teacher.
2. Step the beat while singing the song.
3. Sing the song, clapping the rhythm of the words.
4. Sing the song, alternating between clapping the beat and the word rhythms.
5. Sing the song, step the beat, but stamp on the accented beats (BEAT, beat, BEAT, beat).
6. Sing the song faster, slower, louder, softer, or in higher or lower keys.
   For primary grade children, the teacher may continue the instruction to include:
7. Distinguish beats which have one sound. Call these "ta". Distinguish beats which have two sounds. Call these "ti-ti". Sing song with these rhythm syllables.
8. Identify the higher tones. Call these "sol." Identify lower tones. Call these "mi." Learn hand signs for "sol" and "mi." Sing song, using hand signs.
9. Show the rhythmic notation for the song: I ⊓ I I ⊓ ⊓ ⊓ I I .
10. Show the melodic notation for the song, perhaps on an abbreviated staff: ♩ ♩ ♫ ♩ | ♫ ♫ ♫ ♩ |

Selected from Choksy, 1981.

Figure 7.8. Kodály instructional techniques.

ceived Kodály training scored significantly higher on an auditory discrimination test and on the First-Grade Screening Test than did those who had not received such instruction. No differences were found in a visual-motor integration test, however.

Hurwitz (Hurwitz, Wolff, Bortnick, and Kokas, 1975) also found significant auxiliary effects of Kodály training among first grade children. Investigating the results of Kodály instruction on sequencing and spatial skills (believed to be important in reading achievement), he found that Kodály instruction resulted in higher scores on the Metropolitan Reading Test. Moreover, when these children were tested again at the end of the second grade, the Kodály group's scores were still significantly higher than the scores of groups that had not received Kodály instruction.

The full scope of the Kodály Method cannot be covered here; however, the examples of the careful instruction given to young children remind us that, in order to teach music effectively to young children, one must "make haste slowly." Clearly understood objectives, attention to detail, and much reinforcement of each skill or concept are important aspects of all methods of music instruction. Kodály has reminded us that young children are indeed music learners and that teachers should no longer be content with a "how to amuse them today?" approach to early childhood music education.

THE MANHATTANVILLE MUSIC CURRICULUM PROGRAM: INTERACTION

The methods that have been described thus far all originated in foreign countries. A method that was developed in this country and that provides an innovative, contemporary approach to music learning is the Manhattanville Music Curriculum Project (MMCP). The MMCP, bearing the name of Manhattanville College, where it originated, was a project sponsored by the Arts and Humanities Program of the United States Office of Education during the years 1965–1970.

The purpose of the project was the development of a sequential music learning program from preschool through high school that emphasized a creative approach. The results of the project were *Interaction*, an early childhood/primary music curriculum, and *Synthesis*, which begins at the third grade and extends through the high school grades. These curricula are based on the premise that the most effective way of learning about music is through exploring, manipulating, and organizing the basic material of music—sound. The Manhattanville program does not represent an all-inclusive music curriculum. It focuses upon "creative operations, with discovery, personal exploration, and judgment" (Biasini, Thomas, and Pogonowski, 1970, p. vi). Singing, move-ment, listening, and dramatic activities should be added by the teacher.

The basic belief underlying *Interaction,* the early childhood program that is relevant to our consideration, is that even very young children should "think" in the medium of music in order to understand it; they should manipulate musical sounds like a composer, performer, or con-ductor. This necessitates preparing a special environment and materials so that young children, who cannot read music or work with traditional instruments, can, in some way, work with sound. To accomplish this, a five-phase program was developed. The phases represent the "develop-mental phases of musical exploration" through which children progress from investigation to understanding.

Interaction calls for a laboratory-type classroom. A sound-materials center contains instruments and other materials for creative explo-ration. Activity carrels (semienclosed areas) are set up to provide space for working with the materials; a listening center with records, record player, tape recorder and headsets should also be available. In this type of physical setting, the role of the teacher becomes one of guide, re-source person, facilitator, and stimulator.

Brief descriptions of the phases of the program, all taken from *Interaction* (Biasini et al., 1970), can serve as an introduction to the method.

PHASE ONE: FREE EXPLORATORY ACTIVITIES

The students manipulate and explore sound-producing materials, with-out predetermined goals. They are free to produce sound over and over until they have discovered all the sound-producing possibilities of the materials. Preceding this phase and all other phases, the teacher may stimulate exploration by presenting a group activity.

> Example: Children stand in a circle. A ball of paper is passed from one pupil to the next; each pupil should attempt to make a different sound with the paper ball than that sound which precedes his in the circle. (Biasini et al., p. 42)

PHASE TWO: GUIDED EXPLORATION

The teacher intervenes to encourage the child to extend his discover-ies, for example, classifying the sounds according to timbre, volume, duration, and so forth.

> Example: Ask pupils to close their eyes while an individual makes a sound, such as shuffling feet, opening a drawer or writing on the

chalk board. Class members try to imitate the sound using only paper as a sound source. (p. 54)

PHASE THREE: EXPLORATORY IMPROVISATION

Organize a variety of sounds in combinations and patterns.

> Example: Using a variety of paper (cardboard, straws, etc.), create "sound impressions" of, for example, water dripping from a faucet, a mouse running across the floor. Organize the sounds and tape-record them for listening and identification. (p. 63)

PHASE FOUR: PLANNED IMPROVISATION

Students plan an improvisation or tell a sound story that incorporates a number of sounds.

> Example: Possible topics: "My Jet Plane," "The Mouse That Got Caught." When improvisation is completed, present to class and tape-record it for later listening. (p. 73)

PHASE FIVE: REAPPLICATION

The students explore further possibilities. "What would happen if . . . ?" (Here the teacher suggests ways of changing the improvisation: louder, slower, or softer). Pupils experiment with ideas and revise original work.

Preschool, kindergarten and first-grade children may spend a week, perhaps months, on the first three phases. Beginning experiences may use nonmusical sounds; musical sounds are manipulated in the same way as environmental sounds.

Implementing this curriculum means that teachers must be prepared to teach music in ways far removed from traditional methods. It represents a new way to look at music instruction; for teachers to whom creativity is an important aspect of music learning, *Interaction* provides much food for thought.

SUZUKI TALENT EDUCATION

Talent Education, a method of teaching very young children to play stringed instruments, was originated by Dr. Shinichi Suzuki, a Japanese music educator, in the years following World War II. Although it is not a general music method, it is included in this discussion because of the interest it has aroused among parents and teachers of young children, and because many of the principles on which it is based are applicable to general music teaching.

Suzuki calls his system the "mother tongue" method. Children are taught to play violins and cellos in the way they learn to speak—through imitation and feedback from parents, adults and other children (Figure 7.9). Just as language reading is not involved in learning to speak, so music reading is not involved in learning to play instruments, at least in the beginning stages. Talent Education begins with rote instruction and represents a radical departure from traditional methods of learning to play stringed instruments.

There are other features of the method that set it apart from more traditional approaches. Several are discussed in the following paragraphs.

PARENT INVOLVEMENT

Parents attend all lessons with the child, and, in addition, learn to play the instrument along with the student. In this way, the parent is able to help the child practice correctly at home.

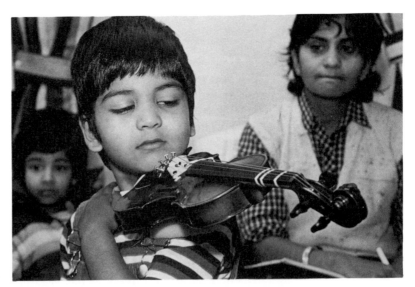

Figure 7.9. In Suzuki Talent Education, children are taught to play violins and cellos through imitation and feedback. Photo courtesy of the Preucil School of Music, Iowa City, Iowa.

MOVEMENT AND PITCH-IMITATION GAMES

Rhythmic movement and singing games are not usually associated with instrumental instruction. Suzuki-trained youngsters, however, learn to march, to turn in place, to move their arms in circular motion, and to bend and move their bodies while playing. All these exercises help to avoid cramped, tense positions. Also, the children engage in pitch-matching activities, singing pitches and melodic patterns given by the teacher. Thus, the music produced on their instruments is associated with music which their voices produce.

REINFORCEMENT

Recordings of the pieces being learned are sent home with the pupils. Children listen to them, move rhythmically with the music, and sing or play along with the recorded music. The "music lesson" does not end when the child leaves the teacher's studio.

CHILD-APPROPRIATE TEACHING STRATEGIES

Various instructional "games" help the child learn proper playing technique. For example, "Footprints are traced for a good stance; collapsed left wrists are tickled; bow hands first learn to shape themselves into rabbits who can wiggle ears and eat carrots and bows" (Tolbert, 1980, p. 136).

NONHURRIED INSTRUCTION

"Patience is not necessary. Mothers should enjoy each step as children learn. Beginners grow slowly, same as mother-tongue education," stated Dr. Suzuki (Tolbert, 1980, p. 136).

Performances by Suzuki-trained students have excited admiration throughout the world. A typical performance may feature dozens of young violinists or cellists, three to eight, playing, in unison, folk songs and baroque and classical string literature with ease, beauty, and finesse.

Some teachers have criticized the method for its rigidity. Musical pieces are learned in a particular sequence, not easily changed. Further, the music in the Suzuki materials tends to be homogeneous in sound. Few modern compositions are included.

STUDIES

Does it accomplish its goals? Little experimental research about the effect of the method on musical development has been published. A feasibility study, for the purpose of developing a model Suzuki program for day-care centers, was conducted by Price (1979). Using an author-constructed performance test to measure achievement, she reported that the overall playing ability of the children was "outstanding" and, further, that the program was favorably received by the children, their parents, and the staff.

Another researcher, Keraus (1973), compared the performances of privately taught students with class-taught students, all of whom had used the Suzuki materials. She found no differences in performance achievement between students (first and third grade pupils) who had received classroom or private instruction.

Suzuki, however, emphasized the importance of musical sensitivity in the lives of children, rather than the development of performance skills. He stated:

> I believe sensitivity and love toward music and art are very important things to all people whether they are politicians, scientists, businessmen or laborers. They are the things that make our lives rich. (Tolbert, 1980, p. 138)

CONCLUSION

Only introductory information has been presented about each method in this chapter. Furthermore, these methods by no means represent the total scope of instructional systems available to today's teachers. These methods are perhaps the best known. They have excited interest among music educators and researchers alike, and they continue to be adapted, improved, and refined to fit our children's need and interests.

But how should one choose a method? Some lines from *Alice in Wonderland* were quoted at the beginning of this chapter. They can serve to remind us that before adapting any method, teachers need to explore, discuss, consider, and evaluate the techniques, materials, and data available about that method. It is taken for granted that all carefully constructed music methodologies have one common goal—the development of musicianship. However, there are many ways to achieve that goal. Some methods may be more compatible with one's musical background, skills, and teaching style than others.

In a study of the status of the arts in preschool education, McDonald (1984) found that teachers whose background had included training and/or experience in a particular arts area felt most successful in planning experiences in that area for their students. This was particularly true for music and, to a lesser extent, for rhythmic movement.

Therefore, teachers need to examine their own abilities and interests. What do you believe is your most "comfortable" teaching style—directing self-discovery activities, interacting with groups of children? Do you feel most comfortable in movement activities, in singing, or in playing instruments? Teachers should discover their own compatible methods of teaching, which may or may not follow a prescribed method. However, we should remember that a method should lead toward identified goals; you should know "where you want to go."

SELECTED SOURCES

THE MONTESSORI METHOD

Miller, J. K. (1981). The Montessori music curriculum for children up to six years of age. *Dissertation Abstracts International, 1981, 41,* 4638A–4639A. (University Microfilms no. 81 09 598).

Montessori, M. (1964). *The advanced Montessori method: The Montessori elementary materials.* Cambridge, MA: Robert Bentley.

THE DALCROZE METHOD

Abramson, R. M. (1973). *Rhythm games* (Book 1). Pittsburgh, PA: Volkwein Bros., Inc.

Aronoff, F. W. (1979). *Music and young children: Expanded edition.* New York: Turning Wheel Press.

Choksy, L.; Abramson, R.; Gillespie, A.; & Wood, D. (1986). *Teaching music in the twentieth century.* Englewood Cliffs, NJ: Prentice-Hall, Inc.

Dorian, M., & Gulland, F. *Telling stories through movement.* Belmont, CA: Fearon Publishers, Inc.

Findlay, E. (1971). *Rhythm and movement: Applications of Dalcroze eurhythmics.* Evanston, IL: Summy-Birchard.

Gell, H. (1973). *Music, movement, and the young child.* Pittsburgh, PA: Volkerin Bros., Inc.

Landis, B., & Carder, P. (1972). *The eclectic curriculum in American music education: Contributions of Dalcroze, Kodaly and Orff.* Reston, VA: Music Educators National Conference.

Rosenstrauch, H. (1964). *Percussion, movement and the child.* Pittsburgh, PA: Volkwein Bros., Inc.

Wax, E., & Roth, S. (1979). *Mostly movement: Stories and activities for musical growth: First steps.* New York: Mostly Movement, Ltd.

THE ORFF APPROACH

Birkenshaw, L. (1982). *Music for fun, music for learning.* St. Louis, MO: Magnamusic-Baton, Inc.

Burnett, M. (1973). *Melody, movement and language.* San Francisco, CA: R & E Research Associates.

Choksy, L.; Abramson, R.; Gillespie, A.; & Wood, D. (1986). *Teaching music in the twentieth century.* Englewood Cliffs, NJ: Prentice-Hall, Inc.

Hall, Doreen. (1960). *Music for children: Teacher's manual.* Mainz: B. Schotts Söhne.

Keetman, G. (1974). *Elementaria* (M. Murray, Trans.). London: Schott and Co., Ltd.

Landis, B., & Carder, P. (1972). *The eclectic curriculum in American music education: Contributions of Dalcroze, Kodaly and Orff.* Reston, VA: Music Educators National Conference.

Regner, H. (Coordinator). (1982). *Music for children: Orff Schulwerk, American Edition. Vol. 1: Preschool.* Schott Music Corp. (American distributor: European-American Music Distributors, P.O. Box 850, Valley Forge, PA.)

THE KODÁLY METHOD

Bacon, D. (1971). *Let's sing together.* West Newton, MA: Kodály Center of America.

Choksy, L. (1974). *The Kodály method.* Englewood Cliffs, NJ: Prentice-Hall, Inc.

Choksy, L. (1981). *The Kodály context.* Englewood Cliffs, NJ: Prentice-Hall, Inc.

Choksy, L., Abramson, R., Gillespie, A., & Wood, D. (1986). *Teaching music in the twentieth century.* Englewood Cliffs, NJ.

Daniel, K. (1981). *Kodály in kindergarten.* Champaign, IL: Mark Foster.

Erdei, P. (Ed.). (1974). *150 American folk songs to sing, read and play.* Farmingdale, NY: Boosey & Hawkes, Inc.

Johnston, R. (1984). *Folk songs North America sings.* Toronto: Caveat Music Publishers, Ltd.

Landis, B., & Carder, P. (1972). *The eclectic curriculum in American music education.* Reston, VA: Music Educators National Conference.

THE MANHATTANVILLE MUSIC CURRICULUM PROGRAM, INTERACTION

Biasini, A.; Thomas, R.; & Pogonowski, L. (1970). *MMCP interaction: Early childhood music curriculum.* Bardonia, NY: Media Materials, Inc.

Thomas, R. B. (1970). *Manhattanville music curriculum program: Final report.* Washington, DC: U. S. Office of Education, Bureau of Research, August 1970. ERIC document ED 045 865.

Thomas, R. B. (1979). *MMCP synthesis.* Bellingham, WA: Americole.

SUZUKI TALENT EDUCATION

Cook, C. A. (1970). *Suzuki Education in Action.* New York: Exposition Press.

Kendall, J. D. (1966). *Talent education and Suzuki: What the American music educators should know about Shinichi Suzuki.* Reston, VA: Music Educators National Conference.

Kendall, J. D. (1973). *Suzuki violin method in American education.* Reston, VA: Music Educators National Conference.

Suzuki, S. (1969). *Nurtured by love.* New York: Exposition Press.

QUESTIONS FOR DISCUSSION/SUGGESTED ACTIVITIES

1. Do the pre- and primary-school music programs of which you are aware reflect any of the methods of music instruction described in this chapter?

2. Teachers are often instructed to use the "best" techniques of a number of methods in their classes. Are there particular difficulties in combining Orff-Kodály, Montessori-Orff, Dalcroze-Kodály or Kodály-Montessori methods that you can identify from the descriptions of the methods provided in this chapter?

3. Plan a rhythmic accompaniment composed of Orff sound-gesture patterns for three of the songs in Chapter 9. Demonstrate it to the class.

4. Try out one of the Dalcrozian exercises described in this chapter. Use piano, percussion instrument, or recording for accompaniment. Present it to the class.

5. Try the MMCP *Interaction* activities described in this chapter. Evaluate them for their effectiveness in developing discriminatory listening skills.

REFERENCES AND SUGGESTED READINGS

Barnet, E. G. (1973). *Montessori and music: Rhythmic activities for young children.* New York: Schocken.

Biasini, A.; Thomas, R.; & Pogonowski, L. (1970). *MMCP interaction: Early childhood music curriculum.* Bardonia, NY: Media Materials, Inc.

Blom, E. (Ed.). (1959). *Grove's dictionary of music and musicians.* New York: St. Martin's Press, Inc.

Boyle, J. D. (1970). The effect of prescribed rhythmical movements on the ability to read music at sight. *Journal of Research in Music Education, 18,* 307–318.

Britton, A. P. (1982). Keokuk to San Antonio . . . 75 years of change. *Music Educators Journal, 68*(6), 42–44.

Burton, L. (Ed.). (1972). *Comprehensive musicianship series.* Menlo Park, CA: Addison-Wesley.

Carobo-Cone, M. (1969). *A sensory-motor approach to music learning. Book 1: Primary concepts.* New York: MCA, Inc.

Choksy, L. (1974). *The Kodály method.* Englewood Cliffs, NJ: Prentice-Hall, Inc.

Choksy, L. (1981). *The Kodály context.* Englewood Cliffs, NJ: Prentice-Hall, Inc.

Choksy, L.; Abramson, R.; Gillespie, A.; & Wood, D. (1986). *Teaching music in the twentieth century.* Englewood Cliffs, NJ: Prentice-Hall, Inc.

Douglas, J. A. (1977). Rhythmic movement and its effect on the music achievement of fourth grade children. *Dissertation Abstracts International, 38,* 6593A. (University Microfilms no. 78 04 685)

Findlay, E. (1971). *Rhythm and movement: Applications of Dalcroze eurhythmics.* Evanston, IL: Summy-Birchard Co.

Fitzmaurice, T. J. (1971). An experimental music program based on Montessorian principles (Doctoral dissertation, Boston University, 1971). *Dissertation Abstracts International, 32,* 2119A.

Gell, H. (1973). *Music, movement, and the young child.* Pittsburgh, PA: Volkerin Bros., Inc.

Gunderson, K. (1980). Suzuki techniques of string instruction. In M. Tolbert (Ed.), *Music of young children: Current issues in music education: A symposium and research conference, Vol. 12* (pp. 135–138). Columbus, OH: The Ohio State University Press.

Hall, D., & Walter, A. (1955). *Music for children.* Mainz: B. Schotts Söhne; U.S.A. distribution, Belwin-Mills Publishing Co.

Harper, A.; Flick, M.; Taylor, K.; & Waldo, R. (1973). Education through music: A breakthrough in early childhood education? *Phi Delta Kappan, 59*(9), 628–629.

Henke, H. H. (1984). The application of Émile Jaques-Dalcroze's solfège-rhythmique to the choral rehearsal. *The Choral Journal, 25*(3), 11–14.

Hurwitz, I.; Wolff, P. H.; Bortnick, B. D.; & Kokas, K. (1975). Nonmusical effects of the Kodály music curriculum in primary grade children. *Journal of Learning Disabilities, 8*(3), 167–174.

Jaques-Dalcroze, É. (1921). *Rhythm, music, and education* (H. F. Rubenstein, Trans.). Great Britain: Hazell Watson and Viney Ltd. for the Dalcroze Society.

Jaques-Dalcroze, É. (1931). *Eurhythmics, art, and education* (F. Rothwell, Trans.; C. Cox, Ed.). New York: A. S. Barnes and Co.

Keene, J. (1982). *A history of music education in the United States.* Hanover and London: University Press of New England.

Kendall, J. (1966). *Talent education and Suzuki.* Reston, VA: Music Educators National Conference.

Keraus, R. K. (1973). An achievement study of private and class Suzuki violin instruction (Doctoral dissertation, University of Rochester, 1973). *Dissertation Abstracts International, 34,* 808A.

Kokas, K. (1969). Psychological testing in Hungarian music education. *Journal of Research in Music Education, 17*(1), 127–134.

Landis, B., & Carder, P. (1972). *The eclectic curriculum in American music education: Contributions of Dalcroze, Kodaly, and Orff.* Reston, VA: Music Educators National Conference.

Mark, M. L. (1979). *Contemporary music education.* New York: Schirmer Books, a Division of Macmillan Publishing Co.

McDonald, D. T. (1984). The creative arts in preschool education. *The Early Childhood Music SRIG Newsletter, 6,* 2–3.

Miller, J. K. (1981). The Montessori music curriculum for children up to six years of age. *Dissertation Abstracts International, 1981, 41,* 4638A–4639A. (University Microfilms No. 81 09 598).

Montessori, M. (1917). *The advanced Montessori method. Vol. 2: The Montessori elementary material.* New York: Stokes.

Montessori, M. (1964). *The advanced Montessori method: The Montessori elementary material.* Cambridge, MA: Robert Bentley.

Montessori, M. (1964a). *The Montessori method: Scientific Pedagogy as applied to child education in the children's houses* (A. E. George, Trans.). Cambridge, MA: R. Bentley.

Montessori, M. (1965). *A Montessori handbook: Dr. Montessori's own handbook* (R. C. Orem, Ed.). New York: G. P. Putnam's Sons.

Orff, C., & Keetman, G. (1950). *Schulwerk.* New York: Associated Music Publ.

Pennington, J. (1925). *The importance of being rhythmic: A study of the principles of Dalcroze eurhythmics applied to general education and to the arts of music, dancing, and acting.* Based on and adapted from *Rhythm, music and education* by É. Jaques-Dalcroze; with an introduction by Walter Damrosch. New York: G. P. Putnam's Sons.

Price, C. V. G. (1979). A model for the implementation of a Suzuki violin program for the day-care center environment: An evaluation of its effectiveness and impact. *Dissertation Abstracts International, 40,* 5357A. (University Microfilms No. 80-07, 813).

Rainbow, E. (1981). A final report on a three-year investigation of the rhythmic abilities of preschool-aged children. *Council for Research in Music Education Bulletin, 66/67,* 69–73.

Richards, M. H. (1964). *Threshold to music.* Palo Alto, CA: Fearon Publ.

Rubin, J. S. (1983). Montessorian music method: unpublished works. *Journal of Research in Music Education, 31*(3), 215–226.

Sandor, F. (Ed.). (1968). *Musical education in Hungary.* Budapest: Editio Musica.

Siemens, M. (1969). A comparison of Orff and traditional instructional methods in music. *Journal of Research in Music Education, 17*(3), 272–285.

Suzuki, S. (1969). *Nurtured by love.* New York: Exposition Press.

Szabo, H. (1969). *The Kodály concept of music education.* New York: Boosey and Hawkes.

Szoni, E. (1974). *Kodály's principles in practice.* New York: Boosey and Hawkes.

Tolbert, M. (Ed.). (1980). *Music of young children: Current issues in music education: A symposium and research conference, Vol. 12.* Columbus, OH: The Ohio State University Press.

Chapter 8

Evaluation of Preschool Music Programs

The success and desired achievement of a program for young children depend on continual and effective evaluation.

—*Eliason and Jenkins, 1981*

"Evaluation is perhaps the least understood and most neglected part of the process of music teaching . . . however, [it] is probably the most important single step of the teaching process" (Illinois Office of Education, 1975, p. 163). In this chapter we will attempt to define evaluation as it applies to early childhood music education, to discuss its role, and to suggest ways to carry it out in early childhood centers, preschools, and kindergartens.

DEFINING EVALUATION

Leonhard and House (1972) defined evaluation in this way: "Evaluation is the process of determining the extent to which the objectives have been attained" (p. 390). Three steps are involved (p. 390):

1. identifying, formulating, and validating objectives
2. collecting data that may reveal current status in relation to the objectives
3. interpreting the data.

Colwell (1970) added one additional step to the process: "the dissemination of the results back into the teaching-learning situation" (p. 4). The addition of this step brings into focus the real purpose of evaluation: improving the music program.

PURPOSES OF EVALUATION

The activities of a preschool or kindergarten music program can be adapted to the needs of individual children only if their developmental progress is measured in some systematic way. Measurement is an important aspect of evaluation. It is not synonymous with evaluation, however. Measurement is a single indicator of achievement at one point in time, such as a test grade or musical performance. Evaluation is a consideration of various related measurements so that a level of achievement in relation to previous levels may be determined. Specific up-to-date evaluation of the learning environment is useful for general curricular planning; such evaluation is essential in planning specific activities for children of various developmental levels or for those with special needs.

Commonly, teachers have relied upon casual observations and their own "feelings" about how children are progressing in their musical development. Casual judgments, however, are often unreliable and do little to provide the information needed to make decisions about the curriculum. Evaluation serves two important purposes: to diagnose status and to provide information about progress toward goals. Evaluation early in the year provides diagnostic information about where both music programs and individual children are—it provides a basis for curricular planning and selection. Evaluation during the year can point up areas of strength of weakness in either programs or individual children so that special emphasis may be given to those areas.

NEED FOR EVALUATION

Evaluation procedures aid in measuring two aspects of early childhood music education: the overall learning environment and the progressive achievement of individual children. When parents ask, "Is the music program measuring up to what a good program ought to be?" teachers need to have factual information. Likewise, when such questions arise as, "Can my child sing in tune?" or "How do my child's musical skills compare with those of most four-year-olds?" then carefully culled information based on various types of measurements obtained throughout the year can provide specific rather than vague answers.

Although we may agree about the benefits of evaluating the progress of both our program and of individual children, the practice of evaluation is not common in many preschools or kindergartens. Perhaps one reason for this situation is the lack of valid and reliable published measuring instruments. However, many methods for gathering evaluative information may be used for gathering data. These include checklists, observational records, and teacher-constructed tests. Each of these methods will be described as they may be applied to evaluation of a music program or evaluation of the musical achievement of individual children.

PROGRAM EVALUATION

In Chapter 4, many aspects of a music learning environment were discussed. While, ultimately, the quality of any program is determined by what takes place between a teacher and a group of students, the philosophy of a school, the planning done by the teacher, and the available materials and equipment will affect the program. The Music Educators National Conference (MENC) has stated that:

> adequate staff and satisfactory facilities and equipment increase the likelihood of excellence to such an extent that it is the responsibility of a professional association to establish standards within its field of competence, and it is a responsibility of a school . . . to seek to achieve those standards. (Music Educators, 1986, p. 16)

Evaluation of a program, therefore, may start, not with the measurement of individual children's musical achievement but with measurement of the music environment planned and prepared for the children. Various aspects of the program that may be measured include:

Philosophy and Goals	Materials and Equipment
Scheduling	Musical Instruments
Staffing and Teaching	Facilities

PHILOSOPHY AND GOALS

A checklist that includes a scale for rating the philosophy and goals of a preschool music program is presented in Figure 8.1. It may help to point up aspects of this program component that are strong or those that need attention.

CURRICULUM

Figure 8.2 continues the evaluation of a music environment in terms of the implementation of the program. The standards for these separate curricular aspects—scheduling, staffing, facilities—were derived from those listed in the MENC document. *The School Music Program: Description and Standards: Early Childhood Music* (Music Educators, 1986).

Instructions: Score each statement using the following scale:
4 = Strong; 3 = Adequate; 2 = Weak; 1 = Very weak or missing

Component	Rating	Practice Standard
Philosophy	_____	1. There exists an articulated philosophical position about the music program.
	_____	2. The philosophy is known to all staff.
	_____	3. The philosophical position is realistically applicable in this setting.
Program Goals	_____	4. Program goals for music have been formulated.
	_____	5. The goals are observable and measurable.
	_____	6. The goals are age-appropriate and reflect the developmental stages of the learners.
	_____	7. The goals encompass a multi-faceted music program, which includes singing, moving, playing instruments, listening to music, and opportunities for individual exploration and creating.
	_____	8. The goals are realistic in terms of your staff and facilities.

Average Score _____

Figure 8.1. Example of a scale for rating a school's music education philosophy and goals.

MATERIALS AND EQUIPMENT

Because a variety of musical experiences is important for children of preschool and kindergarten age, an environment that includes many sound sources, including records, instruments, and listening equipment is needed for a quality program. *The School Music Program: Description and Standards* offers standards by which to evaluate this aspect of a preschool music learning environment. An example of such an evaluation is shown in Figure 8.3.

Instructions: Score each statement using the following scale:
4 = Strong; 3 = Adequate; 2 = Weak; 1 = Very weak or missing

Component	Rating	Practice Standard
Scheduling	_____	1. Music experiences occur every day for all children.
	_____	2. Teachers provide individual music experiences for younger children.
	_____	3. At least 7 percent of the contact time with children is spent in music activities (e.g., at least 21 minutes of music for each five hours of contact time.)
Staffing	_____	4. At least one staff member has some training or background in music.
	_____	5. A music specialist is available for consultation.
Facilities	_____	6. Each classroom has an area designated as a music center in which children have easy access to music materials and equipment.
	_____	7. Each classroom has an area large enough for movement activities.

Average Score _____

Figure 8.2. Example of a scale for rating a school's music curriculum.

EVALUATING CHILDREN'S MUSICAL GROWTH

"What are my children learning about music?" is the ultimate question about any school's music program. The curriculum, the teaching, and the environment may all appear to be satisfactory, but the real effect of all these components can be verified only by evidence of the musical learning of the children. Systematic evaluation, based on separate measures of musical growth, can provide this evidence.

The basic method of determining musical growth is that of criterion-referenced measurements. This method determines the quality of a performance (involving either skills or understandings) by comparing it to preselected standards or criteria. The standards or criteria are based on the program goals established by a school's teachers.

Instructions: Provide a check for each piece of material equipment that is available. Total the number of checks. There are 20 pieces of equipment or materials listed. A score of *16* or better can indicate that your program is strong in this area; a score of *10* or less may indicate areas of weakness.

Component

Equipment and Materials	_____ piano	_____ record player
	_____ headphones	_____ listening center
	_____ cassette recorder that can be operated by the children	
	_____ quality, up-to-date resource book on preschool music	
	_____ music textbook with accompanying recordings	
	_____ set of records or cassette tapes containing a wide variety of musical styles	
Musical Instruments	_____ rhythm drums or tom-toms	
	_____ rhythm sticks (a pair for each child)	
	_____ sandblocks	
	_____ woodblocks or claves	
	_____ tambourines	
	_____ maracas	
	_____ guiros	
	_____ finger cymbals or triangles	
	_____ jingle bells	
	_____ resonator bells or songbells	
	_____ xylophone-type instruments	
	_____ autoharp	
	Total Score _____	

Figure 8.3. Example of a measure for rating a school's musical equipment and materials.

The program goals discussed in Chapter 4 included a number of discrete skills, behaviors, and understandings. Musicality involves all of these; however, achievement in the various areas, even within an individual child, may differ. A child may sing quite accurately but need more experience and time for rhythmic skills to be refined. So, too, do children differ in their ways of demonstrating musical ideas. Some may be able to verbalize their understandings; others may be able to show through movement or instrumental performance what they cannot verbalize.

Because of the various response modes through which we may obtain measurements of musical achievement, any test should have certain consistent characteristics:

1. It should be criterion-referenced
2. It should include each area of music learning
3. It should be referenced to specific instructional objectives
4. It should be diagnostic, referenced to a child's developmental stage
5. It should measure behaviors that represent a child's actual abilities
6. It should be able to be scored consistently
7. It should be conducted periodically so that it contributes to an overall evaluation of musical growth
8. It should be easily administered.

Because tests of young children's musical behaviors do require that teachers exercise their musical judgments in determining test scores, subjectivity is involved. However, teachers who wish to evaluate musical progress using only "perfect" tests and methods are likely not to evaluate at all—a less-than-good decision.

In reviewing the long-range music program goals described in Chapter 4, one can notice that the goal statements begin with verbs: learning to *listen*, to *sing*, to *move*, to *play*, to *develop* music concepts, and to *create* and *value* music. Most of these verbs denote performance. Thus, evaluating the musical development of young children usually means measuring some kind of performance over a period of time.

Figure 8.4 presents a suggested format for charting the musical development of individual children through periodic measurements. If such a chart is kept for each child, the progressive development toward goals in each of the various areas of musical growth will be apparent. It can provide definitive answers to questions concerning the child's interest in music, skill development in areas of singing, listening, rhythmic movement, playing instruments, creating, and progressive understanding of musical concepts.

Such a chart provides a descriptive evaluation of a child's musical progress. This method cannot be rigidly scientific. It can, however, serve systematically to collect periodic data and, if carefully used, can yield a reasonably accurate picture of both the status of a child's musical achievement and the effectiveness of our instruction.

Figure 8.4. Example of a format for evaluating children's music progress.

NAME: _____ Age at initial measurement _____

Instructions: For each attribute listed, score using the following rating scale: 1 = performance does not yet meet criterion; 2 = performance meets minimal levels of criterion; 3 = performance exceeds minimal level of criterion.

Date	Score	Date	Score	Date	Score	Area of Measurement and Objective	
/ /		/ /		/ /		1. Participates freely in music activities.	**AFFECT**
/ /		/ /		/ /		2. Seeks out music activities: sings during play.	
/ /		/ /		/ /		3. Show preferences for certain types of music or music activities.	
/ /		/ /		/ /		1. Sings familiar songs in recognizable fashion.	**SINGING**
/ /		/ /		/ /		2. Accurately imitates melodic patterns.	
/ /		/ /		/ /		3. Sings expressively.	
/ /		/ /		/ /		1. Moves expressively to music.	**MOVING**
/ /		/ /		/ /		2. Accurately imitates rhythmic patterns.	
/ /		/ /		/ /		3. Moves in synchronization (can "keep the beat") with music being performed or heard.	
/ /		/ /		/ /		1. Demonstrates proper technique in holding and playing classroom instruments.	**PLAYING**
/ /		/ /		/ /		2. Accurately imitates rhythmic or melodic patterns on pitched and unpitched instruments.	
/ /		/ /		/ /		3. Shows interest in improvising rhythms and/or melodies on instruments.	
/ /		/ /		/ /		1. Shows, through movement or verbal description, awareness of melodic concepts, including high-low, higher-lower, same-different.	**LISTENING**
/ /		/ /		/ /		2. Shows, through movement or verbal descriptors, awareness of rhythmic concepts, including same-different, fast-slow, faster-slower, short-long (relative duration).	
/ /		/ /		/ /		3. Shows, through movement or verbal descriptors, understanding of dynamic concepts, including loud-soft, louder-softer.	
/ /		/ /		/ /		4. Accurately identifies musical instruments (which have been studied) by sound alone.	
/ /		/ /		/ /		5. Listens to music attentively during class or individual activities.	

Date	Score	Date	Score	Date		Area of Measurement and Objective	
/ /		/ /		/ /		1. Improvises song patterns at play or in class activities.	CREATING
/ /		/ /		/ /		2. Improvises expressive movements to music heard or sung.	
/ /		/ /		/ /		3. Improvises patterns on classroom instruments.	

For such a measuring system to give as accurate a picture of musical growth as is possible among young children, we suggest the following:

1. Use the musical materials included in daily musical activities for the testing materials. The materials for instruction found in Chapter 9 can provide melodic and rhythmic patterns for imitation, songs to be sung, and recorded compositions for measuring listening skills.
2. The "testing" should occur as normal, familiar class or individual activities. An aide can help you record the scores. Children will not feel threatened if testing occurs in this way.
3. Do not misinterpret or misuse the information gathered. Your criteria for scoring the children's performances should be based on your knowledge of what is reasonable to expect of a child at a given age or stage of development.
4. If you feel unable to assign a score to the various behaviors, seek a music specialist either to help you score the performance (perhaps as your "aide") or to discuss what you can realistically expect.

OTHER MUSIC EVALUATION PROCEDURES

The necessity for devising an evaluation format for preschool children arises from the nonexistence of published music tests for children too young to use pencil-and-paper tests. For children in the kindergarten and primary grades, some published tests exist; in addition, some school systems have devised their own methods of measurement for use throughout a school district. These are described in the following sections.

PUBLISHED TESTS

The *Simons Measurements of Music Listening Skills* (Simons, 1976) is designed for group administration to children of ages six, seven, and eight.

Some parts of it have been used successfully with kindergarten children when administered to four or five children at a time and carefully monitored. This criterion-referenced test of fundamental listening skills includes nine subtests of five items each. Children are asked to respond to tape-recorded musical items (short melodies, chords, and rhythm patterns) by marking pictures or numbers on the answer sheets (Figure 8.5). Children need not be able to read to take this test. All the test

(a) "Listen first . . . "

(b) ". . . then fill in the circle."

Figure 8.5. Children respond to tape-recorded musical items by marking pictures or numbers on the answer sheets.

instructions are included on the tape, and the teacher uses overhead transparencies to help explain the testing procedures. The duration of each subtest is five to eight minutes, and the full test should be spread over two or three separate sessions. Data from this test are best used to measure the music listening achievement of groups of children rather than that of individual children.

The *Primary Measures of Music Audiation* (PMMA) (Gordon, 1979) is designed for group administration to children in grades K, 1, 2, and 3. This test was developed by Gordon, whose *Music Aptitude Profile,* designed for those in grade 4 and above, has been widely used for measuring music aptitude.

The PMMA includes a "Tonal" tape recording and a "Rhythm" tape recording, each of which is about twelve minutes long and includes forty items (questions). "The tonal phrases . . . are from two to five tones in length, are all performed at the same tempo and in the same key. . . . The rhythm phrases include tempo beats which may or may not be systematic in number and length" (Gordon, 1979, p. 10). As children listen to the recorded test items, they are asked to identify pairs of musical patterns as the same or different, and to answer by circling a corresponding picture ("same" or "different" illustrations) on an answer sheet. Children need no language, reading, or music reading skills in order to take this test. Percentile norms for each grade level are provided in the test manual so that teachers can compare their pupils' scores with those of others.

In 1982 Gordon's *Intermediate Measures of Music Audiation* (IMMA) was published as an advanced version of the PMMA. It differs from the PMMA in that (1) it is intended for use with a group that includes many children who scored very high on the PMMA, and (2) it is designed for children in grades 1, 2, 3, and 4. The content of the test items is slightly more difficult than that of the PMMA, but the design and format of the two tests are the same.

MUSIC BOOK SERIES TESTS

Silver Burdett Music, a series of music textbooks for grades 1 through 6, included in its 1979 edition a companion set of eighteen music tests and records entitled *Competency Tests,* developed by Colwell (1979). These tests provide a method for periodic assessment of pupil achievement. The teacher's guide for these tests contains full information regarding the tests' design, content, administration, scoring, and interpretation. The following test description is taken from that guide.

Each of the eighteen tests covers the lesson material from about one-third of a graded text, and can be completed in one class period.

Students are asked to listen to music and accompanying questions on a recording, then to respond by filling in circles on an answer sheet. Most of the test items measure students' music-listening skills, such as identifying certain features of the musical examples: rhythm, melody, form, tone color, and others. In some tests, students are required to use their textbooks.

Also included in the teachers' guide is information regarding test reliability, validity, and usability. Users of these tests are urged to study this information because improper interpretation could lead to serious misunderstandings about what the children are learning. The guide also includes clear explanations concerning how the test scores should be interpreted. Study of this material is recommended to those whose training in tests and measurements is limited.

The 1985 edition of the Silver Burdett series, entitled *Music* (Silver Burdett, 1985), also contains a group of music listening tests entitled "What Do You Hear?" These tests are designed to measure the listening skills taught in specific units in the books. In the kindergarten book, short listening tests are interspersed throughout the text. These measure children's ability to discriminate tone color, dynamics, register, tempo, and duration.

All the musical examples and instructions for the test are included on recordings, and reproducible answer sheets are included in the teacher's editions of the books. The answer sheet format is clear and simple. Children respond to the musical examples heard by marking pictures, words, or numbers. The tests in the first four book levels (K, 1, 2, 3) usually contain only four to nine items (questions), and most are two-choice questions. That is, children must decide between two possible answers which is the correct one.

The simplicity and clarity of these tests make them very practical instruments for program evaluation. When tests scores for a full class are combined they provide a good assessment of the listening achievement of a specific grade level. For individual children, however, the test scores on single tests should not be regarded as definitive assessments of this ability, because the brevity of the tests and the small number of choices for each item increase the effect of guessing on the total scores.

Another recent and popular music series, *The Music Book* (Boardman and Andress, 1984), includes evaluation procedures described as "Reports to Parents." Four report forms, one for each quarter of a school year, are provided as "blackline masters," which can be reproduced. The information on the forms provides directions for the teacher in evaluating individual children's performances and understandings of specified tasks. The tasks are based on the material found in lessons and activities of *The Music Book*. The teacher judges the child's responses to the tasks and scores them as "can do" or "not yet." The completed "Report to Parents" shows the teacher's evaluation of the child's attainment of several music learnings.

UNPUBLISHED MEASUREMENTS

Some large school systems have developed their own music evaluation procedures. In May 1985, the Atlanta Public School System initiated tests of music learning for hundreds of children in grades 1 through 7 in order to obtain data that would assist in formulating specific instructional objectives attainable by each grade level. The tests are given to full classrooms of children in one sitting. In grades 1, 2, and 3, this *Test of Musical Concepts* includes only 1, 2, or 3 items for each of the following: melody, harmony, rhythm, tone color, dynamics, and tempo. The brief musical examples and test instructions are recorded on tape: children mark their answers on a computer scoring sheet. The children are asked to select the correct answer from the two given on the tape, or to answer with a question mark if they are unsure of an answer. This method avoids forced-choice answers and reduces the effect of guessing on the total score.

Many other school systems have developed their own testing instruments. This particular test is described to show that music evaluation *is* an ongoing concern in most elementary schools, that it can be accomplished in reasonable ways, and that it is regarded as contributory to planning realistic music program goals and objectives.

Two other measurement techniques that have been used successfully with young children are suggested for teachers' consideration. First, the use of video and audio tape recordings offers a valuable method of evaluating musical growth. Comparisons of performances of individuals, recorded at periodic intervals, vividly display improvement or lack of improvement in specific areas of learning. The motivational value of this type of measurement seems evident. In addition, the accumulated tapes provide an extensive, indisputable record of musical growth that is useful for program or individual evaluation.

Second, Forsythe (1974) and several others have developed methods to measure musical attitudes or preferences of young children by asking them to circle pictures of facial expressions or stick figure drawings in response to questions about music asked aloud by their teachers. "The picture attitude survey was developed as an attempt to avoid the obvious difficulties involved in assessing attitude among children who have limited vocabularies and undeveloped abilities to make fine conceptual discriminations" (Forsythe, p. 39). Examples that may be useful are shown in Figure 8.6.

Teacher asks: "Which one of these faces looks the
most like your face during regular class work?"

Teacher asks: "Which one of these faces looks the
most like your face during music activities (class)?"

Teacher says: "Listen to this record, then circle the face
that looks the most like your face as you listen."

Figure 8.6. Example of a picture attitude survey.

For those who wish to investigate other means of evaluation,
we recommend examination of the materials cited in this chapter's
reference list, especially the books by Andress (1980) and Aronoff (1969).

QUESTIONS FOR DISCUSSION/SUGGESTED ACTIVITIES

1. Review the differences between measurement and evaluation. Which should
   be regarded as the most accurate description of a young child's musical
   achievement? Why?
2. Why is evaluation of a program a necessary part of evaluating children's
   musical growth?
3. Review the various areas of measurement of children's music progress. Which
   areas necessitate the teacher's indirect (out-of-sight) observations, and which
   require direct observations?

4. What is the relationship between criterion-referenced testing and the school's music curriculum?

REFERENCES AND SUGGESTED READINGS

Andress, B. (1980). *Music experiences in early childhood.* New York: Holt, Rinehart & Winston.

Aronoff, F. W. (1969). *Music and young children.* New York: Holt, Rinehart & Winston.

Atlanta Public Schools. *Test of musical concepts—grade 1-3.* (Unpublished). Atlanta, GA.

Boardman, E., & Andress, B. (1984). *The music book.* New York: Holt, Rinehart & Winston.

Braithwaite, J., et al. (1983). *Explorations in early childhood education: The Mt. Druitt early childhood project.* Hawthorn, Victoria, Australia: The Australian Council for Educational Research.

Bredekamp, S. (Ed.). (1986). *Developmentally appropriate practice.* Washington, DC: National Association for the Education of Young Children.

Colwell, R. (1970). *The evaluation of music teaching and learning.* Englewood Cliffs, NJ: Prentice-Hall.

Colwell, R. (1979). *Silver Burdett music competency tests: Teacher's guide.* Morristown, NJ: Silver Burdett.

Eliason, C., & Jenkins, L. (1981). *A practical guide to early childhood education* (2nd ed.). St. Louis: The C. V. Mosby Co.

Forsythe, J. (1974). Evaluation of the project. In *Learning music as a language.* Muscogee Music Project. Columbus, GA: Muscogee County School District.

Georgia State Department of Education. (1980). *Teacher performance assessment instrument.* Atlanta, GA: Division of Staff Development.

Gordon, E. (1979). *Primary measures of music audiation.* Chicago: Music Learning Research Division of G. I. A. Publications.

Gordon, E. (1982). *Intermediate measures of music audiation.* Chicago: G. I. A. Publications.

Gronlund, N. E. (1973). *Preparing criterion-referenced tests for classroom instruction.* New York: Macmillan Company.

Hoepfner, R., & Fink, A. (1973). *Evaluation study of the California state preschool program.* Los Angeles: Center for the Study of Evaluation, UCLA Graduate School of Education.

Illinois State Office of Education. (1975). *Elementary music: Guidelines for elementary music education in Illinois.* Springfield, IL: State Office of Education.

Kokas, K. (July 1968). *Psychological testing in Hungarian music education.* Paper presented at the International Seminar on Experimental Research in Music Education, Reading, England.

Leonhard, C., & House, R. (1972). *Foundations and principles of music education* (2nd ed.). New York: McGraw-Hill.

Locke, W. T. (1979). *Development and implementation of a sequential music program for the kindergarten teacher.* Fort Lauderdale, FL: Nova University.

Music Educators National Conference. (1986). *The School Music Program: Description and Standards.* Reston, VA: MENC.

Oklahoma State Department of Education. (1983). *Growing: Pre-kindergarten through 2nd grade.*

Pond, D. (1981). A composer's study of young children's innate musicality. *Council for Research in Music Education Bulletin, 68,* 1–12.

Shelley, S. (1981). Investigations of the musical capabilities of children. *Council for Research in Music Education Bulletin, 68,* 26–34.

Silver Burdett. "What Do You Hear?" In *Music.* (1985). Morristown, NJ: Silver Burdett Co.

Simons, G. (1976). *Simons measurements of music listening skills.* Chicago, IL: Stoelting Company.

Chapter 9

Materials for Instruction

I give my whole self a shake, shake, shake,
And turn myself about . . .

—*"Looby Loo" (child's song)*

Songs and musical games have been a part of early childhood education for a long time. Group singing has always been recognized as an enjoyable way to help children develop social and participatory skills. Songs help preschoolers learn to follow directions, take turns, and contribute to a group effort. Action songs and finger plays give children the opportunity to refine already-present motor skills and explore new movement patterns. Songs also help children acquire or reinforce non-musical concepts such as directionality, body parts identification, color recognition, and number and letter seriation. Music makes the necessary repetition fun—not tedious drill.

If we use music only for these purposes, however, we are limiting its value and contribution to young children's education. Each song, each musical activity, can lead to improvement in basic musical skills, such as singing, moving, listening, or creating, and to a better understanding of the elements of music—melody, rhythm, dynamics, timbre, harmony, and form. Beginning experiences produce beginning skills and concepts, but these beginnings form the foundation for the more complex and in-depth performances and cognitive understandings that develop from the experiences and teaching we provide.

In Chapter 4, the quality early childhood music program described in *The School Music Program: Description and Standards* (Music Educators National Conference, 1986) was presented. In this chapter, we have attempted to translate the descriptors (types of experiences that are appropriate for various age groups) into actual musical activities. These may serve as models for teachers to plan their own curricular offerings.

For each song and activity in this chapter, a suggested focus, as well as the description of a possible activity, is included. These suggestions are not meant to be prescriptive. Rather, teachers are encouraged to study the songs and experiences given here and formulate their own instructional objectives, which may or may not be derived from the suggestions provided in this chapter.

Although the songs and recordings have been arbitrarily placed in a specific age-group category, a child's song cannot belong to only one group of children. The placement was based on the concept or skill requirement, age-referenced according to the developmental research that has been presented throughout this text. Clearly, there will be children for whom the suggested activities are too complex or inappropriate. Teachers may make their own adjustments.

It is realized that any selected collection of songs cannot represent the musical backgrounds and cultures of all the children in an early childhood center. One of the important tasks of a music educator is to seek out and include music of many cultures, through which a child gains various benefits:

> (1) develops awareness and appreciation for racial and cultural diversity; (2) values the contributions of all ethnic groups; (3) respects his own and others' cultural background; (4) affirms the uniqueness of each individual; (5) learns how to live successfully in a multicultural society; and (6) values and celebrates cultural diversity. (McCullough, 1985, p. 96)

The preschool years, which see progressive ability to give sustained attention to objects and situations, to formulate concepts based on observed similarities and differences, and to organize and categorize ideas on the basis of these similarities and differences, are especially important in musical development.

> It is . . . as if [a child's] toddler years had been spent gathering together the separate tiny pieces which go into a kaleidoscope, and his pre-school years see him able, at last, to put all the pieces into his kaleidoscope mind and shake them around to form new and different patterns at will. (Leach, 1983, p. 422)

This chapter's songs and activities might be described as the separate pieces of the kaleidoscope of "musical experiencing" which, as they are shaken about and put into place, give pleasure and beauty to the process of learning about, thinking about, and producing music.

MUSIC EXPERIENCES FOR INFANTS

Early experiences that include visual, tactile, and kinesthetic stimulation are important in introducing infants to music. In *The School Music*

Program: Description and Standards (Music Educators National Conference, 1986) are descriptions of the type of experiences that should be provided for these youngest learners. The songs and rhymes in this section include multisensory activities that may heighten babies' awareness of rhythmic and pitched sound. They are categorized according to their applicability to the *School Music Program* recommendations, which are displayed in boxed-in units.

> Singing and chanting to them; Rocking, patting, touching and moving with the children to the beat, rhythm patterns, and melodic direction of music heard.

"Here's a Ball"

Here's a ball for Baby,   ⊓ ⊓ ⊓ ≀
Big and soft and round.   ⊓ ⊓ | ≀
Here is Baby's hammer;   ⊓ ⊓ ⊓ ≀
My, how it can pound!   ⊓ ⊓ | ≀
Here is Baby's trumpet;   ⊓ ⊓ ⊓ ≀
Toot, ta-too, ta-toot!   ⊓ ⊓ | ≀
Here's how Baby plays | | ⊓ |
Peek, peek-a-boo! | ⊓ | ≀
Here's a big umbrella   ⊓ ⊓ ⊓ ≀
Keeping Baby dry.   ⊓ ⊓ | ≀
Here's the baby's cradle;   ⊓ ⊓ ⊓ ≀
Rock-a-baby bye.   ⊓ ⊓ | ≀

Suggested Focus: Rhythmic speech, pitch variance.

The Activity: Move the child's arms to (1) trace shape of ball, (2) pound imaginary hammer, (3) play trumpet, (4) hide eyes, (5) form imaginary umbrella, (6) rock baby. Vary the pitch of your speech as you chant the verse with a rhythmic "swing."

"This Little Piggy"

This little piggy went to market;
This little piggy stayed home.
This little piggy had roast beef;
This little piggy had none.
This little piggy cried "Wee, wee, wee!"
All the way home.

Suggested Focus: Rhythmic speech; pitch variance.

The Activity: This toe- or finger-wiggling game, which has always delighted infants and toddlers, should be performed using high/low voice inflection and with a good rhythmic beat.

"Hot Cross Buns"

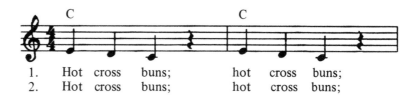

1. Hot cross buns; hot cross buns;
2. Hot cross buns; hot cross buns;

One a pen-ny, two a pen-ny, hot cross buns.
If you have no daugh-ters, give them to your sons.

Suggested Focus: Moving to the melodic rhythm of a song.
The Activity: Clap the infant's hands together to the rhythm of the words of the song. Blow on the child's hands when the rest (𝄽) occurs.

"Pat-a-Cake"

Pat - a - cake, pat - a - cake,   Ba - ker's man;

Bake   me   a   cake   as   fast   as you can;

(spoken)

Pat   it and prick   it   and   mark it with a   "B";

Pop it   in the o - ven for   Ba - by and me!

Suggested Focus: Difference between speech and singing; awareness of different parts (phrases) of a song.

    The Activity: Measures 1–2: Clap child's hands.

                      Measures 3–4: "Stir" the dough (roll child's hands over each other).

                      Measures 5–6: Trace a "B" on baby's tummy.

                      Measures 7–8: Clap child's hand on "Pop."

"The Bus"

Traditional

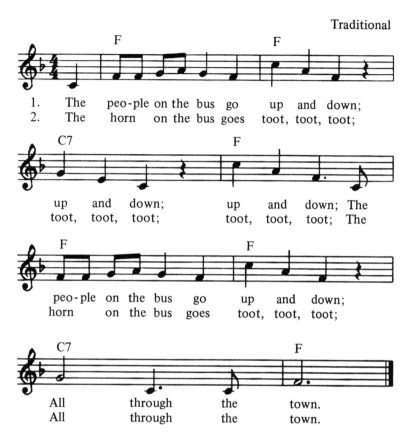

1. The peo-ple on the bus go up and down;
2. The horn on the bus goes toot, toot, toot;

up and down; up and down; The
toot, toot, toot; toot, toot, toot; The

peo-ple on the bus go up and down;
horn on the bus goes toot, toot, toot;

All through the town.
All through the town.

Suggested Focus: Awareness of downward melodic direction.
The Activity: Move the child's arms up and down, or lift child up, then lower, as you sing the words "up and down." Of course, this song should be taught to *all* preschool children and there are many more verses to add for toddlers and older preschoolers.

"Bye, Baby Bunting"

Mother Goose

Bye,   Ba - by Bunt - ing;   Dad - dy's gone a hunt - ing to

get   a   lit - tle   rab - bit   skin   to

wrap his ba - by bunt-ing in.   Bye,   Ba - by Bunt - ing.

Suggested Focus: Rhythmic beat.

The Activity: Perhaps our children's first experience with rhythmic movement occurs when we rock them. Weiser tells us that even the best tempo for rocking babies has been researched. "One researcher found that fast rocking (one time per second) is what babies like best" (1982, p. 214).

Imitating the sounds infants make; Exposing them
to a wide variety of vocal, body, instrumental and
environmental sounds.

"WHAT DO I HEAR?"

Teachers and caregivers help infants attach meaning to their vocalizations by imitating the baby's sounds. The teacher who takes time to engage in one-to-one "musical conversations" with infants encourages more vocalization, more sound exploration, and more awareness of pitch variances in singing and speaking.

However, teachers may encourage their students to explore the expressive possibilities of their voices by imitating environmental and/or musical sounds themselves. The following activities encourage this type of exploration.

1. Investigate a clock. Imitate its "tick-tock"; encourage child to imitate.
2. Watch a metronome tick. Imitate its sound; encourage child to imitate.
3. Listen to a street siren. Imitate its sound; encourage child to imitate.
4. Investigate a small bell. Ring it; allow child to ring it. Imitate its sound; encourage child to imitate.
5. Play individual tones on a piano. Allow child to play tones. Sing the pitches; encourage child to imitate.
6. Pluck a guitar string. Allow child to pluck it. Sing the pitch; encourage child to imitate.
7. Beat a toy drum. Allow child to produce sounds. Imitate them; encourage child to imitate.

Providing exposure to selected recorded music.

The studies of infants' auditory discrimination skills have shown that infants learn to distinguish music that they hear often, especially when it is associated with pleasurable activities. Teachers may choose recordings that they, themselves, enjoy, and they should listen to them often *with* the child. Associative activities and participatory responses may or may not be appropriate. Recorded music should include:

1. tapes of children singing
2. your favorite records
3. recordings of environmental sounds

MUSIC EXPERIENCES FOR TWO- AND THREE-YEAR-OLD CHILDREN

Two- to four-year-old children are in a growth period characterized by rapid language and motor development. During these years, they are action-bound; they must involve their bodies as well as their minds to understand their experiences.

Musically, they enjoy singing and creating songs, and often entertain themselves in this way as they play. They enjoy learning action songs and rhythmic games, but often prefer one-to-one, teacher-child experiences rather than group experiences. They are able to learn and perform quite complex imitative actions.

In *The School Music Program: Description and Standards* (Music Educators, 1986), types of musical skills and understandings appropriate for this age group were identified. The suggested areas of learning served as the format for categorizing the songs and activities in the following section.

PERFORMING/READING

> Sing in a freely improvised style. Sing folk and composed songs. (Pitch and rhythmic precision is not expected.) Recognize the difference between singing and speaking.

"I'm a Little Teapot"

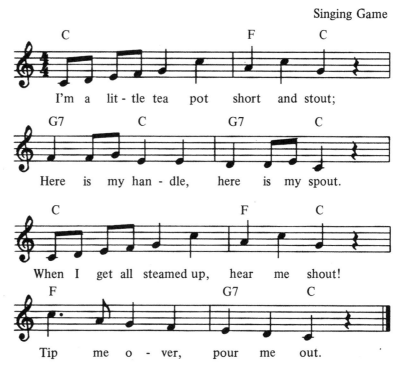

Suggested Focus: Downward movement of the melody on the last phrase.

The Activity: The teapot's handle is formed by placing one hand on one's hip; the spout is the other arm raised with palm down. When "Tip me over, pour me out" is sung, child bends toward "spout."

The game may be performed in circle or randomly spaced formation. The teacher may be the first leader, but individual children should also have turns.

"Eency, Weency Spider"

Singing Game

Suggested Focus: Awareness of like/different phrases.
The Activity: Measures 1–4: "Walk" up arm with fingers of other hand.

Measures 5–8: Raise arms high, let fingers wiggle as arms are lowered.

Measures 9–12: Shape an imaginary "sun" with both arms.

Measures 13–16: Repeat actions of measures 1–4.

"Teddy Bear"

Traditional

Ted-dy Bear, Ted-dy Bear, turn a - round!

Ted-dy Bear, Ted-dy Bear, Touch the ground!

Ted-dy Bear, Ted-dy Bear, show your shoe!

Ted-dy Bear, Ted-dy Bear, that will do!

Ted-dy Bear, Ted-dy Bear, turn out the light!

Ted-dy Bear, Ted-dy Bear, Say good night!

Suggested Focus: Difference between singing and speaking; accurate reproduction of a two-tone song.

The Activity: This song consists of only two different tones, "sol" and "mi," and contains much repetition. After performing the actions suggested by the words, the children may enjoy a game involving "finish the phrase":

Teacher sings: "Teddy Bear, Teddy Bear."

The child sings the phrase of his or her choice or the child says, "Say good-night!"

Discuss the difference between singing and speaking.

"Old MacDonald"

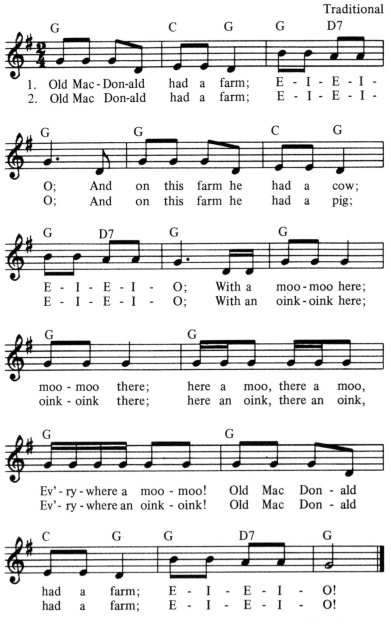

Suggested Focus: Acquiring a repertoire of traditional folk/composed children's songs.

The Activity: Insert names of as many animals as you please!

"Dinah"

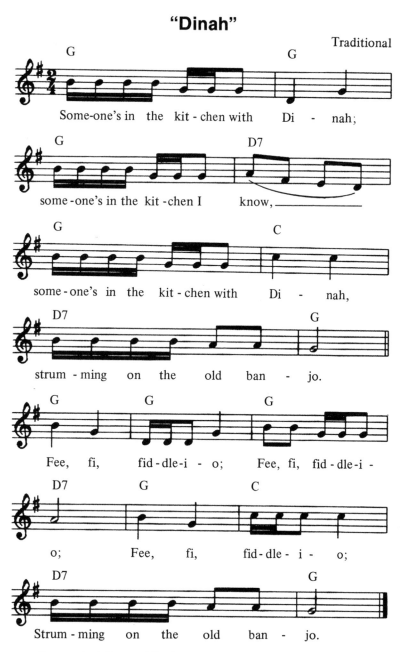

Suggested Focus: Rhythmic beat.

The Activity: While singing the song, strum an imaginary banjo. (Bring a banjo, picture of one, or, best yet, banjo and performer to class.)

"Twinkle, Twinkle, Little Star"

Traditional

1. Twin - kle, twin - kle, lit - tle star.
2. Twin - kle, twin - kle, lit - tle bat.

How I won - der what you are.
How I won - der what you're at!

Up a - bove the world so high;
Up a - bove the world so high;

Like a dia - mond in the sky.
Like a plat - ter in the sky.

Twin - kle, twin - kle, lit - tle star;
Twin - kle, twin - kle, lit - tle bat;

How I won - der what you are!
How I won - der what you're at!

Suggested Focus: Acquiring a repertoire of traditional folk/composed songs.

The Activity: Children develop voco-motor control by singing, over and over again, well-chosen, age-appropriate songs. Songs with limited ranges, descending melodic patterns and much repetition help them in this process. When teaching this song, show the upward and downward movement of the melody with hand levels. Encourage the children to imitate.

*(The second verse is found in Lewis Carroll's *Alice in Wonderland*.)

206

"Humpty Dumpty"

Mother Goose

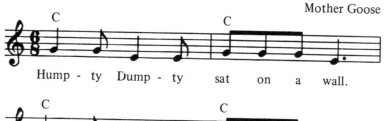

Hump - ty Dump - ty sat on a wall.

Hump - ty Dump - ty had a great fall.

All the king's hor - ses and all the king's men,

Couldn't put Hump-ty to - geth - er a - gain.

Why?____ BE - CAUSE HE'S AN EGG! CRASH!

Suggested Focus: Rhythmic accented beats.

The Activity: Children sit or stand and rock from side to side in time to the song, as if teetering on a wall. After the word "Why?" say the spoken line loudly and then, on the "Crash," all fall flat on floor. A child may provide a cymbal crash at the appropriate moment.

> Play simple rhythm instruments freely and explore
> sounds of rhythm instruments and environmental
> sources. Create sounds on instruments and from other
> sound sources in their environment.

"A Sound Discrimination Activity"

The object of this game is to identify the sounds of familiar objects. The children close their eyes and the leader (the teacher or a child) makes a sound with the object. The group identifies the object. Examples of ways to produce various sounds are:

- crumple a piece of paper
- jingle keys on a key ring
- play a toy drum
- pour water from one container to another
- pound two blocks together
- ring a bell
- play a resonator bell
- shake a tambourine
- tap two pencils together
- turn on a metronome

Suggested Focus: Identification of environmental sounds.

The Activity: Carry through the activity as described. A variation may include moving the object to different places in the room and asking the children not only to identify the object, but also to point to the spot from where the sound comes.

"A Sound Walk"

Many teachers take groups of children on "sound-exploration journeys." With a cassette tape recorder, the sounds (traffic, sirens, rustling of leaves, and so forth) may be recorded. A collection of "sound tapes" can result, with appropriate titles: "Sounds in the Park," "Street Sounds", and the like. Children will enjoy identifying the sounds in later listening sessions.

Suggested Focus: Identification of environmental sounds.

"Charlie Over the Ocean"

Char - lie o - ver the o - cean;

Char - lie o - ver the sea; _____

Char - lie's play - ing an in - stru - ment.

What can it be? _____
(It's a tam - bour - ine. _____)

Suggested Focus: Identification of instrumental sounds.

The Activity: Children sit in a circle. In the center of the circle are a tambourine, a drum, and rhythm sticks (or other combinations). One child is chosen to be "Charlie." Charlie sits in the center of the circle. The circle of children close their eyes and sing the song. After the song is sung, Charlie plays one instrument. Individual children guess what the instrument is, singing its name (last measures of the song) if possible. The child who guesses correctly becomes the next Charlie. (Classroom instruments should be *introduced* singly, one at a time, and one in a session.)

> Walk, run, jump, gallop, clap and "freeze" while an adult responds to the child's movements with sounds on a percussion instrument.

"How Can I Get From Here to There?"

Children watch as one child walks, jumps, runs, gallops, and so on, around the room. Teacher "picks up" the rhythm of the child's movement and plays it on a drum.

Walking may sound like this:

Running may sound like this:

Galloping may sound like this:

Jumping may sound like this:

Suggested Focus: Identification of fast/slow, even/uneven, strong sounds.

The Activity: After the movement activity, the teacher may play the various rhythms of the children's movements and ask the children to describe the movement by vocalizations. The terms "fast/slow," "even/uneven," "strong," should be used by the teacher in discussion of the childrens' descriptions. For a variation, pillows or blocks might be scattered on the floor to make an indoor obstacle course.

CREATING

> Explore the expressive possibilities of their own voices. Improvise songs (or melodic patterns) as they play.

Creativity begins with exploration and experimentation. Young children need to find out how their voices can express ideas, images, moods. They need to explore instruments as well, to find out how they produce sound and how one instrument's sound differs from another's. In this section, several exploratory vocal and instrumental experiences are suggested.

"I Think"

I think it's neat
How a pig likes to eat!
    Oink, Oink, Oink.
I think it's smart
How a dog learns to bark!
    Woof, Woof, Woof.
What do you s'pose
Makes a sound that goes
    Hee-Haw, Hee-Haw, Hee-Haw?

Suggested Focus: Rhythmic speech, pitch variance.
The Activity: The children may decide together which animal's voice should be high, which should be low, which should be *both* high and low. Let individual children have turns at making the sounds.

"Softly"

German Folk Song

Suggested Focus: "Soft," rhythmic singing.

The Activity: The children can rock an imaginary baby while they sing this song. Let them decide whether the song should be sung with "soft voices" or "loud voices." Sing it that way.

"Yankee Doodle"

American Folk Tune

Suggested Focus: Strong rhythmic singing.

The Activity: One *has* to march to this song! Discuss the differences between this song and the previous song, "Softly." Suggest: "Let us sing this song in a *strong* voice as we march."

"Who's That Tapping at My Window?"

(Children sing:)

Who's that tap-ping at my win-dow?

Who's that knock-ing at my door?

(Hider sings:)

I am!   (or pattern of own creation)

(Children sing:)

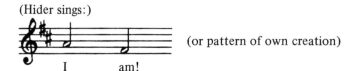

(_____) tap-ping at my win-dow

(_____) knock-ing at my door.

Suggested Focus: Creating melodic patterns.

The Activity: Children close eyes. Teacher chooses one child to hide. When hider is in place, teacher and children sing the first line. The hider then sings answer from hiding place. The children guess who and where hider is, and then sing the last line. A new hider is chosen.

From a Piagetian perspective, hiding games encourage decentering. Although the clue is rather obvious, for three-year-olds, it does not make the game silly: "When three-year-olds hide themselves, . . . they want [to be] found immediately" (Kamii and DeVries, 1980, p. 52). Inferring, from given clues, necessitates decentering; musical games can enhance this process (Figure 9.1).

Figure 9.1. "Who's that tapping at my window?/Who's that knocking at my door?"

"Don't Throw Your Junk"

Suggested Focus: Creating melodic and rhythmic patterns.

The Activity: Four- and almost-four-year-old children enjoy nonsense songs and silly rhymes. Language skills are developing rapidly; these children like to improvise and insert new words in familiar songs. One group of children, after learning this song, delighted in fitting substitute words where the word "junk" occurs. They found that everything from "elephants" to "kangaroos" fitted into this slot! Sometimes the rhythm got slowed down to let the "strange personages" in.

LISTENING/DESCRIBING

> Move spontaneously to music of many types. Improvise movements that indicate awareness of beat, tempo and pitch.

"Musical Chairs"

Musical chairs is a familiar racing game. The usual way of playing this game is for players to march around two lines of chairs placed back to back, numbering one less than the number of players, as long as the music plays. When the music stops, all players attempt to get a chair. The player who does not find a chair is out of the game.

Kamaii and DeVries (1984) suggest that this game, like many childhood group games, may "stimulate children's development in unique ways if used with the insights gained from Piaget's theory" (p. xi). These authors describe this game as one which helps children work out one-to-one numerical relationships. However, the "most valuable part of the game from an educational viewpoint may be the preparation when certain decisions have to be made as to how many chairs to get" (1984, p. 44). Viewed from this perspective, the game may be as educationally useful for preschool children by modifying it so that there are no winners or losers—for example, leaving the same number of chairs as children. "For [young children] . . . the fun of the game is the ritual of marching to music with others and grabbing a chair when the music stops" (Kamii and DeVries, 1984, p. 216).

If the game is played in this manner, music teachers may extend its value by incorporating musical concepts. It is obviously an exercise in distinguishing sound and silence. However, teachers may "stop the music" (either the recording or "live" music played on piano or guitar) at the ends of phrases or sections of the song or composition, thus providing an introduction to structure or form of a piece. Even young children will learn to anticipate when the ending of a phrase or section is going to occur. Another variation: suggest that the children move in "funny ways" while the music is playing.

"Did You Ever See a Lassie?"

Singing Game

1. Did you ev - er see a las - sie, a
2. Did you ev - er see a lad - die, a

las - sie, a las - sie; Did you
lad - die, a lad - die; Did you

ev - er see a las - sie go
ev - er see a lad - die go

this way and that? Go this way and
this way and that? Go this way and

that way, go this way and
that way, go this way and

that way; Did you ev - er see a
that way; Did you ev - er see a

las - sie go this way and that?
lad - die go this way and that?

Suggested Focus: Improvised rhythmic movement.

The Activity: The teacher may be the first leader, but all the children should have a turn at initiating a movement for the class to imitate.

"If You're Happy"

Singing Game

If you're hap - py and you know it, clap your

hands (♩   ♩) If you're hap -py and you know it, clap your

hands (♩   ♩) If you're hap-py and you know it; then your

face will sure - ly show it, if you're

hap - py and you know it, clap your hands (♩   ♩)

Suggested Focus: Rhythmic beat.
The Activity: Insert new directives; for example,

> "pat your knees,"
> "touch your nose,"
> "clap again."

When body movements that make no sound are used as responses, the teacher may direct attention to the beat, which is felt even though not sounded. "How do we know how many times to touch our noses before we sing the next part?" (two silent pulses).

"This Is What"

This   is   what   I   can   do;

Lis - ten,   then   you   do   it,   too!

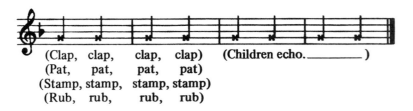

(Clap,   clap,   clap,   clap)   (Children echo._____)
(Pat,   pat,   pat,   pat)
(Stamp, stamp, stamp, stamp)
(Rub,   rub,   rub,   rub)

Suggested Focus: Rhythmic beat, soft/loud sounds.

The Activity: Children echo teacher's body sounds. When the song is well learned, individual children can become the "leaders." In subsequent sessions, direct the children's attention to the relative loudness or softness of the body sounds:

"Which sounds were softer than the others?"

"Let's make our voices match the sounds. When we sing the 'Pat' verse, how shall we make our voices sound?" (and so on).

The concept of "loud/soft" is established early. Teachers may initiate discussion of the effect of dynamic change on the mood of a song.

"Simon Sings High"

Si - mon sings high!

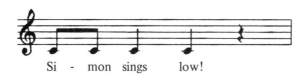

Si - mon sings low!

Suggested Focus: High/low sounds.

The Activity: The leader stands with arms stretched high when singing "Simon sings high" and stoops, with arms down, when singing "Simon sings low." Children imitate (Figure 9.2). When the game has been ritualized, the leader occasionally stoops when singing high, or vice versa. The children must do what the leader sings rather than what the leader actually does. (*Don't* eliminate children from the game who "miss"!)

Figure 9.2. Children stretch arms high when "Simon sings high" and stoop when "Simon sings low." Children choose their own level of participation.

"Ring Around a Rosy"

Singing Game

Ring a-round a ro - sy; Poc-ket full of po - sies;

Ash - es, ash - es, All tum- ble down.

or

All tum - ble down.

Suggested Focus: Higher/lower sounds.

The Activity: The singing game is still a favorite with our youngest preschoolers. The children skip around in a circle, falling to the floor on the last note. After all know the song and game well, the teacher may instruct the children to "tumble down" only if the music tells them to; if it doesn't, they should "freeze" until the song starts again.

"Old Train"

Old train's start - ing   down   the   track.

It   goes   "toot";   I   toot   back!

Click - e - ty, clack - e - ty,   fast down the track.

En - gi - neer waves at   me;   I   wave back!

Suggested Focus: Fast/slow sounds.

The Activity: The game may be played in line formation, each child holding the elbows of the child directly in front. The line moves slowly when the first phrase is sung, and faster on the second phrase. Or, children may be seated, randomly spaced, and do the following actions:

Measures 1-2: Rub palms (or sandblocks) together to match the rhythm of the words: (♩ ♩).

Measures 3-4: On word "toot," reach high and pull an imaginary whistle rope.

Measures 5-6: Rub palms (or sandblocks) as before, matching the faster word rhythm (♫♩).

Measures 7-8: Wave with one hand, then the other.

MUSIC EXPERIENCES FOR FOUR- AND FIVE-YEAR-OLD CHILDREN

Most four- and five-year-old children want to be with other children and enjoy song games and simple line and circle dances. Motor coordination is developing rapidly; vocomotor control enables many to sing accurately and with confidence. They are capable of much conceptual growth and learn best through active participation. *The School Music Program* suggests the following types of musical experiences for this age group.

PERFORMING/READING

> Utilize the singing voice, as distinct from the speaking voice. Match pitches and sing in tune within their own ranges.

In the following section are songs, games, and activities that may be used as pitch-matching exercises. Also included are well-known children's songs pitched in keys to accommodate the comfortable singing ranges of most four- and five-year-old children. Suggested activities are included. Teachers may formulate specific instructional objectives for each song, based on the activity. Songs may be sung for many reasons, however; first and foremost, they should provide pleasure! Only a few songs are presented in this section; teachers should provide *many* more.

"Greeting Songs"

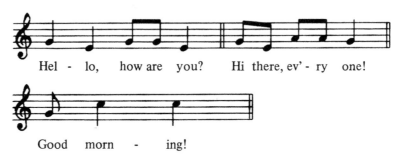

Hel - lo,   how are   you?   Hi there, ev' - ry   one!

Good   morn -   ing!

Suggested Focus: Accurate pitch imitation.

The Activities: The entire class, or individual children in it may echo each greeting. Children need opportunities to hear their individual voices, in a nonthreatening situation, to develop accurate pitch-matching skills.

"One Two"

Suggested Focus: Accurate pitch imitation.

The Activity: The teacher sings the numbers; the group or individual children may complete each phrase.

"Where Is Thumbkin?"

Singing Game

Add verses, with "pointer" (index finger), "long man" (middle finger), "ring man" (fourth finger), and "little man" (pinkie).

Suggested Focus: Accurate pitch imitation.

The Activity: For a pitch-matching exercise, the song may be sung in the following way:

Measure 1: Teacher sings, and holds up one hand.

Measure 2: Children sing, each holding up one hand.

Measure 3: Teacher sings, pointing to thumb with index finger of other hand.

Measure 4: Children sing, each pointing to their thumbs with index finger of other hand.

Measure 5: Teacher sings, moving thumb of one hand up and down.

Measure 6: Children answer, moving thumb up and down.

Measure 7: Teacher sings, moving hand behind back.

Measure 8: Children sing, moving hands behind back.

"People"

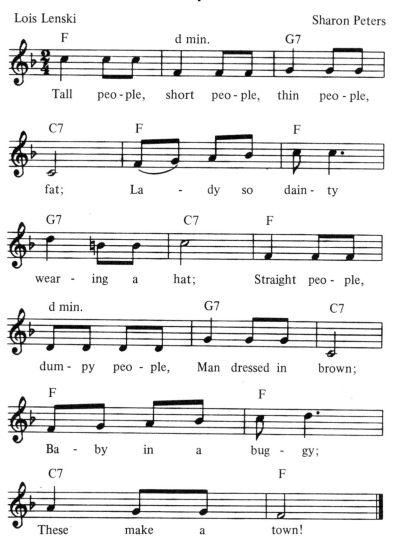

Lois Lenski

Sharon Peters

Poem reproduced by permission of the Lenski Foundation.

Suggested Focus: In-tune singing.

The Activity: Children can assume appropriate physical postures to describe all the folks mentioned in this song! Discussion might focus upon the "high" notes for "tall people" and "not so high" notes for shorter people. "Straight people" have a tune that stays in one place, "dumpy" people "lean lower." Try to initiate discussion of how music can help express what the words of a song say.

"Three Little Pigs"

English Folk Song

Suggested Focus: In-tune singing, with exploration of "high" voices.

The Activity: Can the children sing the "wee, wee, wee" using "high voices?" New verses may be added, describing cats who had kittens, cows who had calves, etc.

2. Now one day one of the three little pigs
   To the other two piggies said he,
   "Why don't we always go oink, oink, oink?
   It's so childish to go wee, wee, wee."

3. These three piggies grew skinny and lean,
   Skinny they might well be.
   For they'd always try to go 'oink, oink, oink'
   And they wouldn't go 'wee, wee, wee!'

4. Now these three piggies, they ups and they dies.
   A very sad sight to see.
   So, don't you ever go oink, oink, oink,
   When you ought to go 'wee, wee, wee.'

"Somebody"

American Folk Song

2. Somebody comes to see me;
   Somebody came last night.
   Somebody asked me to marry (him) (her)
   'Course I said, "All right."

   Suggested Focus: In-tune singing.
   The Activity: Just before the last word is reached, point out a child to sing an "eye-color." Because the note is the tonic of the key, most children will sing the "eye-color" on the correct note. (A feeling for tonality in song phrases is developing during the preschool years.) Then ask the children to find which of their classmates has blue/green/brown eyes!

> Show an awareness of beat, tempo (e.g., fast-slow), dynamics (e.g., loud-soft), pitch (e.g., high-low), and similar and different phrases through movement and through playing classroom instruments.

The activities suggested for the following songs and games provide opportunities for enactive representation of musical concepts.

"What's A Steady Beat?"

Michael Jewell

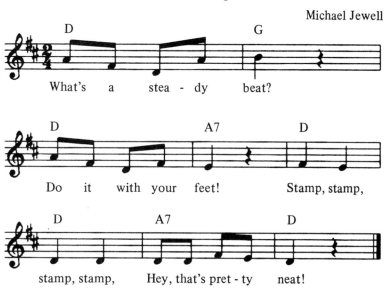

What's a stea - dy beat?

Do it with your feet! Stamp, stamp,

stamp, stamp, Hey, that's pret - ty neat!

2. We've just stamped our feet,
   Now let's clap the beat.
   Clap, clap, clap, clap,
   Hey, that's pretty neat.

3. Now we've done all these,
   So we'll pat our knees,
   Pat, pat, pat, pat,
   Wasn't that a breeze!

Suggested Focus: Rhythmic beat.

The Activity: Young children who are not able to sustain a "steady beat" for an entire song or composition are often able to do so for a limited number of beats.

"Head and Shoulders, Baby"

American Singing Game

Head and shoul-ders, Ba - by, 1, 2,

3; Head and shoul-ders, Ba - by, 1, 2,

3; Head and shoul - ders, head and

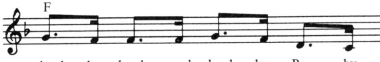

shoul - ders, head and shoul - ders, Ba - by,

1, 2, 3. To the

front, to the back, to the front, to the back, to the
(front clap) (back clap) (front clap) (back clap)

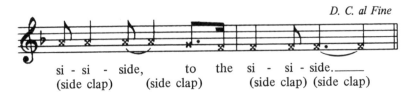

si - si - side, to the si - si - side._____
(side clap) (side clap) (side clap) (side clap)

Suggested Focus: Accented rhythmic beats.

The Activity: Following directions of the words. For a variation, children may name other parts of the body that are "next to" each other—for example, "knees and ankles."

"Engine, Engine"

Engine, engine, number nine;   ⊓ ⊓ ⊓ |
Going down Chicago line.   ⊓ ⊓ ⊓ |
See it sparkle; see it shine!   ⊓ ⊓ ⊓ |
Engine, engine, number nine.   ⊓ ⊓ ⊓ |
Getting fast? Getting slow?   ⊓ | ⊓ |
Listen, listen listen!   ⊓ ⊓ ⊓ ⅔

Suggested Focus: Faster/slower sounds.

The Activity: After children have memorized the four-line chant, chant lines 5 and 6; then rub a pair of sandblocks together, gradually moving them either faster or slower. The children who correctly describe the tempo take turns in producing either "getting faster" or "getting slower" sounds. As a variation, instruct children to chant "Choo, choo" while watching and listening to the sandblock player.

"Oh Dear, What Can the Matter Be?"

English Folk Song

Oh, dear! What can the mat-ter be?

Oh, dear! What can the mat-ter be?

Oh, dear! What can the mat-ter be?

John-ny's so long at the fair! _____

Suggested Focus: Fast/slow sounds.

The Activity: On the words "Oh, dear!" children may bend slowly to one side and then to the other. Patsch (slap the thighs) during the faster melodic rhythm of the other words.

2. He promised he'd buy me a bunch of blue ribbons,
   He promised he'd buy me a bunch of blue ribbons,
   He promised he'd buy me a bunch of blue ribbons
   To tie up my bonny brown hair.

"Skip to My Lou"

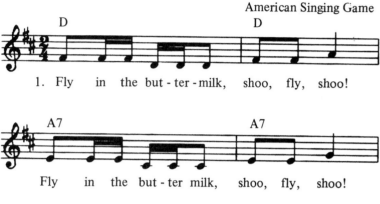

American Singing Game

1. Fly in the but-ter-milk, shoo, fly, shoo!

Fly in the but-ter milk, shoo, fly, shoo!

Fly in the but-ter-milk, shoo, fly, shoo!

Skip to my Lou, my dar - ling!

2. Lost my partner, what'll I do?
   Lost my partner, what'll I do?
   Lost my partner, what'll I do?
   Skip to my Lou, my darling.

3. I'll find another, prettier than you,
   I'll find another, prettier than you,
   I'll find a another, prettier than you,
   Skip to my Lou, my darling.

Suggested Focus: Loud/soft sounds.

The Activity: This song may be used for a traditional circle game, with one child, who is "It," skipping around circle until the last phrase, when he or she chooses a new child to be "It." However, it also may be used to reinforce the loud/soft concept with the following game:

Ask one child, who will be "It," to cover her eyes or leave circle for a moment. Another child, who will be the missing partner, hides somewhere in the room. The children sing verse 2, helping "It" find the missing partner by singing loudly when "It" nears the partner's hiding place, or softly when "It" moves away. When the partner is found, a new child is chosen to be "It."

"Clap Your Hands Up High"

Claire McCoy

Clap   your   hands   up   high!

Stomp your feet down   low!   Pat your knees in the

mid - dle,   mid - dle,   mid - dle   when   the

mu - sic   tells   you   so!

Suggested Focus: High/low/middle sounds.
The Activity: When children have learned the song and accompanying motions the teacher may:

1. Sing the melody without words, using a "la" syllable, while the children perform the actions guided only by the pitches.
2. Reverse measures 1 and 2, 3 and 4. Can children show the "high," "low," or "middle" pitches when sequence is reversed, with only the pitches as cues?

"La, La, Lay"

German Folk Song, tr. Claire McCoy

1. La, la, lay; the sum-mer's here to
2. La, la, lay; the win-ter's here to

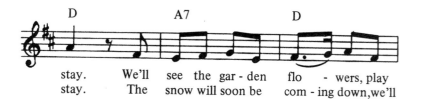

stay. We'll see the gar-den flo - wers, play
stay. The snow will soon be com - ing down, we'll

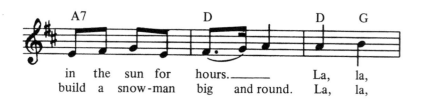

in the sun for hours._____ La, la,
build a snow-man big and round. La, la,

lay; the sum-mer's here to stay!
lay; the win-ter's here to stay!

Suggested Focus: Identification of individual pitch patterns in songs.

The Activity: After the song is well learned, two tone bars (the pitches A and B) can be separated from the set, and a child can play the "La, la, lay" (A, B, A) when the children sing this phrase. Later, the children can sing "A, B, A" instead of "La, la, lay" as they take turns playing the pattern.

"Down by the Station"

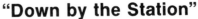

Suggested Focus: Identification of individual pitch patterns in songs.

The Activity: Children can put hand around lips to create an audible "Puff, puff," and reach hand high to pull the whistle rope on "Toot, toot." In addition, the F and high C tone bars may be removed from the set and a child may play them as "Puff, puff, toot, toot" is sung.

The teacher may ask: "Which sounded higher, the 'puffs' or the 'toots'?"

"Favorite Times"

Dennis M. Thomas

1. Au - tumn leaves   are   in   the   air,
2. It's   a   great   time   of   the   year.

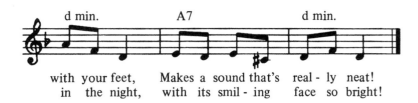

Au - tumn leaves are   ev' - ry - where. Walk - ing through them
Jack - o - lan - terns   will   ap - pear.   You might see   one

with your feet,   Makes a sound that's   real - ly neat!
in   the night,   with its smil - ing   face so bright!

Suggested Focus: Identification of individual pitch patterns in song.
The Activity: After the song has been learned, remove from one set of resonator bells the tones D, E, and F. Place them together: D̄ Ē F̄. From another set, remove D and A. Place them apart from each other: D̄   Ā.

Next, play "D, E, F." Have the children decide where this pattern occurs (on the words "autumn leaves"). Point out that these sounds go up by "steps". Then play "D, A, A." Have the children decide where this pattern occurs (on the words "in the air" and "ev'ry-where"). Show the children that these notes are far apart—some notes in between are not sounded, or "skipped." Individual children may play each pattern (with your help) as the song is sung.

"Tideo"

Singing Game

Suggested Focus: Identification of same/different phrases in songs.

The Activity: Children form circle. One child with bells on ankles or wrists skips or walks around the inside of the circle for the first eight measures. On the phrase, "Jingling, jingling, jingling Jo, Jingle at the windows, Tideo," the child moves to the center of the circle and "dances" in any way he or she chooses to make the bells jingle. Children in the circle imitate. All of the children should have a turn at wearing the bells. Discuss how the song has two different parts; the music tells us when the "jingler" should move inside the circle and start to "dance."

"Brother, Come and Dance With Me"

German Folk Song, tr. Claire McCoy

Bro - ther, come and dance with me;

Take my hand and you will see;

One foot in; One foot back.

Round and round, you've got the knack!

2. With your hands go clip, clip, clap;
   With your feet go trip, trip, trap;
   One foot in . . . . . .

3. With your head go nick, nick, nick;
   With your fingers, tick, tick, tick;
   One foot in . . . . . .

Suggested Focus: Identification of phrases in songs.

The Activity: Each child faces a partner and performs the called-for actions (Figure 9.3). When the children have learned the dance, discuss how many different actions were called for. Point out that there are four parts (phrases), each calling for a different movement.

Figure 9.3. "Brother, come and dance with me."

"Looby Loo"

Singing Game

Here we go Loo - by Loo____

Here we go Loo - by Ly.____

Here we go Loo - by Loo____

All on a Sat - ur - day night.____ I

put my right hand in,____ I

put my right hand out,____ I

give my right hand a shake, shake, shake, and

turn my - self a - bout.____

2. I put my left hand in . . .   4. I put my left foot in . . .
3. I put my right foot in . . .   5. I put my whole self in . . .

Suggested Focus: Identification of two-part structure of a song.
The Activity: In a circle formation, children may dance "looby loo" (improvised in-place movement) or move around in a circle holding hands for the first eight measures. Then follow directions given by the words for the last eight measures. You might suggest that there is a huge bathtub in the middle of the circle; they must "test the temperature" of the water with hands and feet before jumping in.

> Improvise songs spontaneously during many class-
> room and playtime activities. Complete "answers" to
> unfinished melodic phrases by singing or playing
> instruments.

Children acquire the "tools" for improvisation in the many and varied musical experiences we provide for them. If given time and encouragement to explore and refine their ideas, "making up" songs or instrumental tunes is a natural behavior—not one that is unusual or unexpected. The songs and activities in the following section may suggest ways of "triggering" the natural musical creativity of young children.

"One, Two, Three"

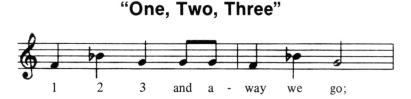

1   2   3   and   a - way   we   go;

Ho,   ho,   ho,   ho,   ho!
(or) time   to   go   out - doors!
(or) now   it's time   to   ____!

Suggested Focus: Expression of original ideas in a musical context.

The Activity: Five-year-old Amy sang this tune on many separate occasions, and the teacher adopted it as a "transition tune" to signal the beginning and ending of activities, as suggested by the substituted words in the last phrase.

Teachers who listen to their students' spontaneous songs, sung while at play or engaged in an interesting task, will discover other original tunes.

CALL/RESPONSE PATTERNS

Who   is   wear - ing   red   to - day?

What   are   your   fav' - rite   things   to   eat?

Suggested Focus: Expression of original ideas in a musical context.

The Activity: Young children often are eager to sing for their friends when it involves answering a question "in song." This type of activity gives valuable experience in fitting words and melodies together. Teachers should not always ask the questions, however; let the children sing questions to the teacher, who will provide "answers" in the pitched keys of the children.

"Who Has the Button?"

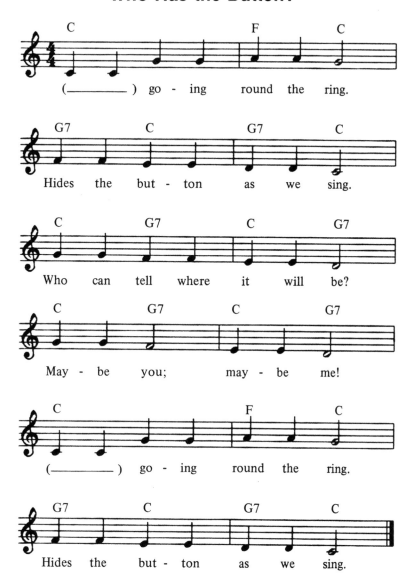

Suggested Focus: Expression of ideas in a musical context.

The Activity: Children are seated in a circle. The teacher sings the song, acting as the first hider, as she passes around the circle, pressing each child's outstretched hands, but letting the button fall in the hands of one child. At the end of the song, the teacher sings

Children volunteer to sing an answer, inserting the name of the child thought to have the button, with a tune of their own: "_____ has the button." If the guesser is wrong the teacher sings the question to other children until the child who has guessed correctly is now "It."

In addition to its value as a singing exercise, this game may be analyzed from the perspective of Piagetian theory. According to Kamii and DeVries (1984) all hiding games encourage decentering.

> In "Button, Button," the (guesser) can study people's hand movements and expressions. For example, he can watch for a look of disappointment or elation as "It" leaves each player. He can also watch closely to see if the hider presses his hands differently for a longer time between any player's palms, and if anyone holds his hands differently after the button has apparently changed hands. (p. 52)

"Megan's Song"

Children's music creations should be shared with parents, teachers, and other children. Andress (1985) described one such sharing experience which occurred in her child-centered preschool music program.

I counted myself most successful one day when 4-year-old Megan loudly informed the group, "Today, I'm going to make up a song." I quickly encouraged her and invited the others to get ready to hear Megan's nice song. She went on to say, "My song is going to be soft, and slow, and it's about putting a baby to sleep." Megan proceeded to sing a very soft, slow, rambling melody about a baby. She smiled broadly, indicating the song was ended. We applauded. Megan had planned her song, sang it according to plan, and had made decisions worthy of a sophisticated composer. (Boswell, 1985, p. 62)

> Utilizes pictures, geometric shapes, and other symbols
> to represent pitch, durational patterns, and simple forms.

Four- and five-year-old children are in the process of learning to substitute symbols for the sensorimotor images of earlier years. The progress in achieving this competency is gradual and develops through many experiences and much reinforcement. In the following song activities, various icons (graphic symbols) are introduced to represent the musical event. Teachers may create many others.

"Simon Sings"

Si - mon sings high!

Si - mon sings low!

Suggested Focus: High/low sounds and their iconic representation.

The Activity: The leader stands with arms stretched high when singing "Simon sings high" and bends over, arms reaching down, when singing "Simon sings low." Children imitate. When the game has been ritualized, the leader occasionally stoops when singing high, or vice versa. The children must do what the leader *sings* rather than what he *does*. (Don't eliminate children from the game who "miss"!)

When the children have become adept at linking the high and low sounds with appropriate actions, prepare a chart, such as one in Figure 9.4

Figure 9.4. Icon chart for playing "Simon Sings."

Discuss which faces represent the high sounds, and which the low. Then play the game pointing to the faces, rather than singing. Ask the children to sing the appropriate words and pitches as you point to the high, or low, icons. Mix the order of sequence.

"One Potato"

1 po - ta - to, 2 po - ta - toes,

3 po - ta - toes, 4; 5 po - ta - toes,

6 po - ta - toes, 7 po - ta - toes, more!

8 po - ta - toes, 7 po - ta - toes,

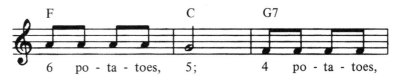

6 po - ta - toes, 5; 4 po - ta - toes,

3 po - ta - toes, 2 po - ta - toes,

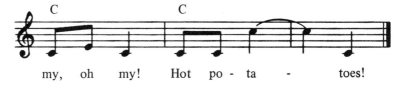

my, oh my! Hot po - ta - toes!

Suggested Focus: Pitches which move higher or lower, with their iconic representations.

The Activity: As the numbers are sung, children build a "stack" of potatoes by placing alternate fists ("potatoes") atop each other as melody moves up, then underneath each other as melody moves down. Clap on "Hot" and shake hands in air (to "cool" them!). Discuss how their fists form a picture of the melody. Make cutout paper potatoes and let the children arrange them to represent the melodic movement of the pitches (Figure 9.5).

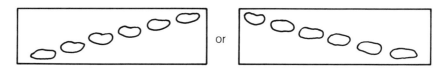

Figure 9.5. Cutout paper potatoes arranged to represent melodic movement of pitches.

"Snowflakes"

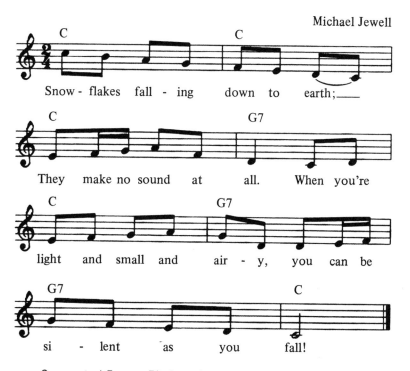

Michael Jewell

Snow - flakes fall - ing down to earth;____

They make no sound at all. When you're

light and small and air - y, you can be

si - lent as you fall!

Suggested Focus: Pitches that move lower, with their iconic representations.

The Activity: Prepare paper snowflakes (cutouts). After the children have learned the song, with appropriate movements as desired, attach the snowflake cutouts to a bulletin board, arranged like this:

Next, hold a set of song bells vertically and let individual children play the bells so the sounds match the visual symbols for "Snowflakes falling down to earth." All children should have the opportunity to play the bells while you point to the snowflake pictures. Call this arrangement a "scale."

"The Balloon Song"

South Africa (adapted)

There were 5 bal - loons,   float -ing in the air;

Float - ing up to - geth-er, with ne - ver a care. A -

long came a sol - dier   march-ing off to war.

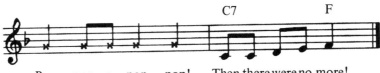

Pop, pop - a, pop, pop!   Then there were no more!
(clap,   clap - a, clap, clap)

Suggested Focus: Rhythmic pattern of long/short sounds and its iconic representation.

The Activity: Children may use rhythm sticks to play the "popping" pattern after they have clapped it. When they can clap or play the pattern with some accuracy, the teacher may wish to introduce rhythm syllables for the notes: for example, "Ta, ti-ti, ta, ta." Sing these syllables in place of the words. Subsequently, a visual representation of the pattern may be presented by arranging rhythm sticks in this manner:

or having children represent the "notes":

"BINGO"

Suggested Focus: Rhythmic pattern of long/short sounds and its enactive and iconic representations.

The Activity: Sing or clap (x):

1st time—	B, I, N, G, O.
2nd time—	x, I, N, G, O.
3rd time—	x, x, N, G, O.
4th time—	x, x, x, G, O.
5th time—	x, x, x, x, O.
6th time—	x, x, x, x, x.

"The pattern disappears from our voices into our hands!" "Which sounds were long? Which sounds were short?"

After the children have identified the short/long sounds, stick notation may be introduced to show the pattern which B, I, N, G, O forms. The children may use rhythm sticks to "build" the pattern.

"The Bear Went Over The Mountain"

Traditional

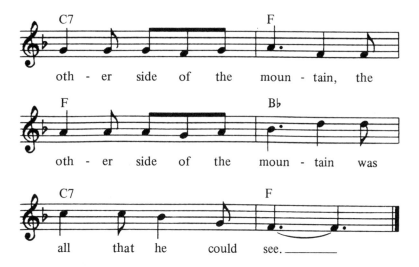

oth - er side of the moun - tain, the

oth - er side of the moun - tain was

all that he could see. _____

Suggested Focus: Same/different phrases, with their iconic representations.

The Activity:

Measures 1–8: Children patsch, 2 beats to a measure, alternately slapping left leg, then right.

Measures 9–12: Stop the patsch; put hand up to shade eyes, turn head from left to right in time to music.

Measures 13–20: Resume patsch movements.

This song has three different parts or sections. The actions will give physical expression to this structure. The teacher may discuss how the actions show "like" and "different" sections and how geometric shapes, such as

could also do this. Prepare a flash card for each shape:

Choose two children to be leaders. When the first section is sung, the child with the circle shape holds up his or her card. For the second section, the triangle is held up. The child holding the circle shape displays it again for the last section of the song.

CREATING

> Explore sound patterns on classroom instruments.
> Express ideas or moods using instruments and
> environmental or body sounds.

Children's creativity manifests itself in their ability to improvise songs, patterns, and rhythms. Experiences with instruments, including free and guided exploration, encourage children to "create." Teachers need to provide opportunities for individual exploration of instruments. Certain group activities may also provide models from which children can "break free" and create their own "compositions." In this section, suggestions are given for encouraging children to give expression to their own ideas on instruments.

"Play a Tune"

Teacher plays a bordun on piano.

Suggested Focus: Expression of original musical ideas on instruments.

The Activity: Individual children are encouraged to play a tune in the treble part of the piano, using only black keys. This activity is better suited to a one-to-one, informal teacher-child musical experience. The important thing to remember is to allow the child to explore. Don't offer too many suggestions. Remember, one note can be a tune!

Xylophones or metallophones may also be used for this activity. The teacher may play a bordun based on a C pentatonic scale:

Arrange an alto xylophone or metallophone to produce a C pentatonic scale. All pitches except the following should be removed:

The child and teacher can now produce satisfactory sounding "duets"!

"Sound Stories"

Suggested Focus: Expression of original ideas on musical instruments.

The Activity: Early childhood educators become adept at spinning tales and improvising stories about the experiences of the children. The addition of instruments for "sound effects" allows for exploration of timbre, without the requirement of the rather sophisticated rhythmic and melodic skills that songs and rhythmic games require. Below is a list of ideas, in the context of sentences that may be used to begin stories, or as exploratory "cues" in themselves.

1. "John went shuffling through the piles of leaves on the sidewalks." (sand blocks)

2. "It was a cold, icy night. The rain was turning to sleet and could be heard on the roof." (maracas)

3. "The cat scampered up the tree and then carefully backed down." (8 tone bars, C, D, E, F, G, A, B, C, or a song bell set)

4. "The heels of mother's shoes made a 'click-clack' sound on the sidewalk as she hurried along." (claves)

5. "The thunder rumbled through the sky." (On an autoharp, sweep a small mallet back and forth over lowest strings.)

LISTENING/DESCRIBING

> Give attention to short musical selections. Respond to musical elements (e.g., pitch, duration, loudness) and musical styles (e.g., march, lullaby) through movement or through playing classroom instruments.

Planning music listening experiences for preschoolers is often difficult because of these children's short attention spans and need for physical movement. In Chapter 5, a music listening program that consisted of classical music for five-year-old children was described (Turnipseed, Thompson, and Kennedy, 1974). The compositions are identified in the following section, entitled "A Music Listening Program: Selected Compositions." Following this listing, five pieces have been singled out, and suggested approaches for preschool are described.

Also included in this section on listening experiences are the names of the compositions used in the Sims (1984) study on creative movement described in Chapter 5. You may wish to include these recordings for listening-involving-movement activities.

"A Music Listening Program: Selected Compositions"

Debussy, C.: "Golliwog's Cakewalk" from the *Children's Corner Suite*

Coates, E.: *Cinderella*

Donaldson, H.: "The Three Billy Goats Gruff" and "The Little Train" from the *Once Upon a Time Suite*

Tchaikovsky, P.: *The Nutcracker Suite*

Dukas, P.: "The Sorcerer's Apprentice"

Jurey, E. B.: *Brother John and the Village Orchestra*

Saint-Saëns, C.: *The Carnival of the Animals*

Grofé, F.: *The Grand Canyon Suite*

Saint-Saëns, C.: "Danse Macabre"

Mussorgsky, M., and Ravel, M.: *Pictures at an Exhibition*

"March of the Toy Soldiers" (from *The Nutcracker Suite* by Peter Tchaikovsky)

Suggested Focus: Rhythmic beat.
The Activity: Form a parade. One child is the leader, and may march as he or she thinks a toy soldier would. Children imitate. Every child should have a turn as a leader.

"Waltz of the Flowers" (from *The Nutcracker Suite* by Peter Tchaikovsky)

Suggested Focus: Rhythmic accent (triple meter).
The Activity: Provide each child with a colored scarf. Children move as they wish to the music, waving the scarves so that they remain aloft. Instruct them to move about, but not to touch each other.

"The Kangaroo" (from *The Carnival of the Animals* by Camille Saint-Saëns)

Suggested Focus: Higher/lower sounds.
The Activity: This composition offers a good opportunity to express through movement the "getting higher/getting lower" shape of the melody. One kindergarten teacher planned the following structured response to the piece and taught it to the youngsters:

Occurrence of upward melodic movement: Children move hands upward beginning at knee-level.

Occurrence of downward melodic movement: Hands move downward.

Occurrence of a "low-high" melodic pattern: Bend low, then stretch high, hands over head.

Occurrence of the end of a phrase: Turn, facing another direction.

"Long-Eared Personages" (from *The Carnival of the Animals* by Camille Saint-Saëns)

Suggested Focus: High/low sounds.
The Activity: This composition is a musical portrait of a mule's voice, with predominant very high and very low sounds. The children may stretch arms high when the violins play in the high register, and thrust them down when other violins quickly "answer" the high notes with two notes played in the low register. The fast tempo and straightforward high/low motifs make it a vigorous and fun way to express "high/low" through physical movement.

"Ballet of the Unhatched Chicks" (from *Pictures at an Exhibition* by Modeste Mussorgsky)

Suggested Focus: Sectional divisions of an instrumental composition.

The Activity: The sections of this composition are separated by a high, relatively long note, which is easily detected. Although the tempo of the piece is quite fast, young children enjoy "dancing" and "freezing" when the long note is heard.

"Music for Creative Movement"

Movement activities form a large part of most early childhood music curricula. If teachers are to form appropriate objectives and plan for the most successful activities for their students, they must have as much information and knowledge as possible about the characteristics and capabilities of the children. (Sims, 1984, pp. 18–19)

Suggested Focus: Influence of musical style on type of movement.
The Activity: Sims' (1984) study of three-, four-, and five-year-old children's creative-movement responses to music, discussed in Chapter 5, used the following compositions. You may wish to include them in your movement-to-music activities.

Gary Haberman: "Fancy Pants" from *Disco for Kids* (Kimbo Educational, Kim 7035)

J. S. Bach: "Air" from *Suite No. 3 in D*

S. Lawrence and B. Hart: "Free to Be . . . You and Me" (Bell Records, 1110)

> Describe with movement or language similarities and differences in music such as loud-soft, fast-slow, up-down-same, smooth-jumpy, short-long, and similar-contrasting. Classify classroom instruments and some traditional instruments by shape, size, pitch and tone quality. Use a simple vocabulary of music terms to describe sounds.

The types of experiences described above provide many suggestions for helping young children learn to listen perceptively to music amd to develop a repertoire of recognized band/orchestral/vocal compositions. For example, careful listening may be encouraged by (1) moving to the music, (2) describing the music (in age-appropriate language), or (3) identifying instruments. The activities in this section may serve to illustrate these methods of working toward the long-range goal, learning to listen perceptively to many types of music.

"Walking Song"* (from *Acadian Songs and Dances* by Virgil Thomson)

Suggested Focus: Similar and contrasting sections.

The Activity: This composition is in ABA form; that is, it has three large sections, the first and last alike. The most obvious contrast between the sections is the tempo, the sequence being fast-slow-fast. The teacher may introduce the piece by giving its title. Preparatory activities might grow from questions such as:

"How many ways can we walk?" (Children demonstrate fast-slow, etc.)

"Let's pretend we're walking along a busy street. How would we walk?" (Children demonstrate ideas.)

"We've come to a toy store. There are lots of toys in the window. How might our walking change?" (Get slower, for example.)

"Now we're past the store. How shall we walk so we won't be late getting home?" (Faster.)

"I'm going to play the 'Walking Song' now. Let's see whether we can walk the way the music tells us, changing when the music changes."

Be sure to follow the activity with a discussion of the three sections—fast, slow, fast—using these terms.

*RCA Adventures in Music Series, Grade 1.

"The Cuckoo in the Deep Wood" (from *Carnival of Animals* by Camille Saint-Saëns)

Suggested Focus: Identification of clarinet and piano timbres.

The Activity: This composition utilizes only two musical instruments—the clarinet and piano. For this reason it lends itself well to an activity emphasizing timbral discrimination.

The following activity describes the way one teacher and her four- to five-year-old students learned to recognize and enjoy this composition.

1. The teacher read a story of a cuckoo who lived in a forest. The children learned to reproduce the cuckoo's call.
2. The recording of the composition was introduced. The children were encouraged to decide what the music was "telling them."
3. A story evolved. The cuckoo call was identified. The children decided the piano chords heard between the calls represented a person walking. A "stage" was set. Rhythm sticks were scattered randomly to represent trees in the forest; a hula hoop became the cuckoo's nest. Children became walkers or birds in the nest.
4. When the piano theme was heard at the beginning of the composition, children "walked in the woods." When the cuckoo call occurred, the children who were the birds in the "nest" popped up and the walkers stopped to listen.

As the composition progresses, the children must listen more closely, for toward the end, the piano's "walking theme" occurs simultaneously with the cuckoo's call; for example, the walkers' and the birds' actions occur at the same time.

Be sure to invite a clarinetist to class if you can. Perhaps the cuckoo's call can be played—the notes are C and A♭.

REFERENCES AND SUGGESTED READINGS

Andress, B. (1985). The practitioner involves young children in music. In J. Boswell (Ed.), *The young child and music: Contemporary principles in child development and music education* (pp. 53–63). Reston, VA: Music Educators National Conference.

Boswell, J. (Ed.). (1985). *The young child and music: Contemporary principles in child development and music education.* Reston, VA: Music Educators National Conference.

Kamii, C., & DeVries, R. (1980). *Group games in early education: Implications of Piaget's theory.* Washington, DC: The National Association for the Education of Young Children.

Leach, P. (1983). *Your baby and child from birth to age five.* New York: Alfred A. Knopf.

McCullough, E. (1985). Multicultural music materials for early childhood music programs. In J. Boswell (Ed.), *The young child and music: Contemporary principles in child development and music education* (p. 96). Reston, VA: Music Educators National Conference.

Music Educators National Conference. (1986). *The school music program: Description and standards.* Reston, VA: MENC.

Sims, W. L. (1984). *Young children's creative movement to music: Categories of movement, rhythmic characteristics, and reactions to change.* Research paper presented at the Music Educators National Conference, Chicago, IL.

Turnipseed, J. P.; Thompson, A.; & Kennedy, N. (1974). *Utilization of a structured classical music listening program in the development of auditory discrimination skills of preschool children.* Research paper presented at the Music Educators National Conference, Atlantic City, NJ.

Weiser, M. G. (1982). *Group care and education of infants and toddlers.* St. Louis: The C. V. Mosby Co.

Appendix A

Teacher Skills: Using Instruments

Using classroom instruments skillfully adds to the effectiveness of any early childhood music program. Children are attracted by the sight and sound of musical instruments, and they enjoy music lessons where they are used. This is an important reason for teachers to take time to develop some beginning skills. However, learning to play a classroom instrument is not just for the children but for the teacher, as well. Acquiring some skills in playing autoharp or barred-instrument accompaniments, or recorder melodies, can help you grow musically.

The following sections of this chapter give introductory information about some of the instruments commonly found in early childhood centers and kindergartens. Perhaps these introductions will enable you to self-start, and, when you need further instruction, to seek out self-help books and/or workshops.

THE AUTOHARP

One of the most useful accompanying instruments in our classrooms is the autoharp. It is easily played by both teachers and students; it provides very satisfactory accompaniments for children's singing; it is portable; and it requires little knowledge of music theory to produce satisfactory accompaniments.

The autoharp is a zitherlike instrument. Accompanying chords are produced by pressing a single chord bar and strumming across the strings. The teacher need only follow the chord symbols (letter names of the chords) above the melody line of a song to know which chord bar to press. Strumming with the steady beat of the song produces a satisfactory accompaniment.

HOLDING THE INSTRUMENT

There are two common ways to hold an autoharp while playing accompaniments. One may position it in the lap or on a table, with the longest side of the instrument closest to the body. The right hand (or more dextrous one) strums the strings in the area to the left of the chord bars. The left hand presses the chord bars. The right hand crosses over the left hand so that there is greater freedom for strumming.

The autoharp may also be held in folksinger's position, where it is held upright against the body. One end may rest in the lap. In this position, the left hand approaches the chord bars from the left; the right hand strums the strings with a downward motion (low to high pitched strings).

USING THE CHORD BARS

Autoharps commonly have twelve or fifteen chord bars, although there are models that have as many as twenty-one and as few as five. The five-chord instruments are child-size and useful for young children; some teachers have their kindergarten students accompany class singing of songs which use only one or two chords.

Figure A.1 is a drawing of a fifteen-chord-bar arrangement on an autoharp. There are three types of chords: major (Maj.), minor (Min.) and seventh (Sev.) chords. When playing an accompaniment, be sure to notice not only the letter symbol for the chord (G, F, C, etc.) but also the type-of-chord designation (Maj., Min., Sev.). You might compare

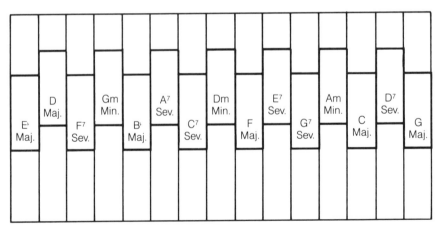

Figure A.1. Autoharp bar chords.

the G Maj., G Min., and G[7] Sev. chords. They do not sound alike and, generally, one cannot substitute for another. If only the chord letter designation in a song is given, the major chord should be played; for example, given "G", the G major chord should be played.

PLAYING THE CHORDS

The chord symbols, appearing as capital letters with "type" designation, are written above the melody line of a song. All of the songs in Chapter 9 have chord symbols for appropriate accompaniment.

Most children's songs need only two or three different chords for an accompaniment. Bars are arranged so that the chords needed for songs in common key tonalities are adjacent to each other for easy fingering.

"Chord sets" consist of the chords that generally belong together when accompanying songs. The most frequently used chord is that built on the first note of the scale the song is based on (often, the song ends on this note). This is the I chord. The next most used chord is usually the one built on the fifth note of the scale—the V[7] chord. The third chord in most chord sets is the IV chord, built on the fourth step of the scale. When the autoharp is played in the lap or table position, the performer places the left index finger on the I chord; the V[7] chord of that key will be found under the middle finger and the IV chord under the ring finger. The chart in Figure A.2 may clarify this arrangement.

As you develop proficiency in playing in these keys, song accompaniments that require other fingering patterns will not be difficult.

FINDING THE STARTING PITCH

To locate the beginning pitch of a song, find the string of the correct pitch on the pitch chart under the strings to the right of the chord bars. Pluck the note in the middle octave range. It also helps to strum the I chord of the song to establish both pitch and key of the song. Strumming the I chord in the tempo of the song provides a satisfactory introduction to most songs.

STRUMMING

A steady, even strum can be produced like this:

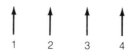

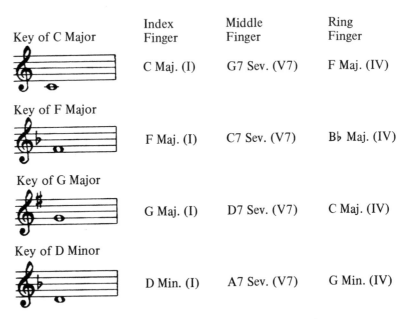

Key of C Major	Index Finger	Middle Finger	Ring Finger
Key of C Major	C Maj. (I)	G7 Sev. (V7)	F Maj. (IV)
Key of F Major	F Maj. (I)	C7 Sev. (V7)	B♭ Maj. (IV)
Key of G Major	G Maj. (I)	D7 Sev. (V7)	C Maj. (IV)
Key of D Minor	D Min. (I)	A7 Sev. (V7)	G Min. (IV)

Figure A.2. Autoharp fingering patterns for chords.

You may vary the pattern by strumming the bass octave strings for the accented beats and the high octave strings for the others, like this:

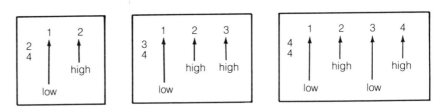

Fingernails and thumbs may be used for strumming, but they are likely to grow tender and sore! Picks may be purchased. Felt picks give a soft, modulated accompaniment; plastic picks a louder, more twangy sound. Paper clips or small triangular pieces of cardboard work, too.

TUNING THE AUTOHARP

Autoharps should be checked periodically to see whether they are in tune. A change of weather or rough treatment can cause the strings to loosen or tighten, producing nontuneful chords! Local music store repairmen can usually tune the instruments; most music specialists can help you also. If you have had some experience in tuning instruments, you may wish to tune it yourself with the tuning key provided. Start with the lowest F string, and tune all the Fs to a piano pitch, then the Gs, etc. Be very careful, for only a fraction of a turn can raise or lower a string's pitch to a considerable degree. Too much tension breaks strings!

THE RECORDER

The recorder is a small, flutelike instrument that is the ancestor of the woodwind instruments in our modern orchestras and bands. Recorders come in various sizes: sopranino, soprano, alto, tenor, and bass. Soprano recorders are most frequently used in the schools. Plastic soprano recorders, which are quite inexpensive, are available; however, wood recorders, which produce a better tone, are now relatively inexpensive. You will find many beginning instruction books at music stores.

Because of its soft, flutelike sound, the soprano recorder provides a good model of musical sound for children. A teacher may use it in sound-discrimination games: "I'll play a high sound. Marc, can you sing

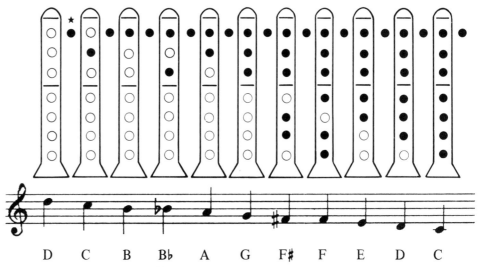

Figure A.3. Recorder fingering chart.

the high sound?" Or "I'll play a long sound. Billy, can you hum this long sound?" The melodies of familiar songs can be played: "I'll play a song we all know. Can you tell me which song it is and sing the words?" As the teacher's playing skill progresses, improvised tunes, played as a child strums an autoharp chord or plays a bordun on a xylophone, add to the musical interest of a lesson.

HOLDING THE RECORDER

To produce the best possible tone, the recorder is held at a 45 degree angle. Chin should be held up, and only the tip of the mouthpiece is inserted between the lips, slightly in front of the teeth. Very little air is needed to produce a tone; too much air will result in a shrill whistle. The left-hand fingers cover the holes on the top section of the instrument; the left thumb covers the hole in back. Right-hand fingers cover the lower four holes; the right thumb rests on the back of the recorder. Fingering is shown in Figure A.3.

PLAYING THE RECORDER

As has been stated, only a breath of air is needed to produce a tone. Each tone should be articulated with the tongue. This is done by forming the syllable "too" and beginning each tone with this "tongueing" as the note is fingered. Experimentation will enable you to produce a satisfactory tone with minimum practice. Remember, in European countries, many four-year-olds learn to play the recorder!

BARRED INSTRUMENTS

Xylophones, metallophones, and glockenspiels are part of the instrumental ensemble developed by Carl Orff for his method of instruction. Mention has been made in various parts of this book about teachers' accompanying rhythm chants or improvised tunes ("sol-mi" or "sol-mi-la" tunes) with borduns.

A bordun accompaniment may be played on a xylophone or metallophone by striking simultaneously the first and fifth tones of the scale the song or chant is based on. If a child plays the instrument, the teacher may remove all the bars except the ones needed for the bordun. Figure A.4 identifies the notes in the keys of C, F, G, and D that would be used for bordun accompaniments. The sol-mi pitches that might constitute the chant in a particular key are shown, also.

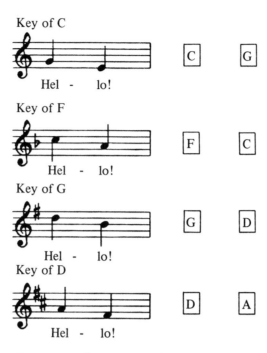

Figure A.4. Borduns in C, F, G, and D.

PENTATONIC SCALES

Children may improvise melodies over a bordun using the notes of a pentatonic scale. Figure A.5 shows how the barred instruments should be set up to produce pentatonic scales in the keys of C, F, G, and D. A pentatonic melodic pattern played by a child may also be used as an ostinato accompaniment for pentatonic songs. Pentatonic melodies do not use the fourth or seventh steps of the scale (Figure A.6).

MALLET TECHNIQUE

The mallets used for playing the barred instruments should be held loosely enough so that they will bounce lightly when the bar is struck. If the mallet is held rigidly, the sound will not ring, but will be muffled.

BODY PERCUSSION

In many activities books, especially those containing Orff activities, suggested body percussion rhythms are "notated" as accompaniments

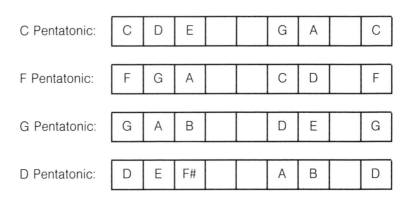

C Pentatonic:	C	D	E			G	A		C
F Pentatonic:	F	G	A			C	D		F
G Pentatonic:	G	A	B			D	E		G
D Pentatonic:	D	E	F#			A	B		D

Suggested Improvisatory Experience: Teacher plays bordun on C and G. Child improvises melodic patterns using notes of C pentatonic scale.

Figure A.5. Pentatonic scales.

Figure A.6. An Orff bass xylophone, with bars removed to form a pentatonic scale.

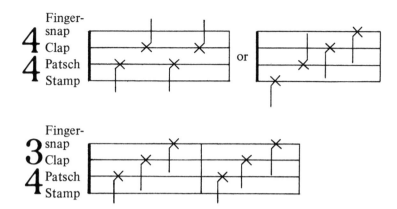

Figure A.7. Body-Percussion Rhythms

to songs. The notation may look like that shown in Figure A.7. The body-rhythms in the first example would work for a song with a $\frac{2}{4}$ or $\frac{4}{4}$ meter signature; the ones in the second example could be used to accompany a song or chant in $\frac{3}{4}$ or slow $\frac{6}{8}$ meter.

Songs and Movement Activities: Sources

compiled by Claire McCoy

SONG BOOKS

Beall, Pamela Conn, and Nipp, Susan Hagen
Wee Sing
Wee Sing and Play
Wee Sing Silly Songs
Wee Sing around the Campfire
Price/Stern/Sloan Publishers, Inc., 410 North La Cienega Blvd., Los Angeles, CA 90048 1985

Children's songs and fingerplays, which are a part of every child's growing-up years. Traditional tunes with autoharp/guitar chord accompaniments. Cassette tape optional.

Feierabend, John M.
Music for Very Little People
Boosey Hawkes, Inc., 200 Smith St., Farmingdale, NY 11735 1986

This collection contains 50 songs and rhythmic activities for interactive experiences between adults and infants and toddlers. Bouncing, tickling, wiggling, tapping, and clapping song activities are included as well as lullabies and quiet songs. Cassette tape optional.

Glazer, Tom
Eye Winker, Tom Tinker, Chin Chopper: Fifty Musical Fingerplays
Do Your Ears Hang Low?: Fifty More Musical Fingerplays
Doubleday and Company, Inc., Garden City, NY 1973, 1980

These collections contain familiar finger play songs, familiar finger plays newly set to music, and some folk songs with new finger plays. Tasteful piano accompaniments for the songs are supplied along with chord symbols.

Glazer, Tom
Music for Ones and Twos: Songs and Games for the Very Young Child
Doubleday and Co., Inc., Garden City, NY 1983

Songs about the very young child's everyday experiences, using the child's vocabulary, are found in this collection. Most of the songs are composed, but some traditional songs are included. The songs are notated with piano accompaniments and chord symbols.

Harrop, Beatrice
Sing Hey Diddle Diddle: 66 Nursery Rhymes with Their Traditional Tunes
A. C. Black, 35 Bedford Row, London, England 4JH

Attractive layouts and many color plates make this collection a treat for the eye. The simple piano and guitar harmonizations provided for the nursery tunes are in good keys for preschool singers.

Jenkins, Ella
The Ella Jenkins Song Book for Children
Oak Publications, New York 1966

This compilation of original and traditional songs and chants includes piano and chord accompaniments along with comments on each of the songs.

Kenney, Maureen
Circle round the Zero
Magnamusic-Baton, Inc., 10370 Page Industrial Boulevard, St. Louis, MO 63132
1983

Jump rope chants, clap pattern songs, ball-bouncing games, counting-out rhymes, call and response songs, elimination games, and singing games collected from city playgrounds have been notated and compiled in this book.

McLaughlin, Roberta, and Wood, Lucille
The Small Singer
Bowmar Records, Dist.: Belwin Mills Publ. Corp. 15800 N.W. 48th Ave. Miami, FL 33014(N) 1969

This book, filled with traditional songs, newly composed songs, nursery rhymes, holiday songs, and songs for special activities, should be included in any basic library of children's songbooks. The songs are in reasonable ranges; chords and piano accompaniments are included. Movement and instrumental activities are suggested for some songs.

Nelson, Esther
Musical Games for Children of All Ages
Dancing Games for Children of All Ages
Sterling Publishing Co., Inc., New York 1983, 1984

Both books contain musical games suitable for children age 4 or older; songs with piano accompaniments and directions for the games are provided.

Musical Games includes jump rope, ball bouncing, and pat-a-cake games. Many songs are new lyrics set to familiar tunes. Several rhymes in Spanish are included. The musical material in *Dancing Games* comes primarily from the repertoire of folk songs and traditional children's songs. However, some of the songs are written in keys that would make joining in difficult for young children.

Nelson, Esther
The Silly Songbook
The Funny Songbook
Sterling Publishing Co., Inc., New York 1981, 1984

Humorous traditional songs and familiar tunes with contrived humorous lyrics—the type of songs considered "camp songs"—can be found in these collections. Some of the songs exceed a comfortable singing range for preschool children. Chords and simple piano accmpaniments are provided.

Scelsa, Greg, and Millang, Steve
The Youngheart Autoharp Songbook
Oscar Schmidt International 1982

The alphabet, days of the week, months of the year—topics appropriate for young children—are some of the subjects of the songs in this book. However, because the songs are fairly long and the melodies often exceed the comfortable singing range of most preschool children, the songs may be more successfully sung by adults rather than children. The collection includes composed songs and arrangements of traditional songs with melody lines, chords, and teaching suggestions. The book also includes basic instructions for playing the autoharp.

Shotwell, Rita
Rhythm and Movement Activities for Early Childhood
Alfred Publishing Co., 1533 Morrison St., P.O. Box 5964, Sherman Oaks, CA 91413 1984

Activities that make use of singing, finger plays, and simple rhythm instruments are described in this book; directions for the games and ideas for variations on the games are given. While most of the song melodies are provided, some of the activities assume knowledge of the song. Some of the chants are written without suggested rhythms.

Williams, Raylene
Sing a Little Song
6284 Thistlebrook Dr., Memphis, TN 38115 1983

This small collection includes fourteen songs written to be used with children from birth to six years of age. The songs lie within the comfortable singing range for most young children; as the child's singing voice develops, the child should easily be able to join the adult in the songs. The book includes the melodies and chords for the songs as well as suggestions for using the songs.

Wirth, M.; Stassevitch, V.; Shotwell, R.; and Stemmler, P.
Musical Games, Fingerplays and Rhythmic Activities for Early Childhood
Parker Publishing Co., Inc., West Nyack, NY 1983

This large collection of musical games, chants, finger plays, and games for developing listening skills was compiled with the classroom teacher in mind. Suggested age ranges, necessary materials, and directions for the activities are clearly laid out. Notated melodies and chord symbols are provided for the songs.

MOVEMENT

Barlin, Anne, and Barlin, Paul
The Art of Learning through Movement
Bowmar/Noble Publishers, Inc. 1978

Releasing a child's potential for expressive movement is the goal of the activities described in this book. Stories and fantasies are used as vehicles for involving children in movement. Much of the material in this book can be used with children as young as 4 years old. Illustrative photographs and recorded accompaniments are included.

Stecher, M.; McElheny, H.; and Greenwood, M.
Music and Movement Improvisations, vol. 4 of *Threshold*
Early Learning Library
Macmillan Publishing Co., Inc., New York 1972

This book aims to sensitize the teacher to students' spontaneous explorations with sound and movement and gives suggestions for turning those explorations into learning experiences without excessive structure. Helpful ideas for involving shy children and handling problem situations are provided along with a selected bibliography and list of songs and records.

Wax, Edith, and Roth, Sydell
Mostly Movement: Book 1, First Steps
Mostly Movement: Book 2, Accent on Autumn
Mostly Movement, Ltd., New York 1979, 1982

These books are intended to help teachers of students, ages 3 to 8, teach music through storytelling. The books follow a clear and helpful WHAT, WHY, HOW format. The books are indexed according to musical subjects. Book 1 contains three longer dramatizations and other shorter activities; musical examples with piano accompaniment are incorporated. Topics of interest in autumn are found in the stories and songs out of which the learning activities of Book 2 grow.

KODÁLY AND ORFF APPROACHES

Bradford, Louise
Sing It Yourself: 220 Pentatonic American Folk Songs
Alfred, 15335 Morrison St., Sherman Oaks, CA 91403 1978

Teachers who are looking for authentic American folk literature for young children will find this book very helpful. The songs are grouped according to the intervals that comprise the songs; the songs are also indexed by subject matter. Notated melody lines, some suggestions for using the songs, and a bibliography are included in the book. The songs are compatible with the Orff and Kodály approaches to music education.

Burnett, Millie
Melody, Movement, and Language: A Teacher's Guide of
Music in Game Form for the Pre-School and Primary Grades
Music Innovations, Box 1, Allison Park, PA 15101 1973

Music concepts for the young child are introduced with activities that begin with words and chants, then extend to movement, instruments, and songs. Complete instructions for implementing these activities and notated melodies with chord symbols are included in this book. The author also provides a valuable introduction and bibliography.

Daniel, Katinka Scipiades
Kodály in Kindergarten
Mark Foster, Champaign, IL 1981

Yearlong goals for ear training and rhythm training, monthly lesson outlines, and sequenced individual lesson plans are provided in this book. The singing games, finger plays, and songs used in the lesson plans are notated in stick notation and solfège syllables.

Hein, M.A.; Choksy, L.; and Dalton, K.
The Singing Book, Beginning Level
Renna/White Associates, San Francisco

For teachers who wish to use the Kodály approach with young children, this book provides teaching suggestions, many songs comprised of the scale tones of sol, mi, and la with additional songs including do and re, and illustrations of graphic notation suitable for young children. The song repertoire is made up of traditional folk songs and singing games.

Kersey, Robert
Just Five
Just Five Plus Two
Belwin-Mills, Melville, NY 1972, 1975

These two collections contain notated melodies of international and American folk songs and singing games. The first book is devoted exclusively to pentatonic melodies; the second book progresses to songs using the full scale and some altered tones. The range and scale degrees of each song are identified.

Regner; Hermann, ed.
Music for Children, Orff-Schulwerk
American edition Vol. 1—Preschool Based on Carl Orff-Gunild Keetman *Music für Kinder.* Schoot, London 1982

This volume provides an excellent introduction to using the Orff approach with young children. In addition to notated songs, detailed explanations for combining those songs with movement and instrumental activities can be found. To deepen the teacher's understanding of the Orff approach, articles on the topics of movement, speech and song, improvisation, listening, poetry and rhymes, and parental involvement are included.

Nash, Grace
Primary/Pre-Primary Songs and Verses and Orff Instruments
Swarwout Productions, Scottsdale, AR 1978

Songs with appealing texts for preschool children, singing games, and suggestions for the use of movement and instruments are found in this book. The scale tones used in each song are identified.

Nash, G.; Jones, G.; Potter, B.; and Smith, P.
The Child's Way of Learning: A Handbook for Building Creative Teaching Experiences
Alfred Publishing Co., Inc., 15335 Morrison St., Sherman Oaks, CA 91403 1977

Based on the philosophy that active learners are better learners, these movement, rhythm, and singing activities are designed to bolster students' self-image and help in acquisition of academic skills. Detailed instructions, notated melodies, and suggestions for the use of Orff instruments are provided for the teaching strategies. The ideas in this book were intended for use at levels K through 6. A helpful introduction and bibliography are included.

Saliba, Konnie
Jelly Beans and Things
Cock-A-Doodle Tunes, Box 311, Cordova, TN 38018 1982

Ideas for the use of movement and instruments are included along with the eighteen composed songs in this collection. Children in the age group for which these songs are intended—ages 5 to 8—should enjoy the texts.

RECORDS

Bowmar Records
Dist.: Belwin-Mills Publ. Corp. 15800 N.W. 48th Ave. Miami, FL 33014(N)

Wood, Lucille
The Small Listener

The short selections in this collection, drawn predominantly from the classical and romantic repertoire, illustrate a variety of rhythms, meters, and moods. The teaching suggestions provided are appropriate for kindergarten.
The Small Player

Nursery songs, folk songs, and classical pieces are interestingly orchestrated and arranged to highlight the rhythmic aspect of the music. The teacher's guide gives suggestions for helping children experiment with rhythm instruments and movement.
The Small Singer

Interesting arrangements with a variety of timbres provide the backgrounds for the adult soloists on these albums.

Educational Activities, Inc. Box 392, Freeport, NY 11520
Palmer, Hap

The lively, popular sound of the Hap Palmer records is very appealing to children. These imaginative songs make learning fun.

AR713 *Baby Songs*
AR533 *Creative Movement and Rhythmic Expression*
AR581 *Easy Does It*
  motor skill development
AR556 *The Feel of Music*
  relates music concepts to movement
AR517 *Feelin' Free: A Personalized Approach to Vocabulary and Language Development*
AR543 *Getting to Know Myself*
AR545 *Homemade Band*
AR514 *Learning Basic Skills through Music*, Vol. I
AR522 *Learning Basic Skills through Music*, Vol. II
AR526 *Learning Basic Skills through Music*, Vol. III
AR521 *Learning Basic Skills through Music*, Vol. IV
AR594 *Learning Basic Skills through Music*, Vol. V
AR523 *Modern Tunes for Rhythm Instruments*
AR546 *Movin'*
AR584 *Sea Gulls*
  music for rest and relaxation
AR597 *Tickly Toddle*
  for use with very young children
AR555 *Walter the Waltzing Worm*
  designed to increase children's vocabulary and movement skills
AR576 *Witches' Brew*
  language development

Jenkins, Ella

AR595 *I Know the Colors of the Rainbow*

Zeitlin, Patty, and Berman, Marcia

AR551 *Spin, Spider, Spin* 1974

Songs in the folk tradition focus on the appreciation of nature. Although the songs are intended primarily for listening, children can easily join in the frequent refrains.

Folkways Records
632 Broadway, New York 10012

Jenkins, Ella

FC7544 *And One and Two*
   designed to help children develop listening skills as they participate in singing and movement
FC7638 *Call-and-Response Rhythmic Group Singing*
FC7679 *Counting Games and Rhythms for the Little Ones*
FC7630 *Early Childhood Songs*
   vocal and instrumental versions of traditional songs for young children
FC7662 *Growing Up with Ella Jenkins*
FC7631 *Little Johnny Brown*
   children are invited to participate in activities designed to encourage development of steady beat and memory
FC7543 *My Street Begins at My House*
FC7660 *Nursery Rhymes with Ella Jenkins*
FC7566 *Play Your Instrument and Make a Pretty Sound*
FC7653 *Rhythms of Childhood*
FC7655 *Songs and Rhythms from Near and Far*
FC7680 *Rhythm and Game Songs for the Little Ones*, Vol. 2
FC7546 *This-A-Way, That-A-Way: Cheerful Songs and Chants*
FC7652 *This Is Rhythm*
FF302 *This Is Your Year*
   special issues for the International Year of the Child
FC7666 *We Are America's Children*
FC7664 *You'll Sing a Song and I'll Sing a Song*

Troubadour Records Ltd.

Raffi

Rise and Shine

This album contains a mix of newly composed songs and traditional songs. Some of the simple songs could be sung by preschool children, but many of the songs are too complex for young children to sing.

SPECIAL EDUCATION

Janiak, William
Songs for Music Therapy
Kimbo Educational 1978

The 25 songs in this collection emphasize body awareness and movement. Several of the songs are meant to be personalized with students' names. The songs could be easily learned by children and are appropriate for use with preschool or special education students. Teaching suggestions are included along with the melody and guitar chords for each song.

Walden, David, and Birkenshaw, Lois
The Goat with the Bright Red Socks, recording and songbook Berandol Music Ltd., 11 Saint Joseph St., Toronto, Canada 1980

These fun songs are written about subjects appropriate for use with special education and preschool children: body parts, numbers, colors, transportation, nutrition, and family living. The ranges of these songs are also appropriate. The book includes melodies with chords and some suggestions for movement and variations on the songs.

MUSIC TEXTBOOK SERIES

Music series texts offer a well-rounded music program for children of kindergarten age; a balance of singing, playing, listening, and movement activities are provided. In addition to the notated songs, recording of those songs and music for listening are provided.

American Book Company
135 W. 50th St.
New York, NY 10020

New Dimensions in Music: Music for Early Childhood, by Robert A. Choate
Follett Publishing Co.
1010 West Washington Blvd.
Chicago, IL 60607

Discovering Music Together: Early Childhood, by Charles Leonhard

Ginn and Co.
191 Spring St.
Lexington, MAS 02173

The Magic of Music: Kindergarten, by Lorrain Watters

Holt, Rinehart and Winston
383 Madison Ave.
New York, NY 10017

   The Music Book: Kindergarten, by Eunice Boardman

Macmillan Publishing Co., Inc.
866 Third Ave.
New York, NY 10022

   The Spectrum of Music with Related Arts: Kindergarten, by Mary Val Marsh

Silver Burdett Co.
250 James St.
Morristown, NJ 07632

   Silver Burdett Music: Early Childhood, by Elizabeth Crook

BOOKS ABOUT MUSIC IN EARLY CHILDHOOD

Andress, Barbara
Music Experiences in Early Childhood
Holt, Rinehart and Winston, New York 1980

A research-based, hands-on, discovery approach to early childhood music is presented in this book. Theoretical and very specific practical information can both be found: chapter topics include educational theory, movement, singing, playing, evaluation, and teacher performance skills. The appendixes provide resource lists, guitar chords, and songs for use during the day.

Lawrence, Marjorie
What? Me Teach Music?: A Classroom Teacher's Guide to Music in Early Childhood
Alfred Publishing Co., Inc., 15335 Morrison St., Sherman Oaks, CA 1982

This book is intended to be used as a "pick up and use" guide for the person with no music background. Terminology is explained for the nonmusician, and bar instruments are used to aid the teacher in learning melodies. Based on the Orff and Kodály approaches, solfège and two-, three-, and four-note songs are used.

Wood, Donna
Move, Sing, Listen, Play
Gordon V. Thompson Limited, Toronto, Canada 1982

Wood outlines the stages of child development and corresponding musical development in her book. Songs and activities appropriate to the developmental stages are included.

Glossary of Musical Terms

Accelerando: Gradually getting faster.

Accent: A tone or a beat that is louder and receives more emphasis.

Action song: A song that involves body movement in addition to singing.

Autoharp: A chording instrument used to accompany songs.

Bass clef: The clef used to designate notes below middle C, in which the F below middle C is notated on the fourth line.

Beat: The recurring rhythmic pulse heard or sensed throughout a song or composition.

Bells: Metal bars arranged in scale formation on a frame and struck with a mallet.

Bordun: A "drone" produced by the first and fifth tones of a scale sounded simultaneously.

Canon: A musical form in which all parts are the same, but start at different times. Like a round, except that some adjustment is made so that all parts end together.

Chant: A repeated phrase, spoken rhythmically.

Chord: Three or more tones sounded simultaneously.

Coda: An ending that is added to a song or composition.

Contour: The shape of a melody, determined by the rise and fall of the pitches.

Crescendo: Gradual increase in loudness.

"Cuckoo" call: The "sol-mi," descending minor third interval found in many children's vocal improvisations.

Decrescendo: Gradual increase in softness.

Dissonance: The simultaneous sound of tones that are discordant to a listener.

Duration: The length of time a note or chord is held.

Dynamics: The degrees of loudness and softness of a song or composition.

Eighth note: A note with a solid head, a stem, and a flag. Lasts half as long as a quarter note.

Finger plays: A series of finger, hand, or arm movements suggested by the words of a song.

Form: The design of repetition or contrast in the phrases or sections of a song or composition.

Half note: A note with an open head and stem. Lasts twice as long as a quarter note.

Half step: The smallest pitch interval possible on a keyboard instrument (e.g., F to F♯).

Hand signs: A series of hand positions, each one denoting a different step of a scale.

Harmony: Two or more tones played or sung at the same time.

Improvisation: A spontaneously created musical performance.

Interval: The distance from one pitch to another.

Key: The tonality, or perceived relationship of tones to one another. Songs that gravitate to the note C, for example, are said to be in the key of C.

Key signature: An arrangement of sharps and flats at the beginning of each line of music, which denotes the tonality or key.

Measure: The division of rhythms into a specified number of beats, separated by a vertical line called a measure bar.

Meter: The basic grouping of beats, usually in a measure. Basic meter groupings of many songs are in two, three, four, or six beats.

Meter signature: The two numbers at the beginning of a piece that indicate the number of beats in a measure (the top number) and the kind of note that represents the pulse (the bottom number).

Metronome: A mechanical device that produces steady beats, the speed of which can be regulated.

Middle C: The C nearest to the middle of the piano keyboard.

Music literature: A body of musical compositions.

Ostinato: A rhythmic or melodic pattern that is played repeatedly, often to form an accompaniment to a song or composition.

Patsch (**German**): To slap the top of the thighs with one's hands.

Pentatonic scale: A five-tone scale. There are many five-tone scales, but the one most common to folk music is the one that uses steps 1, 2, 3, 5, and 6 of the major scale.

Phrase: A musical thought or idea, often compared to a sentence in language.

Pitch: The highness or lowness of a musical sound.

Pulse: Another term for rhythmic beat.

Quarter note: A note with a filled-in head and a stem. It often represents the basic pulse or beat of a song or composition.

Range: The distance between the highest and lowest notes of a song, composition, voice, or instrument.

Register: The general pitch range of a song or voice.

Repertoire: A body of music that has been studied and learned.

Rhythm: The organization of sounds, silences, and patterns into different groupings.

Rhythm syllables: A series of speech sounds assigned to notes of varying duration.

Rondo: A musical form with a recurring theme that is alternated between contrasting sections (e.g., A, B, A, C, A)

Rote song: A song learned by imitation rather than note-reading.

Scale: A series of tones ascending or descending according to a prescribed pattern of intervals.

Seventh chord: A chord of four tones, each a third apart.

Skip: A musical interval consisting of notes more than one alphabet letter-name away from one another (e.g., C to G).

Solfège: Use of the "do-re-mi" system for identifying pitches.

Step: A musical interval one alphabet letter-name away from another (e.g., C to D).

Stick notation: A simplified form of rhythmic notation showing just note stems (e.g., | | ⊓ |).

Tempo: The speed at which a song or composition is performed.

Timbre (pronounced "tam-bur"): the tonal quality characteristic of a voice or instrument.

Tonal center: The beginning pitch of a scale, or the note to which a melody gravitates or "comes home."

Tonic: Another term for tonal center.

Treble clef: The clef that designates the G above middle C on the second line of the staff.

Triple meter: Music in which the rhythmic groupings are felt in threes (e.g., BEAT, beat, beat).

Unison: Singing or playing the same melody at the same time.

Index